Better Homes and Gardens®

365
Last-Minute
MEALS

D1450723

Meredith® Books
Des Moines, Iowa

365 LAST-MINUTE MEALS

Editor: Jessica Saari
Contributing Project Editor: Mary Williams
Contributing Writers: Ellen Boeke, Annie Krumhardt
Contributing Graphic Designer: Matthew Eberhart, Evil Eye
    Design, Inc.
Cover Designer: Renee E. McAtee
Design Coordinator: Diana Van Winkle
Copy Chief: Terri Fredrickson
Copy Editor: Kevin Cox
Publishing Operations Manager: Karen Schirm
Senior Editor, Asset & Information Management:
    Phillip Morgan
Edit and Design Production Coordinator: Mary Lee Gavin
Editorial Assistant: Cheryl Eckert
Book Production Managers: Pam Kvitne,
    Marjorie J. Schenkelberg, Rick von Holdt, Mark Weaver
Contributing Photographer: Scott Little
Contributing Copy Editor: Lisa Bailey
Contributing Proofreaders: Alison Crouch,
    Sarah Enticknap, Candy Meier
Contributing Indexer: Elizabeth Parson
Test Kitchen Director: Lynn Blanchard
Test Kitchen Product Supervisor: Marilyn Cornelius
Test Kitchen Home Economists: Elizabeth Burt, R.D., L.D.;
    Juliana Hale; Maryellyn Krantz; Greg Luna; Laura Marzen,
    R.D.; Jill Moberly; Dianna Nolin; Colleen Weeden;
    Lori Wilson

Meredith® Books
Executive Director, Editorial: Gregory H. Kayko
Executive Director, Design: Matt Strelecki
Managing Editor: Amy Tincher-Durik
Executive Editor: Jennifer Darling
Senior Editor/Group Manager: Jan Miller
Marketing Product Manager: Toye Cody

Publisher and Editor in Chief: James D. Blume
Editorial Director: Linda Raglan Cunningham
Executive Director, Marketing: Kevin Kacere
Executive Director, New Business Development: Todd M. Davis
Executive Director, Sales: Ken Zagor
Director, Operations: George A. Susral
Director, Production: Douglas M. Johnston
Director, Marketing: Amy Nichols
Business Director: Jim Leonard

Vice President and General Manager: Douglas J. Guendel

Better Homes and Gardens® Magazine
Editor in Chief: Gayle Goodson Butler
Deputy Editor, Food and Entertaining: Nancy Hopkins

Meredith Publishing Group
President: Jack Griffin
Senior Vice President: Karla Jeffries

Meredith Corporation
Chairman of the Board: William T. Kerr
President and Chief Executive Officer: Stephen M. Lacy

In Memoriam: E.T. Meredith III (1933–2003)

Our Better Homes and Gardens® Test Kitchen seal on the back cover of this book assures you that every recipe in *365 Last-Minute Meals* has been tested in the Better Homes and Gardens® Test Kitchen. This means that each recipe is practical and reliable, and meets our high standards of taste appeal. We guarantee your satisfaction with this book for as long as you own it.

All of us at Meredith® Books are dedicated to providing you with the information and ideas you need to create delicious foods. We welcome your comments and suggestions. Write to us at: Meredith Books, Cookbook Editorial Department, 1716 Locust St., Des Moines, IA 50309-3023.

Pictured on the front cover (clockwise from top left):
Chicken-Biscuit Pie (page 159), Ranch-Style Chicken Salad (page 253), Bacon Cheeseburgers (page 318), Texas Chili Made Easy (page 18)
Pictured on the back cover (from left to right):
Chicken Fingers (page 251), Asian Chicken Salad (page 346), Individual Sicilian Meat Loaves (page 103)

Table of Contents

Introduction

So many meals to cook, so little time ... it's easy to see why take-out and frozen dinners have become so popular! When supper has to be on the table after work and before soccer practice, preparing a homemade dinner can seem like a near impossibility. But worry no more! With 365 Last-Minute Meals, you'll learn that preparing weeknight dinners doesn't have to be time-consuming or difficult, and that quick meals can be truly delicious. Each recipe in this book can be on your family's table—start to finish—in 30 minutes or less, so you won't be confined to your kitchen for hours on end. And because each recipe calls for seven ingredients or less (excluding salt, pepper, water, nonstick cooking spray, and optional items), you won't spend precious time tracking down unusual ingredients in the supermarkets.

Variety in meals is important—especially when you have kids. That's why this book provides a different dinner for every day of the year! Try a new dish every night and never again will you hear the words, "Oh no, not *that* again!" Additionally, the book has been organized according to seasons, enabling you to use the freshest, most in-season ingredients possible. To ensure your success, each recipe has been tested and approved in the Better Homes and Gardens® Test Kitchen, so you know they'll work the first time and every time.

What about side dishes? No problem! Each recipe comes with a menu full of fast and easy serve-along suggestions to create a complete meal. These side dishes utilize the convenience products and dishes available on supermarket shelves and in the deli and bakery. See page 6 for more simple side dish ideas.

Let this book inspire you to cook meals with all the down-home goodness of a made-from-scratch meal—without all the effort. A new and exciting meal can be on your family's table every night of the year. Now let's get cookin'!

What's for Dinner?

Meal planning is often the hardest part of cooking weeknight dinners. Use these tips to ease the process:

- It's important to plan ahead. At the beginning of the week, make a list of meals you would like to make during the week.

- Can any of your meal ideas be frozen and saved for a busy day? If so, make a double (or triple) batch and freeze the extra. You'll be glad you did.

- Certain meals can be "recycled." Leftovers such as pasta make delicious, entirely new meals. For example, if you have a spaghetti meal one night, cook extra pasta so you can create a spaghetti pie or lo mein dish later in the week. Keep this in mind when planning your weeknight dinners—it can save you plenty of time.

- When you shop, be smart. As you plan your meal strategy for the week, jot down a list of the ingredients you'll need from the grocery store. Then organize your list according to the layout of the grocery store you shop at. This will get you in and out of the store quickly. Here's a list of headings to start with.

- **Meat, fish, and poultry**
- **Produce**
- **Frozen ingredients**
- **Pantry items**
- **Dairy**

TOOLS OF THE TRADE

Countless cooking tools exist nowadays, but which ones do you really need? Begin by stocking your kitchen with the basic equipment to prepare weeknight meals. Add additional tools as you see fit. For example, if you use a particular tool often, such as a spatula, buy two. Or if you like to make soups and stews, invest in a Dutch oven or stock pot. Here are lists of cooking tools, from the basics to more specialized equipment.

MUST-HAVE BASICS:

- **Baking dish:** 13x9 inch
- **Blender**
- **Broiler pan**
- **Can opener**
- **Chef's knife:** 8 to 10 inches
- **Colander**
- **Four-sided grater/shredder**
- **Kitchen shears**
- **Large spoons**
- **Measuring cups:** one set for liquid and one set for dry ingredients
- **Measuring spoons**
- **Meat thermometer**
- **Mixing bowls** in various sizes
- **One large soup pot:** about 5 quarts
- **Paring knife**
- **Spatulas**
- **Strainer**
- **Two cutting boards:** one plastic, one wooden
- **Two nonstick skillets:** one large, one small
- **Two saucepans:** one large, one small
- **Vegetable peeler**
- **Whisk**
- **Wooden spoons**

FUN-TO-HAVE TOOLS:

- **Dutch oven:** Can be used on the burner and in the oven.
- **Food processor:** Makes quick work of pureeing, mincing, and mixing.
- **Heavy-duty stand mixer:** Mixes large quantities of dough.
- **Ice cream scoopers:** Use to create uniform-size cookies and meatballs.
- **Immersion blender:** Allows you to blend food in any pot, pan, or dish.
- **Lemon squeezer:** Helps you get the most juice out of citrus.
- **Microplane grater:** Supersharp grater that quickly grates cheese or zests citrus.
- **Pizza slicer:** Use it to slice pita bread and tortillas, in addition to pizza.
- **Salad spinner:** Makes quick work of washing and drying salad greens and veggies.
- **Serrated knife:** Slices bread and tomatoes perfectly every time.
- **Slow cooker:** Simmers food for hours while the cook is out and about.
- **Tongs:** Turns foods easily.

BRINGING ORDER TO DISORDER

Time for a Refrigerator Raid

- Begin by throwing away items you never use or anything that is old.
- Take a look at your condiments. If you have doubles of some items (e.g., yellow mustard or ketchup), combine the bottles and throw away the extra.
- Organize the fridge by putting similar items together. Designate areas of the fridge for certain types of food. It's a good rule of thumb to keep dairy items, meats, and vegetables on separate shelves. Also be sure to label and date leftovers and keep them in one spot in the fridge.

Bye-Bye, Freezer Frustration!

- Starting immediately, label and date EVERYTHING you store in your freezer. This way you'll never be left with mystery packages.
- Rummage through the contents of your freezer looking for old freezer-burnt items. If you see ice crystals covering the surface of the food, toss it. If you cannot identify the food in a package, throw it away—chances are, you'll never use it if you don't know what it is.
- Divide your freezer into sections: dessert foods, vegetables, meats, and breads. This will cut down on time you spend searching out what you need for a recipe.

Keep Cupboards Coordinated

- Group similar items together. Keep all canned vegetables in one place. Put all starches, such as pasta and rice, in one area.
- Place bottled items, such as oils or vinegars, on a tray. This makes it easy to slide them out to find what you're looking for. It also prevents drips and spills from pooling in your cupboards.
- Keep baking ingredients, such as flours, sugars, baking powder, and so on, on one shelf in your cupboard. If you're tight on space, store these items in stackable plastic airtight containers (labeled and dated, of course).
- Face all package labels forward so you can see them.
- Stagger heights. Place tall foods behind shorter foods so you are able to see everything.
- Alphabetize your herbs and spices. If kitchen space permits, invest in a lazy Susan.

A Place to Start

Before you even begin cooking, there are a few steps you can follow to save yourself time and effort. Check out these pointers to make cooking a fun and creative venture rather than a chore.

- Coordinate cooking times. Before you begin cooking, think about the side dishes you plan to serve with your meal. Will your side dish take longer to cook than the main dish? Be sure to start the meal component that will take the longest first.

- When you bring home groceries, wash your fresh vegetables, herbs, and greens. You'll save time while cooking by having these ingredients ready to use.

- Read through your week's recipes in advance. This will allow you to familiarize yourself with the cooking techniques you'll be performing throughout the week. Also, you won't forget important steps, such as marinating a day ahead.

- Set all your ingredients for a dish out on the counter before you begin cooking. This way you know you'll have everything you need for the recipe.

- Have all the ingredients fit the description on the recipe's ingredient list. For example, if your recipe calls for a chopped green pepper, chop the green pepper before you start cooking the dish.

Stress-Free Serve-Alongs

Side dishes can make or break the meal—but that doesn't mean they have to be time-consuming. Enlist the help of the numerous convenience products that line today's supermarket shelves. When choosing sides, think about what flavors and textures will best complement your main dish. If your main dish is robust in flavor, go for a milder side dish. Or if you're serving soup, stew, or chili, serve something drier alongside, such as bread or crackers. Here are some products that make quick side dishes.

- **Fresh breads from your grocery store bakery:** These are great for dipping in soups, stews, and saucy dishes.

- **Frozen bread dough:** It can be easily transformed into breadsticks, focaccia bread, or just a plain loaf.

- **Frozen egg rolls:** These are a fun accompaniment to an Asian dish, such as stir-fry.

- **Frozen french fries:** Kids love fries! And they go great with a variety of dishes—such as hamburgers, chicken, steaks, and chops. Or serve them as a tasty snack.

- **Frozen vegetables:** Whether you purchase mixed or a single variety, seasoned or unseasoned, just toss them in the microwave for a quick, no-fuss side.

- **Meat counter items:** Check out the prepared sides—such as vegetable kabobs, stuffed mushrooms, or baked potatoes—your grocery's meat counter offers.

- **Precut vegetables:** These save you two steps—washing and chopping.

- **Prewashed salad greens:** Just toss the greens into a bowl with your favorite dressing for a vitamin-rich side salad.

- **Refrigerated cooked pasta:** From tortellini to linguine, pasta is a favorite serve-along with so many dishes. Since this type is already cooked, all you have to do is heat it!

- **Refrigerated mashed potatoes:** A snap to prepare, these are the perfect complement to any type of meat.

- **Rice and rice blends:** With so many varieties available, you can find a flavor that rounds out just about any meal.

Speed Through Cleanup

Cleaning up the kitchen may be a pain, but it's a necessary part of the process. To minimize the time you'll spend tidying up, use these helpful tips:

- Clean as you go. Keep your sink full of warm, soapy water, ready to soak dirty dishes.

- Line pans with foil or parchment paper and coat with nonstick cooking spray.

- Use resealable bags, instead of bowls, to marinate meats.

- When measuring sticky ingredients, such as honey, coat measuring cups with nonstick cooking spray.

- Start a family ritual of cleaning the kitchen together after every meal. You'll be surprised how fast the kitchen can be tidied when everyone chips in.

EMERGENCY SUBSTITUTIONS

These equivalents come in handy when you're in a bind.

Bread crumbs: 1 cup = ¾ cup cracker crumbs

Broth: 1 cup = 1 bouillon cube + 1 cup boiling water

Butter: 1 cup = 1 cup margarine

Celery: ½ cup, chopped = 1 tablespoon dried celery flakes

Cornstarch: 1 tablespoon = 2 tablespoons flour

Flour: 2 tablespoons = 1 tablespoon cornstarch

Fresh herbs: 1 tablespoon = 1 teaspoon dried

Garlic: 1 clove = ⅛ teaspoon garlic powder

Lemon juice: 1 tablespoon = ½ teaspoon white vinegar

Mustard: 1 tablespoon, prepared = 1 teaspoon dry mustard

Onion: 1 medium onion, chopped = 2 tablespoons dried onion flakes

Sour cream: 1 cup = 1 cup plain yogurt

Yogurt: 1 cup = 1 cup sour cream or buttermilk

Fall

1

Beef Tenderloin with Blue Cheese and Walnuts

START TO FINISH:
20 MINUTES

MAKES:
4 SERVINGS

4   beef tenderloin steaks, cut 1 inch thick (about 1 pound)
½   teaspoon garlic salt
     Nonstick cooking spray
⅓   cup dairy sour cream
3   tablespoons crumbled blue cheese
3   tablespoons chopped walnuts, toasted

1. Trim fat from steaks. Sprinkle steaks with garlic salt. Lightly coat an unheated large skillet with nonstick cooking spray. Preheat skillet over medium-high heat. Add steaks; reduce heat to medium. Cook to desired doneness, turning once halfway through cooking. Allow 10 to 13 minutes for medium rare (145°F) to medium (160°F). Transfer steaks to dinner plates.

2. Meanwhile, in a small bowl stir together sour cream and blue cheese. Spoon sour cream mixture on top of steaks. Sprinkle with walnuts.

Per serving: 264 cal., 17 g total fat (6 g sat. fat), 81 mg chol., 255 mg sodium, 2 g carbo., 0 g fiber, 26 g pro.

MENU
Hot cooked wild rice
Roasted acorn squash wedges
Pear tart

Tenderloins with Rosemary and Port

2

START TO FINISH:
20 MINUTES

MAKES:
4 SERVINGS

4   beef tenderloin steaks, cut 1 inch thick (about 1 pound)
1   tablespoon olive oil or cooking oil
1½ teaspoons snipped fresh rosemary or ½ teaspoon dried rosemary, crushed
⅓   cup port wine
⅓   cup water
¼   cup whipping cream

1. Trim fat from steaks. Sprinkle both sides of steaks with *salt* and *black pepper*. In a large skillet heat oil over medium-high heat. Add steaks; reduce heat to medium. Cook for 10 to 13 minutes for medium rare (145°F) to medium (160°F), turning once halfway through cooking. Remove steaks from skillet, reserving drippings; cover steaks to keep warm.

2. For sauce, add rosemary to drippings in skillet. Cook and stir for 1 minute to loosen any brown bits in bottom of skillet. Carefully stir port and water into skillet. Bring to boiling. Boil, uncovered, about 3 minutes or until mixture is reduced by half. Stir in whipping cream. Return to boiling; boil gently for 2 to 3 minutes or until slightly thickened. Spoon sauce over steaks.

Per serving: 295 cal., 18 g total fat (7 g sat. fat), 90 mg chol., 132 mg sodium, 3 g carbo., 0 g fiber, 24 g pro.

MENU
Crusty country bread
Spinach salad with balsamic vinaigrette
Roasted potatoes

3

Coriander-Studded Tenderloin Steak

PREP:
10 MINUTES

BROIL:
12 MINUTES

MAKES:
4 SERVINGS

4   beef tenderloin steaks, cut 1 inch thick (about 1 pound)
1   tablespoon reduced-sodium soy sauce
1   tablespoon olive oil
1   tablespoon snipped fresh chives
1   teaspoon bottled minced garlic (2 cloves)
½   teaspoon coriander seeds or cumin seeds, crushed
½   teaspoon celery seeds
½   teaspoon black pepper

1. Preheat broiler. Trim fat from steaks. Sprinkle steaks lightly with *salt.* In a small bowl combine soy sauce, oil, chives, garlic, coriander seeds, celery seeds, and pepper. Brush the mixture onto both sides of each steak.

2. Place meat on the unheated rack of a broiler pan. Broil 3 to 4 inches from the heat for 12 to 14 minutes for medium rare (145°F) or 15 to 18 minutes for medium (160°F), turning once halfway through broiling.

Per serving: 164 cal., 9 g total fat (3 g sat. fat), 42 mg chol., 256 mg sodium, 1 g carbo., 0 g fiber, 18 g pro.

MENU
Mashed sweet potatoes
Roasted Brussels sprouts
Cranberry sauce

Peppery Steak with Bordelaise Sauce

4

START TO FINISH:
25 MINUTES

MAKES:
4 SERVINGS

1¼ cups water
1 cup packaged sliced fresh mushrooms
½ cup finely chopped onion (1 medium)
1 0.87- to 1.2-ounce package brown gravy mix
¼ cup dry red wine
4 beef ribeye, top loin, or tenderloin steaks, cut ¾ inch thick (about 1½ pounds)
2 teaspoons garlic-pepper seasoning
2 tablespoons olive oil

1. For sauce, in a medium saucepan bring water to boiling. Add mushrooms and onion. Reduce heat. Cook, covered, for 3 minutes. Stir in dry gravy mix and red wine. Cook, uncovered, about 3 minutes or until thickened, stirring occasionally. Cover; keep warm.

2. Meanwhile, trim fat from steaks. Rub garlic-pepper seasoning into both sides of each steak. In a large skillet heat oil over medium-high heat. Add steaks; reduce heat to medium. Cook to desired doneness, turning once halfway through cooking. Allow 7 to 9 minutes for medium-rare (145°F) to medium (160°F). Serve the steaks with the sauce.

Per serving: 366 cal., 18 g total fat (5 g sat. fat), 81 mg chol., 954 mg sodium, 7 g carbo., 1 g fiber, 39 g pro.

MENU
Steamed mixed vegetables
Candied sweet potatoes
Chocolate silk pie

5

Sauteed Sirloin and Mushrooms

START TO FINISH:
30 MINUTES

MAKES:
4 SERVINGS

1   to 1¼ pounds boneless beef top sirloin steak, cut ¾ inch thick
¾   teaspoon cracked black pepper
1   tablespoon butter or margarine
¾   cup beef broth
1   tablespoon teriyaki sauce, soy sauce, or hoisin sauce
1¾   cups packaged sliced fresh mushrooms
1   small onion, cut into very thin wedges

1. Trim fat from steak. Cut steak into 4 serving-size portions. Sprinkle both sides of steaks with pepper; pat pepper into meat with fingers. In a large skillet heat butter over medium-high heat. Add steaks; reduce heat to medium. Cook steaks in hot butter to desired doneness, turning once halfway through cooking. Allow 9 to 11 minutes for medium-rare (145°F) to medium (160°F). Remove steaks from skillet, reserving drippings; cover steaks to keep warm.

2. Carefully add beef broth and teriyaki sauce to drippings in skillet. Cook and stir until bubbly, stirring to scrape up brown bits. Stir in mushrooms and onion. Cook, uncovered, over medium heat for 8 to 10 minutes or until most of the liquid evaporates. Transfer steaks to dinner plates; top with mushroom mixture.

Per serving: 191 cal., 8 g total fat (3 g sat. fat), 62 mg chol., 403 mg sodium, 3 g carbo., 1 g fiber, 26 g pro.

MENU
Sourdough rolls
Buttered lima beans
Mashed potatoes

Barbecued Beef Sandwiches

6

START TO FINISH:
20 MINUTES

MAKES:
4 SANDWICHES

1   tablespoon cooking oil
1   medium onion, sliced and separated into rings
12 ounces packaged beef stir-fry strips
⅔ cup bottled barbecue sauce
1   teaspoon lemon juice or vinegar
4   hoagie buns, split and toasted
3   slices Monterey Jack cheese with jalapeño peppers or Monterey Jack cheese, quartered

1. In a large skillet heat oil over medium–high heat. Add onion; cook onion about 3 minutes or until tender. Add beef strips. Cook and stir for 2 to 3 minutes or until meat is slightly pink in center.

2. Stir in barbecue sauce and lemon juice. Cook over medium heat until heated through, stirring occasionally. Spoon beef mixture onto hoagie bun bottoms. Top with cheese and bun tops.

Per sandwich: 689 cal., 22 g total fat (9 g sat. fat), 76 mg chol., 1,257 mg sodium, 82 g carbo., 4 g fiber, 37 g pro.

MENU
Corn chips
Baked beans
Coleslaw (from a deli)

7

Hamburger Stroganoff

START TO FINISH:
25 MINUTES

MAKES:
3 TO 4 SERVINGS

12 ounces ground beef

½ teaspoon bottled minced garlic (1 clove) or ⅛ teaspoon garlic powder

1½ cups water

1½ cups half-and-half, light cream, or milk

1 4-ounce can (drained weight) sliced mushrooms, drained

1 1.5-ounce package stroganoff sauce mix

4 ounces dried medium egg noodles (2 cups)

1. In a large saucepan cook ground beef and garlic over medium heat until meat is brown. Drain off fat.

2. Stir the water, half-and-half, mushrooms, and dry stroganoff sauce mix into meat mixture in skillet. Bring to boiling. Stir in noodles. Reduce heat. Simmer, covered, for 6 to 8 minutes or until noodles are tender, stirring occasionally.

Per serving: 528 cal., 34 g total fat (16 g sat. fat), 132 mg chol., 949 mg sodium, 31 g carbo., 1 g fiber, 23 g pro.

MENU
Dinner rolls
Steamed peas and carrots
Baked apples

Chili-Burger Supper

8

START TO FINISH:
20 MINUTES

MAKES:
4 SERVINGS

1   cup dried elbow macaroni or penne pasta
1   pound ground beef
½   teaspoon chili powder
1   11.25-ounce can condensed chili beef soup
1   14.5-ounce can diced tomatoes, undrained
½   cup shredded cheddar cheese (2 ounces)
    Dairy sour cream (optional)
    Sliced green onion (optional)

1. Cook pasta according to package directions; drain well.

2. Meanwhile, in a large skillet cook ground beef over medium heat until meat is brown. Drain off fat. Add chili powder to beef in skillet; cook and stir for 1 minute.

3. Add soup, undrained tomatoes, and cooked pasta to beef mixture in skillet. Cook and stir over medium heat until the mixture is bubbly. Sprinkle with cheese. If desired, serve with sour cream and green onion.

Per serving: 501 cal., 23 g total fat (11 g sat. fat), 94 mg chol., 948 mg sodium, 38 g carbo., 7 g fiber, 33 g pro.

MENU
Onion rings (frozen)
Coleslaw (from a deli)
Hot fudge sundaes

9 Italian Beef Soup

START TO FINISH:
25 MINUTES

MAKES:
6 SERVINGS

1   pound ground beef
2   14-ounce cans beef broth
1   16-ounce package frozen broccoli and/or cauliflower
1   14.5-ounce can diced tomatoes, undrained
1   5.5-ounce can (¾ cup) tomato juice
1   cup dried rotini, wagon wheel, or other small pasta
½   cup purchased basil pesto

1. In a 4-quart Dutch oven cook beef over medium heat until brown. Drain off fat. Stir in beef broth, frozen vegetables, undrained tomatoes, and tomato juice.

2. Bring to boiling; stir in pasta. Reduce heat. Simmer, covered, about 10 minutes or until vegetables and pasta are tender. Stir in pesto.

Per serving: 317 cal., 16 g total fat (5 g sat. fat), 54 mg chol., 905 mg sodium, 20 g carbo., 4 g fiber, 21 g pro.

MENU
Crusty Italian bread
Cheesecake with desired
fruit preserves

Snappy Joes

10

START TO FINISH:
25 MINUTES

MAKES:
6 SERVINGS

1 pound ground beef or uncooked ground turkey
½ cup chopped green sweet pepper
⅓ cup chopped onion (1 small)
1 cup shredded cabbage with carrot (coleslaw mix)
1 8-ounce can tomato sauce
½ cup hot-style or regular bottled barbecue sauce
6 whole wheat hamburger buns, split and toasted, or 6 baked potatoes

1. In a large skillet cook ground meat, sweet pepper, and onion over medium heat until meat is brown and vegetables are tender. Drain off fat.

2. Stir cabbage with carrot, tomato sauce, and barbecue sauce into meat mixture in skillet. Bring to boiling; reduce heat. Simmer, uncovered, for 10 minutes. Serve the meat mixture in buns or over baked potatoes.

Per serving: 277 cal., 8 g total fat (3 g sat. fat), 43 mg chol., 710 mg sodium, 29 g carbo., 2 g fiber, 21 g pro.

MENU
Multigrain chips
Red and green grapes
Brownies

11

Texas Chili
Made Easy

START TO FINISH:
20 MINUTES

MAKES:
6 SERVINGS

12   ounces ground beef

1   15-ounce can pinto beans, undrained

1   cup bottled salsa

½   cup beef broth

1   teaspoon chili powder

½   teaspoon ground cumin

     Dairy sour cream (optional)

1. In a large skillet cook ground beef over medium heat until brown. Drain off fat.

2. Stir undrained beans, salsa, beef broth, chili powder, and cumin into meat in skillet. Bring to boiling; reduce heat. Simmer, covered, for 10 minutes. Spoon into bowls. If desired, top with sour cream.

Per serving: 178 cal., 8 g total fat (3 g sat. fat), 36 mg chol., 442 mg sodium, 12 g carbo., 4 g fiber, 15 g pro.

MENU

Texas toast

Vegetable tray with
sour cream dip

Apple pie

White and Green Chili

12

START TO FINISH:
30 MINUTES

MAKES:
4 SERVINGS

1 pound unseasoned meat loaf mix (⅓ pound each ground beef, pork, and veal), lean ground beef, or ground pork

⅓ cup chopped onion (1 small)

2 15-ounce cans Great Northern beans or white beans, rinsed and drained

1 16-ounce jar green salsa

1 14-ounce can reduced-sodium chicken broth

1½ teaspoons ground cumin

2 tablespoons snipped fresh cilantro

¼ cup dairy sour cream (optional)

1. In a 4-quart Dutch oven cook ground meat and onion over medium heat about 5 minutes or until brown. Drain off fat. Add beans, salsa, broth, and cumin. Bring to boiling; reduce heat. Simmer, covered, for 15 minutes.

2. To serve, stir 1 tablespoon of the cilantro into the chili. Divide chili among 4 soup bowls. Sprinkle with remaining cilantro. If desired, top with sour cream.

Per serving: 440 cal., 15 g total fat (5 g sat. fat), 81 mg chol., 1,256 mg sodium, 41 g carbo., 13 g fiber, 32 g pro.

MENU
Corn chips
Mixed greens salad with desired dressing
Pumpkin pie

13

Beef and Three-Cheese Tortellini Salad

START TO FINISH:
30 MINUTES

MAKES:
4 SERVINGS

2   cups refrigerated or frozen cheese-filled tortellini (about 9 ounces)
8   ounces cooked beef or cooked ham, cut into thin strips (1½ cups)
1   cup packaged Colby Jack or cheddar cheese cubes
1   cup packaged broccoli florets
1   small yellow summer squash or zucchini, halved lengthwise and sliced (1 cup)
½   cup bottled Parmesan Italian salad dressing
     Leaf lettuce
     Cherry tomatoes, halved (optional)

1. Cook tortellini according to package directions. Drain tortellini. Rinse with cold water; drain again.

2. In a large bowl combine tortellini, meat strips, cheese, broccoli, and squash. Drizzle salad dressing over beef mixture; toss gently to coat. Quick-chill in the freezer for 10 minutes or until ready to serve (or chill in the refrigerator for 4 to 24 hours).

3. To serve, line 4 salad plates with leaf lettuce. Divide beef mixture among plates. If desired, garnish with cherry tomatoes.

Per serving: 498 cal., 28 g total fat (12 g sat. fat), 97 mg chol., 822 mg sodium, 30 g carbo., 3 g fiber, 31 g pro.

MENU
Focaccia
Fresh pear slices and cheese plate

14

Easy Pot Roast with Fruit

START TO FINISH:
25 MINUTES

MAKES:
4 SERVINGS

1 17-ounce package refrigerated cooked beef pot roast with juices
1 tablespoon butter or margarine
2 tablespoons minced shallot
2 tablespoons tarragon vinegar
2 cups fresh fruit wedges (such as apples, plums, and peaches)
1 teaspoon snipped fresh tarragon (optional)

1. Remove meat from package, reserving juices. In a large skillet melt butter over medium heat. Add shallot and cook in hot butter for 1 minute. Add pot roast; reduce heat. Simmer, covered, about 10 minutes or until heated through.

2. In a small bowl stir together reserved meat juices and tarragon vinegar. Pour over meat. Spoon fruit on top. Cover; heat for 2 minutes more. Sprinkle with snipped tarragon.

Per serving: 230 cal., 8 g total fat (3 g sat. fat), 72 mg chol., 386 mg sodium, 15 g carbo., 2 g fiber, 23 g pro.

MENU
Multigrain rolls
Hot cooked noodles
Steamed broccoli

15

Chipotle Brisket Sandwiches

START TO FINISH:
15 MINUTES

MAKES:
6 SANDWICHES

1 pound refrigerated cooked beef with barbecue sauce

1 to 2 canned chipotle peppers in adobo sauce, chopped

½ of a 16-ounce package shredded cabbage with carrot (coleslaw mix) (about 4 cups)

⅓ cup bottled coleslaw dressing

6 kaiser rolls, split and toasted

1. In a large saucepan combine beef with barbecue sauce and chipotle peppers. Cook and stir about 5 minutes or until heated through.

2. Meanwhile, in a large bowl combine coleslaw mix and coleslaw dressing.

3. To serve, spoon beef mixture onto roll bottoms. Top with coleslaw mixture and roll tops.

Per sandwich: 406 cal., 17 g total fat (5 g sat. fat), 37 mg chol., 1,050 mg sodium, 47 g carbo., 2 g fiber, 16 g pro.

MENU
Multigrain chips
Fresh apple and pear slices
Tapioca pudding

Easy Meatball Panini

16

START TO FINISH:
25 MINUTES

MAKES:
4 SANDWICHES

16 frozen Italian-style cooked meatballs (about 1 pound)

1 15-ounce can pizza sauce

4 Italian rolls or hoagie buns

4 slices provolone cheese

1 cup loosely packed large basil or spinach leaves

1. Preheat broiler. In a large saucepan combine meatballs and pizza sauce. Cook, covered, over medium-low heat about 10 minutes or until heated through, stirring occasionally.

2. Meanwhile, cut a thin slice from the tops of the rolls; hollow out rolls leaving a ¼- to ½-inch-thick shell. (Discard or save bread from rolls for another use.) Place hollowed-out rolls and roll tops, cut sides up, on a baking sheet. Broil 3 to 4 inches from the heat for 1 to 2 minutes or until lightly toasted. Remove roll tops from baking sheet.

3. Spoon meatballs and sauce into toasted roll shells. Top with cheese. Broil about 1 minute more or until cheese is melted. To serve, place basil leaves on top of cheese and replace roll tops.

Per sandwich: 740 cal., 38 g total fat (18 g sat. fat), 98 mg chol., 1,570 mg sodium, 63 g carbo., 8 g fiber, 36 g pro.

MENU
Potato chips
Pasta salad (from a deli)
Chocolate chip cookies

17

Saucy Meatball Sandwiches

START TO FINISH:
20 MINUTES

MAKES:
6 SANDWICHES

18 frozen Italian-style cooked meatballs (about 1 ounce each)
1 26- to 28-ounce jar red pasta sauce
½ cup coarsely chopped onion (1 medium)
6 hoagie buns, split and toasted
1 cup shredded Italian 4-cheese blend (4 ounces)

1. In a large saucepan combine frozen meatballs, pasta sauce, and onion. Bring to boiling; reduce heat. Simmer, covered, about 10 minutes or until meatballs are heated through, stirring occasionally.

2. Spoon hot meatball mixture onto bottom halves of rolls. Spoon any remaining sauce over the meatballs. Sprinkle cheese over the meatballs. Top with bun halves. Let stand for 1 to 2 minutes before serving.

Per sandwich: 802 cal., 36 g total fat (14 g sat. fat), 74 mg chol., 2,293 mg sodium, 88 g carbo., 9 g fiber, 32 g pro.

MENU
Corn chips
Carrot and celery sticks
Hot fudge sundaes

Pork with Apples

18

START TO FINISH:
25 MINUTES

MAKES:
4 SERVINGS

1   pound pork tenderloin

2   tablespoons olive oil, butter, or margarine

1   teaspoon bottled minced garlic (2 cloves)

1   20-ounce can sliced apples, drained

2   teaspoons snipped fresh thyme or ½ teaspoon dried thyme, crushed

1. Trim fat from meat. Cut meat crosswise into ½-inch slices. Set aside.

2. In a 12-inch skillet heat olive oil over medium-high heat. Add garlic; cook for 15 seconds. Add pork slices; reduce heat to medium. Cook about 4 minutes or until pork slices are no longer pink and juices run clear, turning once halfway through cooking. Add drained apples and thyme. Cover and cook about 1 minute or until apples are heated through.

Per serving: 292 cal., 11 g total fat (2 g sat. fat), 73 mg chol., 61 mg sodium, 24 g carbo., 2 g fiber, 24 g pro.

MENU
Hot cooked noodles
Steamed green beans
Cinnamon ice cream with caramel sauce

19

Cranberry-Sauced Pork and Sweet Potatoes

START TO FINISH:
20 MINUTES

MAKES:
4 SERVINGS

4   boneless pork loin chops, cut ¾ inch thick (about 1 pound)
    Nonstick cooking spray
1   17-ounce can vacuum-pack sweet potatoes
1   tablespoon butter or margarine
1   cup orange juice
¼   cup dried cranberries

1. Trim fat from chops. Sprinkle chops lightly with *salt* and *black pepper*. Lightly coat an unheated large skillet with cooking spray. Preheat skillet over medium-high heat. Add chops; reduce heat to medium. Cook for 8 to 12 minutes or until chops are 160°F, turning once halfway through cooking.

2. Meanwhile, place sweet potatoes in a medium saucepan. Mash with a potato masher. Stir in butter. Cook and stir over medium heat until potatoes are heated through. If desired, season to taste with salt and black pepper.

3. Remove chops from skillet, reserving drippings; cover chops to keep warm. Add orange juice and cranberries to drippings in skillet. Bring to boiling; reduce heat. Simmer, uncovered, about 7 minutes or until liquid is reduced by half. Transfer chops to dinner plates; spoon sauce over chops. Serve with mashed sweet potatoes.

Per serving: 341 cal., 8 g total fat (4 g sat. fat), 78 mg chol., 226 mg sodium, 38 g carbo., 3 g fiber, 27 g pro.

MENU
Whole wheat rolls
Steamed mixed vegetables
Apple and cranberry crisp

Peppered Pork Chops and Pilaf

20

START TO FINISH:
25 MINUTES

MAKES:
4 SERVINGS

4   boneless pork loin chops, cut ¾-inch thick
2   teaspoons seasoned pepper blend
1   tablespoon olive oil
3   cups vegetables, such as broccoli, carrots, mushrooms, onions, and/or sweet peppers, cut into bite-size pieces
1   14-ounce can chicken broth
2   cups uncooked instant brown rice
¼   cup bottled roasted red sweet pepper, drained and cut into strips

1. Trim fat from chops. Sprinkle both sides of meat with seasoned pepper blend. In a large skillet heat oil over medium-high heat. Add chops; reduce heat to medium. Cook chops for 8 to 12 minutes or until 160°F, turning once halfway through cooking. Remove chops from skillet, reserving drippings; cover chops to keep warm.

2. Add vegetables, broth, and uncooked rice to skillet. Bring to boiling; reduce heat. Simmer, covered, for 5 to 7 minutes or until rice is done and vegetables are crisp-tender. Return pork chops to skillet; cover and heat through. Garnish with roasted red pepper strips.

Per serving: 304 cal., 9 g total fat (2 g sat. fat), 47 mg chol., 607 mg sodium, 31 g carbo., 4 g fiber, 25 g pro.

MENU
Sourdough bread
Spinach and tomato salad with vinaigrette dressing
Cinnamon ice cream

21 Maple-Glazed Pork Chops

START TO FINISH:
20 MINUTES

MAKES:
4 SERVINGS

4   boneless pork loin chops, cut about ¾ inch thick
4   tablespoons butter or margarine, softened
2   tablespoons pure maple syrup or maple-flavor syrup
⅓   cup chopped pecans, toasted

1. Trim fat from chops. Sprinkle both sides of chops with *salt* and *black pepper.* In a 12-inch skillet melt 1 tablespoon of the butter over medium-high heat. Add chops; reduce heat to medium. Cook the chops for 8 to 12 minutes or until chops are 160°F, turning once halfway through cooking. Transfer chops to dinner plates.

2. Meanwhile, in a small bowl combine the remaining 3 tablespoons butter and the maple syrup. Spread butter mixture evenly over chops. Let stand for 1 minute or until melted. Sprinkle with pecans.

Per serving: 333 cal., 23 g total fat (10 g sat. fat), 98 mg chol., 310 mg sodium, 8 g carbo., 1 g fiber, 23 g pro.

MENU
Multigrain rolls
Roasted acorn squash wedges
Steamed broccoli spears

Pork Chops with Pear Sauce

22

4   boneless pork loin chops, cut ¾ inch thick
½   teaspoon salt
½   teaspoon black pepper
1   tablespoon olive oil
¼   cup butter or margarine
3   tablespoons pure maple syrup or maple-flavor syrup
3   tablespoons peach, apricot, or plum preserves or jam
1½ teaspoons snipped fresh basil or ½ teaspoon dried basil, crushed
3   medium pears, cored and thinly sliced

1. Trim fat from chops. Season chops with salt and pepper. In a 10-inch skillet heat oil over medium-high heat. Add chops; reduce heat to medium. Cook chops for 8 to 12 minutes or until 160°F, turning once halfway through cooking. Remove chops from skillet; cover chops to keep warm.

2. For sauce, in the same skillet melt butter over medium heat. Stir in maple syrup, peach preserves, and basil. Add pears. Cook, covered, about 3 minutes or just until pears are tender and heated through, occasionally spooning sauce over pears. Serve pear sauce over chops.

Per serving: 495 cal., 23 g total fat (11 g sat. fat), 108 mg chol., 437 mg sodium, 40 g carbo., 4 g fiber, 32 g pro.

MENU
Mixed greens salad with vinaigrette dressing
Dutch apple pie

23 Oven-Fried Pork Chops

PREP:
10 MINUTES

BAKE:
20 MINUTES

OVEN:
425°F

MAKES:
4 SERVINGS

3   tablespoons butter or margarine

1   egg

2   tablespoons milk

1   cup packaged corn bread stuffing mix

4   pork loin chops, cut ½ inch thick

1. Preheat oven to 425°F. Place butter in a 13x9x2-inch baking pan; place in the preheated oven about 3 minutes or until butter melts.

2. Meanwhile, in a shallow dish beat egg with a fork; stir in milk. Place dry stuffing mix in another shallow dish. Dip pork chops into egg mixture. Coat both sides with stuffing mix. Place chops in the baking pan with the butter.

3. Bake, uncovered, for 10 minutes. Turn chops. Bake for 10 to 15 minutes more or until 160°F and juices run clear.

Per serving: 326 cal., 16 g total fat (8 g sat. fat), 131 mg chol., 392 mg sodium, 17 g carbo., 0 g fiber, 26 g pro.

MENU
Crusty dinner rolls
Steamed peas
Applesauce

Pork and Sweet Potato Stir-Fry

24

START TO FINISH:
25 MINUTES

MAKES:
4 SERVINGS

1½ cups uncooked instant white rice
¼ cup thinly sliced green onion (2)
1 large sweet potato (about 12 ounces)
1 medium tart apple (such as Granny Smith)
12 ounces packaged pork stir-fry strips
2 to 3 teaspoons Jamaican jerk seasoning
1 tablespoon cooking oil
⅓ cup water

1. Prepare rice according to package directions. Stir half of the green onion into the cooked rice.

2. Meanwhile, peel sweet potato. Cut into quarters lengthwise, then thinly slice crosswise. Place in a microwave-safe pie plate or shallow dish. Cover with vented plastic wrap. Microwave on 100% power (high) for 3 to 4 minutes or until tender, stirring once. Remove core from apple; cut apple into 16 wedges. Sprinkle meat strips with Jamaican jerk seasoning; toss to coat.

3. In a wok or large skillet heat oil over medium-high heat. Add meat and stir-fry for 2 minutes (add more oil if necessary during cooking). Add apple and remaining green onion. Stir-fry for 1 to 2 minutes more or until no pink remains.

4. Stir in sweet potato and water. Bring to boiling; reduce heat. Simmer, uncovered, for 1 minute. Serve immediately over hot cooked rice mixture.

Per serving: 365 cal., 9 g total fat (2 g sat. fat), 38 mg chol., 131 mg sodium, 54 g carbo., 3 g fiber, 16 g pro.

MENU
Warm pita bread
Spinach salad with desired dressing
Figs and dates

25

Quick Pork and Bean Soup

START TO FINISH:
30 MINUTES

MAKES:
4 SERVINGS

2 tablespoons cooking oil

12 ounces packaged pork stir-fry strips

1 cup chopped onion (1 large)

2 cups water

1 11.5-ounce can condensed bean with bacon soup

1½ cups sliced carrot (3 medium)

1 teaspoon Worcestershire sauce

¼ teaspoon dry mustard

1. In a large skillet heat oil over medium-high heat. Add pork and onion; cook and stir for 3 to 4 minutes or until no pink remains in meat.

2. Stir in water, soup, carrot, Worcestershire sauce, and dry mustard. Bring to boiling; reduce heat. Simmer, covered, for 15 minutes.

Per serving: 312 cal., 13 g total fat (3 g sat. fat), 52 mg chol., 678 mg sodium, 23 g carbo., 6 g fiber, 24 g pro.

MENU
Crusty rolls
Coleslaw (from a deli)
Chocolate cake

Cavatappi with Tomatoes and Ham

26

START TO FINISH:
30 MINUTES

MAKES:
4 SERVINGS

1 medium onion, cut into ¼-inch slices

12 red and/or yellow cherry and/or pear tomatoes, halved

8 ounces dried cavatappi or gemelli pasta

¼ teaspoon crushed red pepper (optional)

2 ounces thinly sliced cooked ham, cut into strips

3 tablespoons thinly sliced fresh basil

2 tablespoons garlic-flavor olive oil or olive oil

1. Preheat broiler. Place onion slices on the foil-lined rack of an unheated broiler pan. Broil onion slices 4 inches from heat for 5 minutes. Add tomato halves to pan; broil about 5 minutes more or until edges are brown.

2. Meanwhile, cook pasta according to package directions, adding crushed red pepper (if desired) to the water. Drain well. Return pasta to pan; cover and keep warm.

3. Cut up onion slices. Toss onion pieces and tomato halves with pasta. Add ham, basil, and olive oil; toss to mix.

Per serving: 341 cal., 11 g total fat (2 g sat. fat), 16 mg chol., 381 mg sodium, 47 g carbo., 2 g fiber, 13 g pro.

MENU
Country Italian bread
Caesar salad
Pumpkin cake

27

Ham and Beans with Spinach

START TO FINISH:
20 MINUTES

MAKES:
4 SERVINGS

2   15-ounce cans Great Northern beans

1   tablespoon olive oil

1   tablespoon bottled minced garlic (6 cloves)

2   cups cooked smoked ham cut into bite-size strips

3   cups chopped packaged prewashed fresh spinach

1. Drain beans, reserving liquid. In a large nonstick skillet heat olive oil over medium heat. Add garlic; cook and stir for 1 minute. Add beans and ham to skillet. Cook about 5 minutes or until heated through, stirring occasionally.

2. Stir spinach into bean mixture in skillet; cover and cook for 2 to 5 minutes more or until greens are wilted. If desired, thin mixture with some of the reserved bean liquid.

Per serving: 324 cal., 8 g total fat (2 g sat. fat), 39 mg chol., 1,443 mg sodium, 33 g carbo., 11 g fiber, 29 g pro.

MENU
Breadsticks
Mashed sweet potatoes
Sauteed apples with cinnamon ice cream

Grilled Ham-on-Rye Special

28

PREP:
15 MINUTES

COOK:
4 MINUTES

MAKES:
4 SANDWICHES

¼ cup bottled Thousand Island salad dressing

1 teaspoon yellow mustard

1 cup packaged shredded cabbage with carrot (coleslaw mix)

1 tablespoon butter or margarine

8 slices rye, marble rye, or whole wheat bread

4 ounces thinly sliced cooked ham

4 ounces thinly sliced Swiss, mozzarella, or Colby cheese

1. In a small bowl stir together salad dressing and mustard. Stir in shredded cabbage with carrot; mix well.

2. Spread a thin layer of butter on one side of each bread slice; turn bread over. Top 4 of the bread slices with half of the ham. Add cabbage mixture, spreading evenly; top with cheese and remaining ham. Top with remaining bread slices, butter side up.

3. Heat a large skillet or griddle over medium-low heat. Place sandwiches in skillet. Cook for 2 to 3 minutes or until golden. Turn sandwiches over; cook for 2 to 3 minutes more or until bread is golden and cheese starts to melt.

Per sandwich: 409 cal., 21 g total fat (9 g sat. fat), 54 mg chol., 1,023 mg sodium, 37 g carbo., 5 g fiber, 18 g pro.

MENU
Potato chips
Dill pickles
Fresh pear slices and dried dates

29 Ham and Cheese Quesadillas

START TO FINISH:
20 MINUTES

MAKES:
4 SERVINGS

¾ cup shredded Swiss, Monterey Jack, or cheddar cheese (3 ounces)

4 7- to 8-inch whole wheat, spinach, tomato, or plain flour tortillas

3 ounces thinly sliced cooked ham

⅔ cup chopped tomato

2 tablespoons sliced green onion (optional)

1. Sprinkle cheese over half of each tortilla. Top with ham, tomato, and, if desired, green onion. Fold tortillas in half, pressing together gently.

2. In a 10-inch nonstick skillet cook quesadillas, two at a time, over medium heat for 1½ to 2 minutes per side or until light brown. Cut into wedges.

Per serving: 260 cal., 10 g total fat (5 g sat. fat), 31 mg chol., 699 mg sodium, 29 g carbo., 3 g fiber, 13 g pro.

MENU
Tortilla chips with salsa
Refried beans
Spanish rice (from a mix)

Creamy Ham and Vegetable Chowder

30

START TO FINISH:
20 MINUTES

MAKES:
4 SERVINGS

1½ cups water

2 carrots, peeled and cut into ½-inch pieces

1 cup refrigerated diced potatoes

1 medium onion, cut into chunks

1 10.75-ounce can reduced-fat and reduced-sodium condensed cream of celery soup

1 cup cubed cooked ham

1 cup frozen peas

½ of an 8-ounce jar process cheese dip (½ cup)

1. In a large saucepan bring water to boiling. Add carrot, potato, and onion. Return to boiling; reduce heat. Simmer, covered, for 8 minutes. Add soup, ham, peas, and cheese dip. Cook and stir for 4 to 5 minutes or until heated through.

Per serving: 244 cal., 11 g total fat (6 g sat. fat), 48 mg chol., 1,201 mg sodium, 27 g carbo., 4 g fiber, 11 g pro.

MENU
Breadsticks
Romaine salad with desired dressing
Chocolate cupcakes

31

Sausage and Cavatelli Skillet

START TO FINISH:
20 MINUTES

MAKES:
4 SERVINGS

8 ounces dried cavatelli (about 1¾ cups)

1 pound bulk Italian sausage or ground beef

¾ cup chopped green sweet pepper (1 medium)

1 20-ounce jar pasta sauce with mushrooms

1 cup shredded mozzarella cheese (4 ounces)

1. Cook pasta according to package directions; drain well. Return pasta to pan; cover and keep warm.

2. Meanwhile, in a large skillet cook meat and sweet pepper until meat is brown. Drain off fat. Stir in pasta sauce; cook about 2 minutes or until heated through. Stir in drained pasta. Sprinkle with cheese. Cover and cook about 2 minutes more or until cheese is melted.

Per serving: 677 cal., 32 g total fat (13 g sat. fat), 93 mg chol., 1,469 mg sodium, 60 g carbo., 4 g fiber, 32 g pro.

MENU
Focaccia
Deli marinated-vegetable salad
Apple cake

Hot and Saucy Tortellini

32

START TO FINISH:
25 MINUTES

MAKES:
4 SERVINGS

7   to 8 ounces dried cheese-filled tortellini (about 1¾ cups)
8   ounces bulk Italian sausage
1   16-ounce jar salsa
1   13- to 14-ounce jar red pasta sauce
2   tablespoons snipped fresh cilantro

1. Cook tortellini according to package directions; drain well. Return tortellini to pan; cover and keep warm.

2. Meanwhile, in a large skillet cook sausage until brown; drain off fat. Stir salsa and pasta sauce into sausage in skillet. Bring to boiling; reduce heat. Simmer, covered, for 5 minutes. Stir cooked tortellini and 1 tablespoon of the cilantro into sauce mixture; heat through. Sprinkle individual servings with the remaining 1 tablespoon cilantro.

Per serving: 450 cal., 20 g total fat (5 g sat. fat), 38 mg chol., 1,848 mg sodium, 42 g carbo., 3 g fiber, 21 g pro.

MENU
Crusty Italian bread
Caesar salad
Carrot cake

33

Sausage, Bean, and Spinach Soup

START TO FINISH:
25 MINUTES

MAKES:
4 SERVINGS

8 ounces hot or mild bulk pork sausage

½ cup chopped onion (1 medium)

2 19-ounce cans white kidney (cannellini) beans, rinsed and drained

2 cups coarsely chopped packaged prewashed spinach or coarsely chopped escarole

1 14-ounce can reduced-sodium chicken broth

¼ cup dry white wine or reduced-sodium chicken broth

1 tablespoon snipped fresh thyme or 1 teaspoon dried thyme, crushed

¼ cup finely shredded Parmesan cheese (1 ounce) (optional)

1. In a large saucepan cook sausage and onion over medium heat about 5 minutes or until sausage is brown and onion is tender. Drain off fat.

2. Add beans, escarole (if using), chicken broth, wine, and dried thyme (if using). Bring to boiling; reduce heat. Simmer, covered, for 5 minutes. Stir in spinach and fresh thyme (if using). Heat through. If desired, sprinkle individual servings with Parmesan cheese.

Per serving: 357 cal., 16 g total fat (5 g sat. fat), 41 mg chol., 1,021 mg sodium, 39 g carbo., 13 g fiber, 25 g pro.

MENU
Multigrain rolls
Cheesecake with
raspberry jam

Nuevo Pork and Bean Sandwiches

34

START TO FINISH:
20 MINUTES

MAKES:
6 SANDWICHES

6   ounces chorizo sausage or bulk Italian sausage
1   16-ounce can refried beans
1   4.5-ounce can diced green chile peppers, drained
3   8-inch pieces baguette-style French bread, split and toasted
1   cup red and/or green sweet pepper strips
½   cup shredded Monterey Jack cheese (2 ounces)

1. Remove casings from sausage, if present. In a large skillet cook sausage over medium heat until brown. Drain sausage well in a colander; wipe skillet with paper towels. Return sausage to skillet. Stir in refried beans and chile peppers. Heat through.

2. Preheat broiler. Spread sausage mixture on bottom halves of bread. Place on the unheated rack of a broiler pan. Top with sweet pepper strips and cheese.

3. Broil about 4 inches from the heat for 1 to 2 minutes or until cheese is melted. Replace top halves of bread. Cut each portion in half crosswise.

Per sandwich: 311 cal., 15 g total fat (6 g sat. fat), 7 mg chol., 865 mg sodium, 53 g carbo., 4 g fiber, 20 g pro.

MENU
Tortilla chips with salsa
Avocado slices
Hot fudge sundaes

35 Black Bean and Kielbasa Soup

START TO FINISH:
15 MINUTES

MAKES:
5 SERVINGS

2   15- to 18.5-ounce cans ready-to-serve black bean soup

1   14.5-ounce can diced tomatoes with garlic and onion, undrained

12 ounces cooked, smoked Polish sausage, halved lengthwise and cut into ½-inch slices

1   cup frozen whole kernel corn

1. In a large saucepan stir together soup, undrained tomatoes, sausage, and corn. Bring to boiling; reduce heat. Simmer, covered, about 10 minutes or until heated through.

Per serving: 414 cal., 22 g total fat (7 g sat. fat), 48 mg chol., 1,624 mg sodium, 36 g carbo., 13 g fiber, 18 g pro.

MENU

Corn bread

Mixed greens salad with desired dressing

Purchased pumpkin pie

Corn and Bacon Chowder 36

START TO FINISH:
25 MINUTES

MAKES:
4 TO 6 SERVINGS

5 slices bacon, chopped
1 medium onion, halved and thinly sliced
2 cups milk
2 cups frozen whole kernel corn
1 10.75-ounce can condensed cream of mushroom soup
1 cup diced cooked potato
¼ teaspoon black pepper

1. In a large saucepan cook bacon until crisp. Remove bacon with a slotted spoon, reserving 2 tablespoons of the drippings in the saucepan. Drain bacon on paper towels; set aside.

2. Cook onion rings in reserved drippings over medium heat until tender. Stir in milk, corn, soup, potato, and pepper.

3. Bring to boiling; reduce heat. Simmer, uncovered, for 2 to 3 minutes. Remove from heat. Top individual servings with crumbled bacon.

Per serving: 329 cal., 18 g total fat (7 g sat. fat), 24 mg chol., 750 mg sodium, 34 g carbo., 2 g fiber, 11 g pro.

MENU
Rye or pumpernickel bread
Spinach salad with desired dressing
Blonde brownies

37 Hot Apple and Cheese Sandwiches

START TO FINISH:
25 MINUTES

MAKES:
4 SANDWICHES

1 medium apple or pear
4 whole wheat or plain English muffins, split
2 tablespoons Dijon-style mustard
4 slices Canadian-style bacon
4 slices Swiss cheese
Apple chunks (optional)

1. Core apple and thinly slice crosswise to form rings. Spread cut sides of English muffin halves with mustard.

2. Top 4 of the muffin halves with a slice of bacon, 1 or 2 apple rings, and a slice of cheese. Top with remaining muffin halves, cut sides down.

3. Heat a large nonstick skillet or griddle. Place sandwiches in skillet or on griddle. Cook over medium-low heat for 9 to 10 minutes or until sandwiches are golden brown and cheese starts to melt, turning once halfway through cooking. If desired, garnish sandwiches with apple chunks.

Per sandwich: 303 cal., 11 g total fat (6 g sat. fat), 40 mg chol., 851 mg sodium, 34 g carbo., 3 g fiber, 20 g pro.

MENU
- Multigrain chips
- Dill pickles
- Carrot and celery sticks with vegetable dip
- Cookies

Canadian Bacon Pizza

38

PREP:
15 MINUTES

BAKE:
15 MINUTES

OVEN:
350°F

MAKES:
4 TO 6 SERVINGS

1   16-ounce package Italian bread shell (such as Boboli brand)
1   6-ounce jar marinated artichoke hearts
1   5.2-ounce container semisoft cheese with garlic and herb
1   3.5-ounce package pizza-style Canadian-style bacon (1½-inch-diameter slices)
1   medium sweet pepper, cut into bite-size strips

1. Preheat oven to 350°F. Place the bread shell on a large baking sheet. Drain artichoke hearts, reserving 1 tablespoon of the marinade. Coarsely chop artichokes; set aside.

2. In a small bowl combine cheese and reserved marinade. Spread half of the cheese mixture over bread shell; top with Canadian bacon, sweet pepper, and artichoke hearts. Spoon remaining cheese mixture by teaspoons over toppings.

3. Bake about 15 minutes or until heated through.

Per serving: 529 cal., 24 g total fat (9 g sat. fat), 54 mg chol., 1,136 mg sodium, 58 g carbo., 2 g fiber, 23 g pro.

MENU
Mixed greens salad with desired dressing
Lemon cake

39 Lamb Chops with Cinnamon Apples

START TO FINISH:
25 MINUTES

MAKES:
4 SERVINGS

8 lamb loin chops, cut 1 inch thick
1 tablespoon butter or margarine
1 tablespoon water
3 medium red cooking apples, cored and sliced (3 cups)
1 tablespoon packed brown sugar
¼ teaspoon salt
¼ teaspoon ground cinnamon

1. Trim fat from chops. In a large skillet melt butter over medium-high heat. Add chops; reduce heat to medium. Cook for 9 to 11 minutes for medium (160°F), turning once halfway through cooking. Remove chops from skillet, reserving drippings. Cover chops to keep warm.

2. Add water to skillet. Cook until bubbly, stirring to loosen any brown bits in bottom of skillet. Add apple slices. Cook about 5 minutes or until apples are tender, stirring occasionally. Add brown sugar, salt, and cinnamon. Cook and stir about 2 minutes or until sugar dissolves. Spoon apple mixture over chops.

Per serving: 394 cal., 14 g total fat (6 g sat. fat), 153 mg chol., 287 mg sodium, 19 g carbo., 4 g fiber, 47 g pro.

MENU
Warm pita bread
Roasted butternut squash chunks
Coconut ice cream with honey

Apple-Dijon Chicken

40

START TO FINISH:
30 MINUTES

MAKES:
4 SERVINGS

4   skinless, boneless chicken breast halves
2   tablespoons butter or margarine
1   medium tart cooking apple (such as Granny Smith), cut into thin wedges
⅓   cup whipping cream
2   tablespoons Dijon-style mustard

1. Butterfly cut each chicken breast half by cutting horizontally from one long side of the breast almost to, but not through, the opposite long side of the breast. Lay the breast open. Sprinkle both sides of chicken breasts with *salt* and *black pepper.*

2. In a large skillet melt 1 tablespoon of the butter over medium-high heat. Add 2 of the chicken breasts; cook for 4 to 6 minutes or until chicken is no longer pink (170F°), turning to brown evenly. Remove chicken from skillet; cover to keep warm. Repeat with remaining chicken.

3. Melt remaining 1 tablespoon butter in skillet. Add apple; cook and stir about 3 minutes or until tender. Add whipping cream and mustard to skillet. Cook and stir until heated through and slightly thickened. Season to taste with additional salt and pepper. Serve sauce and apples over chicken.

Per serving: 342 cal., 16 g total fat (9 g sat. fat), 142 mg chol., 407 mg sodium, 6 g carbo., 1 g fiber, 40 g pro.

MENU
Rice pilaf (from a mix)
Roasted Brussels sprouts
Chocolate silk pie

41

Chicken Breasts with Mozzarella

START TO FINISH:
30 MINUTES

MAKES:
4 SERVINGS

1   6-ounce package long grain and wild rice pilaf mix
1   cup packaged fresh broccoli florets
¼   cup thinly sliced green onion (2)
1   tablespoon olive oil or cooking oil
4   Italian-style or butter-garlic-marinated skinless, boneless chicken breast halves
1   medium tomato, cored, halved and thinly sliced
4   slices mozzarella cheese (3 ounces)

1. Prepare rice mix according to package directions, adding broccoli the last 5 minutes of cooking. Stir in green onion and set aside.

2. Meanwhile, preheat broiler. In a large broilerproof skillet heat oil over medium-high heat. Add chicken; reduce heat to medium. Cook for 8 to 12 minutes or until no longer pink (170°F), turning occasionally to brown evenly. If necessary, reduce heat to medium-low to prevent overbrowning. Remove skillet from heat.

3. Arrange halved tomato slices on chicken breast halves. Top with cheese. Broil chicken 3 to 4 inches from heat about 1 minute or until cheese is melted and brown. Serve chicken with rice mixture.

Per serving: 363 cal., 10 g total fat (4 g sat. fat), 73 mg chol., 1,269 mg sodium, 38 g carbo., 3 g fiber, 31 g pro.

MENU
Sourdough bread
Spinach salad with vinaigrette dressing
Apple pie

Chicken Veronique

42

START TO FINISH:
20 MINUTES

MAKES:
4 SERVINGS

4   skinless, boneless chicken breast halves
¼   teaspoon salt
¼   teaspoon black pepper
¼   cup butter
1   cup seedless red grapes, halved
3   tablespoons sherry vinegar or red wine vinegar
¼   teaspoon dried thyme, crushed

1. Sprinkle chicken with salt and pepper. In a large skillet melt 2 tablespoons of the butter over medium-high heat. Add chicken; reduce heat to medium. Cook for 8 to 12 minutes or until no longer pink (170°F), turning occasionally to brown evenly. Remove chicken from skillet; cover to keep warm.

2. For sauce, add the remaining 2 tablespoons butter, grapes, vinegar, and thyme to hot skillet. Cook until slightly thickened, stirring to loosen any brown bits in bottom of skillet. Serve sauce over chicken.

Per serving: 301 cal., 15 g total fat (8 g sat. fat), 115 mg chol., 348 mg sodium, 7 g carbo., 0 g fiber, 33 g pro.

MENU
French baguette slices
Hot cooked fettuccine
Steamed broccoli spears

43

Chicken and Shells Soup

START TO FINISH:
30 MINUTES

MAKES:
4 SERVINGS

2 14-ounce cans reduced-sodium chicken broth (3½ cups)

1 teaspoon dried Italian seasoning, crushed

½ teaspoon bottled minced garlic (1 clove)

12 ounces skinless, boneless chicken breast halves, cut into bite-size pieces

¾ cup dried small shell macaroni

¾ cup frozen peas

¼ cup thinly sliced green onion (2)

1. In a medium saucepan combine chicken broth, Italian seasoning, and garlic; bring to boiling. Add chicken and pasta. Return to boiling; reduce heat. Simmer, uncovered, for 8 to 9 minutes or until pasta is tender and chicken is no longer pink, stirring occasionally.

2. Add frozen peas and green onion; cook about 2 minutes more or until peas are crisp-tender.

Per serving: 211 cal., 2 g total fat (0 g sat. fat), 49 mg chol., 546 mg sodium, 21 g carbo., 2 g fiber, 27 g pro.

MENU

Mixed greens salad with desired dressing

Toasted garlic bread

Rice pudding with raisins

Chicken with Cranberry Sauce

44

START TO FINISH:
25 MINUTES

MAKES:
4 SERVINGS

1   tablespoon butter, margarine, or olive oil
4   skinless, boneless chicken breast halves
½   of a 16-ounce can (1 cup) whole cranberry sauce
2   tablespoons honey
½   teaspoon ground ginger

1. In a large skillet melt butter over medium-high heat. Add chicken; reduce heat to medium. Cook over medium heat for 8 to 12 minutes or until no longer pink (170°F), turning occasionally to brown evenly. If necessary, turn heat to medium-low to prevent overbrowning. Remove skillet from heat. Remove chicken from skillet, reserving drippings. Cover chicken to keep warm.

2. For sauce, add cranberry sauce, honey, and ginger to drippings in skillet. Cook and stir over medium-low heat until heated through. Serve sauce with chicken.

Per serving: 330 cal., 5 g total fat (2 g sat. fat), 90 mg chol., 127 mg sodium, 36 g carbo., 1 g fiber, 33 g pro.

MENU
Mashed sweet potatoes
Steamed green beans
Pecan pie

45 Chicken with Herb Rub

START TO FINISH:
20 MINUTES

MAKES:
4 SERVINGS

½ cup snipped fresh mint

2 tablespoons sesame seeds

2 to 4 teaspoons fennel seeds, crushed

2 teaspoons dried thyme, crushed

1 teaspoon salt

¼ teaspoon black pepper

4 skinless, boneless chicken breast halves

1 tablespoon olive oil or cooking oil

1. For rub, in a small bowl combine mint, sesame seeds, fennel seeds, thyme, salt, and pepper. Sprinkle rub evenly over chicken; rub in with your fingers.

2. In a large skillet heat oil over medium-high heat. Add chicken; reduce heat to medium. Cook for 8 to 12 minutes or until no longer pink (170°F), turning occasionally to brown evenly.

Per serving: 228 cal., 8 g total fat (1 g sat. fat), 82 mg chol., 662 mg sodium, 2 g carbo., 1 g fiber, 34 g pro.

MENU
Roasted potatoes
Steamed mixed vegetables
Pumpkin bars

Chicken with Dried Fruit and Honey

46

START TO FINISH:
25 MINUTES

MAKES:
4 SERVINGS

8   skinless, boneless chicken thighs
½   teaspoon pumpkin pie spice or ¼ teaspoon ground ginger
1   tablespoon butter or margarine
1   cup mixed dried fruit bits
⅓   cup water
¼   cup honey

1. Sprinkle 1 side of each chicken thigh with pumpkin pie spice. In a 12-inch skillet melt butter over medium-high heat. Add chicken thighs; reduce heat to medium. Cook about 4 minutes or until brown, turning occasionally.

2. Stir fruit bits, water, and honey into skillet. Bring to boiling; reduce heat. Simmer, covered, for 10 to 15 minutes or until chicken is no longer pink (180°F).

Per serving: 381 cal., 9 g total fat (4 g sat. fat), 149 mg chol., 171 mg sodium, 41 g carbo., 0 g fiber, 35 g pro.

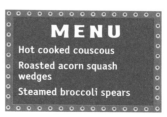

MENU
Hot cooked couscous
Roasted acorn squash wedges
Steamed broccoli spears

47

Golden Skillet Chicken

START TO FINISH:
20 MINUTES

MAKES:
4 SERVINGS

4   skinless, boneless chicken breast halves

1   10.75-ounce can condensed golden mushroom soup

¾   cup reduced-sodium chicken broth

½   of an 8-ounce tub cream cheese spread with chive and onion

2   cups hot cooked angel hair pasta or thin spaghetti

1. Heat a large nonstick skillet over medium-high heat for 1 minute. Add chicken; reduce heat to medium. Cook for 8 to 12 minutes or until no longer pink (170°F), turning occasionally to brown evenly. Remove chicken from skillet; cover to keep warm.

2. For sauce, add soup, chicken broth, and cream cheese to hot skillet. Cook and stir over medium heat until combined and mixture is heated through. Serve chicken and sauce over hot cooked pasta.

Per serving: 520 cal., 14 g total fat (8 g sat. fat), 113 mg chol., 906 mg sodium, 51 g carbo., 2 g fiber, 43 g pro.

MENU
Whole wheat rolls
Roasted Brussels sprouts
Cheesecake with caramel sauce

Chicken with Black Beans and Rice

48

2 tablespoons cooking oil

1 pound skinless, boneless chicken breast halves, cut into 2-inch pieces

1 6- to 7.4-ounce package Spanish rice mix

1¾ cups water

1 15-ounce can black beans, rinsed and drained

1 14.5-ounce can diced tomatoes, undrained

Sour cream, sliced green onion, and lime wedges (optional)

1. In a 12-inch skillet heat 1 tablespoon of the oil over medium-high heat. Add chicken; cook and stir until chicken is brown. Remove chicken from skillet.

2. Add rice mix and remaining 1 tablespoon oil to skillet; cook and stir for 2 minutes over medium heat. Stir in seasoning packet from rice mix, the water, beans, and undrained tomatoes; add chicken. Bring to boiling; reduce heat. Simmer, covered, for 15 to 20 minutes, or until rice is tender and chicken is no longer pink. Remove skillet from heat. Let stand, covered, for 5 minutes.

3. If desired, serve with sour cream, green onion, and lime wedges.

Per serving: 424 cal., 9 g total fat (2 g sat. fat), 66 mg chol., 1,080 mg sodium, 52 g carbo., 6 g fiber, 37 g pro.

MENU

Warm flour tortillas

Spinach salad with desired dressing

Cinnamon ice cream topped with warm apple pie filling

49

Chicken and Salsa Soup

START TO FINISH:
25 MINUTES

MAKES:
4 SERVINGS

1¾ cups water

1   14-ounce can reduced-sodium chicken broth

8   ounces skinless, boneless chicken breast halves or thighs, cut into bite-size pieces

1   to 2 teaspoons chili powder

1   11-ounce can whole kernel corn with sweet peppers, drained

1   cup chunky salsa

3   cups broken tortilla chips

½   cup shredded Monterey Jack cheese with jalapeño peppers (2 ounces)

1. In a 3-quart saucepan combine water, chicken broth, chicken, and chili powder. Bring to boiling; reduce heat. Simmer, covered, for 8 minutes. Add drained corn. Simmer, uncovered, about 5 minutes more or until chicken is no longer pink. Stir in salsa; heat through.

2. To serve, ladle soup into bowls. Top with crushed tortilla chips and sprinkle with the cheese.

Per serving: 284 cal., 6 g total fat (3 g sat. fat), 45 mg chol., 1,153 mg sodium, 27 g carbo., 3 g fiber, 22 g pro.

MENU

Corn bread sticks

Mixed greens salad with desired dressing

Cookies

Chicken and Pasta with Pesto Dressing

50

START TO FINISH:
30 MINUTES

MAKES:
4 SERVINGS

6 ounces dried wagon wheel macaroni or rotini (about 2 cups)

12 ounces skinless, boneless chicken breast halves, cut into 1-inch pieces

½ cup dairy sour cream

¼ cup refrigerated pesto sauce

1 cup chopped fresh vegetables, such as red, yellow, or green sweet pepper; broccoli; zucchini; or cucumber

⅓ cup chopped tomato (1 small)

¼ cup pine nuts or chopped walnuts, toasted (optional)

1. Cook pasta according to package directions, adding chicken the last 5 to 6 minutes of cooking. Cook until pasta is tender but firm and chicken is no longer pink. Drain pasta and chicken. Rinse with cold water; drain again.

2. In a large bowl stir together sour cream and pesto. Add pasta mixture, chopped fresh vegetables, and tomato. Toss to coat. If desired, sprinkle with nuts.

Per serving: 392 cal., 14 g total fat (5 g sat. fat), 65 mg chol., 218 mg sodium, 37 g carbo., 3 g fiber, 28 g pro.

MENU
Focaccia
Caesar salad
Cappuccino with biscotti

51

Mushroom and Tomato Pesto Pizza

PREP:
15 MINUTES

BAKE:
10 MINUTES

OVEN:
400°F

MAKES:
4 SERVINGS

1   12-inch Italian bread shell (such as Boboli brand)

½   cup purchased dried tomato pesto

1   cup shredded pizza cheese (4 ounces)

1   6-ounce package refrigerated Italian-seasoned cooked chicken breast strips

1½ cups sliced fresh shiitake, crimini, and/or button mushrooms

1. Preheat oven to 400°F. Place the bread shell on a 12-inch pizza pan. Spread pesto over bread shell. Sprinkle with half of the cheese. Top with the chicken strips and mushrooms. Sprinkle with remaining cheese.

2. Bake for 10 to 15 minutes or until pizza is heated through and cheese is melted.

Per serving: 585 cal., 24 g total fat (8 g sat. fat), 55 mg chol., 1,382 mg sodium, 64 g carbo., 4 g fiber, 33 g pro.

MENU
Pasta salad (from a deli)
Lemon cake with vanilla
ice cream

Golden-Crusted Chicken Pies

52

PREP:
15 MINUTES

BAKE:
12 MINUTES

OVEN:
375°F

MAKES:
4 SERVINGS

¾ cup milk

4 teaspoons all-purpose flour

¼ teaspoon black pepper

1 10.75-ounce can condensed minestrone soup

2 cups cubed cooked chicken or turkey (about 10 ounces)

1 3-ounce package cream cheese, cubed

1 package (5) refrigerated buttermilk or country-style biscuits

1. Preheat oven to 375°F. In a screw-top jar combine milk, flour, and pepper. Cover and shake well. In a medium saucepan stir milk mixture into minestrone soup. Cook and stir over medium heat until thickened and bubbly. Stir in chicken and cream cheese. Heat through, stirring to melt cream cheese.

2. Pour hot chicken mixture into 4 ungreased 10-ounce custard cups. Separate the biscuits; cut biscuits into quarters. Arrange 5 biscuit quarters on top of each custard cup.

3. Bake, uncovered, for 12 to 15 minutes or until biscuits are golden.

Per serving: 415 cal., 20 g total fat (8 g sat. fat), 92 mg chol., 1,139 mg sodium, 31 g carbo., 3 g fiber, 28 g pro.

MENU
Steamed mixed vegetables
Red and green grapes
Shortbread cookies and spiced apple cider

53 Pasta and Bean Chicken Soup

START TO FINISH:
25 MINUTES

MAKES:
5 SERVINGS

3½ cups reduced-sodium chicken broth

1 19-ounce can white kidney (cannellini) beans or one 15-ounce can
Great Northern beans, rinsed and drained

1 14.5-ounce can diced tomatoes with onion and garlic or diced tomatoes
with basil, oregano, and garlic, undrained

2 cups chopped cooked chicken (10 ounces)

1½ cups thinly sliced carrot (3)

1 cup water

1 cup dried ditalini or tiny bow ties (4 ounces)

¼ cup purchased pesto

1. In a large saucepan combine chicken broth, beans, undrained tomatoes, chicken, carrot, water, and pasta.

2. Bring to boiling; reduce heat. Simmer, covered, about 10 minutes or until pasta is tender but still firm. Stir in pesto.

Per serving: 323 cal., 12 g total fat (1 g sat. fat), 46 mg chol., 914 mg sodium, 33 g carbo., 5 g fiber, 25 g pro.

MENU
Focaccia
Apple cake

Curried Chicken Soup

54

START TO FINISH:
20 MINUTES

MAKES:
5 SERVINGS

5   cups water

1   3-ounce package chicken–flavor ramen noodles

2   to 3 teaspoons curry powder

1   cup packaged sliced fresh mushrooms

2   cups cubed cooked chicken (10 ounces)

⅔   cup coarsely chopped apple (1 medium)

1   8-ounce can sliced water chestnuts, drained

1. In a large saucepan combine water, the flavoring packet from the ramen noodles, and the curry powder. Bring to boiling.

2. Break up noodles and stir into mixture in saucepan; add mushrooms. Return to boiling; reduce heat. Simmer, uncovered, for 3 minutes.

3. Stir in chicken, apple, and water chestnuts; heat through. Season to taste with *salt* and *black pepper*.

Per serving: 179 cal., 6 g total fat (1 g sat. fat), 50 mg chol., 329 mg sodium, 13 g carbo., 2 g fiber, 18 g pro.

MENU
Warm pita bread
Pineapple sorbet with toasted coconut

55

Chicken and Vegetable Soup

START TO FINISH:
25 MINUTES

MAKES:
4 SERVINGS

1   16-ounce package frozen Italian vegetables (zucchini, carrots, cauliflower, lima beans, and Italian beans)

1   14.5-ounce can Italian-style stewed tomatoes, undrained

1   12-ounce can vegetable juice

1   cup chicken broth

1½ cups chopped cooked chicken (about 8 ounces)

1. In a large saucepan combine frozen vegetables, undrained tomatoes, vegetable juice, and chicken broth.

2. Bring to boiling; reduce heat. Simmer, covered, about 10 minutes or until vegetables are tender. Stir in chicken; heat through.

Per serving: 206 cal., 5 g total fat (1 g sat. fat), 47 mg chol., 784 mg sodium, 18 g carbo., 4 g fiber, 18 g pro.

MENU
Sourdough rolls
Cheese plate
Baked apples

Simply Ramen Chicken Soup

56

START TO FINISH:
15 MINUTES

MAKES:
4 SERVINGS

2   14-ounce cans reduced-sodium chicken broth
2   3-ounce packages chicken-flavor ramen noodles
½   teaspoon dried oregano or basil, crushed
1   10-ounce package frozen cut broccoli
2   cups shredded cooked chicken or turkey (about 10 ounces)
¼   cup sliced almonds, toasted

1. In a large saucepan combine chicken broth, seasoning packets from ramen noodles, and oregano. Bring to boiling.

2. Break up noodles. Add noodles and broccoli to mixture in saucepan. Return to boiling; reduce heat. Simmer, uncovered, for 3 minutes. Stir in chicken; heat through. Sprinkle individual servings with almonds.

Per serving: 416 cal., 18 g total fat (2 g sat. fat), 62 mg chol., 1,300 mg sodium, 32 g carbo., 3 g fiber, 30 g pro.

MENU
Egg rolls (frozen or takeout)
Almond cookies and chocolate ice cream

57 Hot Sandwich Loaf

PREP:
10 MINUTES

BAKE:
15 MINUTES

OVEN:
375°F

MAKES:
6 SANDWICHES

¼ cup creamy Dijon-style mustard blend

1 tablespoon prepared horseradish (optional)

1 unsliced loaf Italian bread (about 12 inches long)

1 6-ounce package Swiss cheese slices

2 2.5-ounce packages very thinly sliced smoked chicken or smoked turkey

1 2.5-ounce package very thinly sliced pastrami

1. Preheat oven to 375°F. In a small bowl stir together the mustard blend and, if desired, horseradish; set aside. Cut bread loaf into 1-inch slices by cutting from the top to, but not through, the bottom crust. (You should have 11 pockets.)

2. To assemble loaf, spread a scant tablespoon of the mustard blend on both sides of every other pocket in the bread loaf, starting with the first pocket on one end. Place the bread loaf on a baking sheet. Divide cheese slices, chicken slices, and pastrami slices among the pockets.

3. Bake about 15 minutes or until heated through. To serve, cut bread loaf into sandwiches by cutting through the bottom crusts of the unfilled pockets.

Per sandwich: 389 cal., 14 g total fat (7 g sat. fat), 48 mg chol., 1,004 mg sodium, 42 g carbo., 2 g fiber, 21 g pro.

MENU
Corn chips
Potato salad (from a deli)
Relish tray (olives, pickles, raw vegetables)

Nutty Turkey Tenderloins

58

PREP:
10 MINUTES

BAKE:
18 MINUTES

OVEN:
375°F

MAKES:
4 SERVINGS

2   turkey breast tenderloins (about 1 pound)
¼   cup creamy Dijon-style mustard blend
1   cup corn bread stuffing mix
½   cup finely chopped pecans
2   tablespoons butter, melted

1. Preheat oven to 375°F. Split each turkey breast tenderloin in half horizontally to make 4 turkey steaks. Brush turkey generously with the mustard blend. In a shallow dish combine dry stuffing mix and pecans; dip turkey in stuffing mixture, turning to coat both sides. Place in a shallow baking pan. Drizzle with melted butter.

2. Bake, uncovered, for 18 to 20 minutes or until turkey is no longer pink (170°F).

Per serving: 395 cal., 21 g total fat (5 g sat. fat), 84 mg chol., 566 mg sodium, 21 g carbo., 1 g fiber, 30 g pro.

MENU
Steamed peas and carrots
Mashed potatoes
Pumpkin bars

59 Turkey Steaks with Cranberry-Orange Sauce

START TO FINISH:
30 MINUTES

MAKES:
4 SERVINGS

2 turkey breast tenderloins (about 1 pound)
2 tablespoons butter or margarine
1 6-ounce package quick-cooking long grain and wild rice mix
1 10-ounce package frozen cranberry-orange relish, thawed
2 tablespoons orange liqueur or orange juice

1. Split each turkey tenderloin in half horizontally to make 4 turkey steaks. Sprinkle turkey with *salt* and *black pepper.* In a large skillet melt butter over medium-high heat. Add turkey; reduce heat to medium. Cook for 15 to 18 minutes or until no longer pink (170°F), turning occasionally to brown evenly.

2. Meanwhile, cook rice mix according to package directions.

3. Remove turkey from skillet; cover to keep warm. Remove skillet from heat; cool for 2 minutes.

4. For sauce, carefully add cranberry-orange relish to drippings in skillet; stir in liqueur. Return skillet to heat; cook and stir over low heat until heated through. Spoon sauce over turkey. Serve with rice.

Per serving: 481 cal., 8 g total fat (4 g sat. fat), 84 mg chol., 941 mg sodium, 68 g carbo., 31 g pro.

MENU
Stuffing (from mix)
Steamed green beans
Purchased pecan pie

Five-Spice Turkey Stir-Fry

60

START TO FINISH:
25 MINUTES

MAKES:
4 SERVINGS

1   4.4-ounce package beef lo-mein noodle mix

12   ounces turkey breast tenderloin, cut into thin bite-size strips

¼   teaspoon five-spice powder

¼   teaspoon salt

¼   teaspoon black pepper

2   tablespoons cooking oil

½   of a 16-ounce package frozen sweet pepper and onion stir-fry vegetables

2   tablespoons chopped honey-roasted peanuts or plain peanuts

1. Prepare noodle mix according to package directions; set aside. In a small bowl toss together turkey strips, five-spice powder, salt, and pepper; set aside.

2. Pour 1 tablespoon of the oil into a wok or large skillet. Heat over medium-high heat. Carefully add frozen vegetables to wok; cook and stir for 3 minutes. Remove vegetables from wok. Add remaining 1 tablespoon oil to hot wok. Add turkey mixture; cook and stir for 2 to 3 minutes or until turkey is no longer pink. Return vegetables to wok. Cook and stir about 1 minute more or until heated through.

3. To serve, divide noodle mixture among 4 dinner plates. Top with turkey mixture; sprinkle with peanuts.

Per serving: 314 cal., 11 g total fat (2 g sat. fat), 76 mg chol., 670 mg sodium, 26 g carbo., 3 g fiber, 27 g pro.

MENU

Spring rolls
(frozen or takeout)

Figs and dates

61 Parmesan-Sesame-Crusted Turkey

PREP:
15 MINUTES

COOK:
8 MINUTES

MAKES:
4 SERVINGS

½ cup finely shredded Parmesan cheese (2 ounces)

¼ cup sesame seeds

1 egg, lightly beaten

4 turkey breast slices, cut ½ inch thick

¼ teaspoon salt

¼ teaspoon black pepper

1 tablespoon olive oil or cooking oil

1. In a shallow dish or pie plate combine Parmesan cheese and sesame seeds. Place egg in another shallow dish or pie plate. Dip turkey slices into egg; coat with cheese mixture. Sprinkle each turkey slice with salt and pepper.

2. In a large skillet heat oil over medium-high heat. Add turkey slices; reduce heat to medium. Cook for 8 to 10 minutes or until turkey is no longer pink (170°F), turning occasionally.

Per serving: 498 cal., 28 g total fat (13 g sat. fat), 171 mg chol., 1,336 mg sodium, 3 g carbo., 1 g fiber, 57 g pro.

MENU
Buttermilk biscuits
Mashed potatoes
Steamed mixed vegetables

Turkey Burgers with Cranberry Sauce

62

PREP:
12 MINUTES

BROIL:
11 MINUTES

MAKES:
4 BURGERS

⅓   cup herb-seasoned stuffing mix, crushed

2   tablespoons milk

1   tablespoon snipped fresh sage or ½ teaspoon dried sage, crushed

¼   teaspoon salt

1   pound uncooked ground turkey
     Lettuce leaves

4   whole wheat hamburger buns, split and toasted

½   cup whole cranberry sauce

1. Preheat broiler. In a large bowl combine stuffing mix, milk, sage, and salt. Add ground turkey; mix well. Shape into four ½-inch patties.

2. Place patties on the unheated rack of a broiler pan. Broil 4 to 5 inches from the heat for 11 to 13 minutes or until internal temperature registers 165°F on an instant-read meat thermometer, turning once halfway through broiling.

3. Arrange lettuce leaves on bottom halves of buns. Top with patties and cranberry sauce. Add top halves of buns.

Per burger: 350 cal., 11 g total fat (3 g sat. fat), 71 mg chol., 503 mg sodium, 37 g carbo., 3 g fiber, 28 g pro.

MENU
Multigrain chips
Broccoli salad (from a deli)
Praline ice cream with gingersnaps

63

Mock Monte Cristo Sandwiches

PREP:
10 MINUTES

BAKE:
15 MINUTES

OVEN:
400°F

MAKES:
6 HALF SANDWICHES

6   slices frozen French toast

2   tablespoons honey mustard

3   ounces sliced cooked turkey breast

3   ounces sliced cooked ham

3   ounces thinly sliced Swiss cheese

1. Preheat oven to 400°F. Lightly grease a baking sheet; set aside. To assemble sandwiches, spread 1 side of each of the frozen French toast slices with honey mustard. Layer 3 of the toast slices, mustard sides up, with turkey, ham, and cheese. Cover with remaining toast slices, mustard sides down. Place sandwiches on prepared baking sheet.

2. Bake for 15 to 20 minutes or until sandwiches are heated through, turning sandwiches once halfway through baking. To serve, cut each sandwich in half diagonally.

Per half sandwich: 221 cal., 9 g total fat (4 g sat. fat), 75 mg chol., 704 mg sodium, 21 g carbo., 1 g fiber, 14 g pro.

MENU
Kettle-cooked potato chips
Three-bean salad
(from a deli)
Vegetable tray
with vegetable dip

One-Pot Chicken and Pasta Dinner

64

START TO FINISH:
30 MINUTES

MAKES:
4 SERVINGS

8   ounces dried linguine or spaghetti, broken in half
3   cups packaged small broccoli florets
1   8-ounce tub cream cheese spread with roasted garlic, chive, and onion
      or cream cheese spread with garden vegetables
1   cup milk
¼   teaspoon black pepper
1   6-ounce package refrigerated chopped cooked chicken
    Milk (optional)

1. In a Dutch oven cook pasta according to package directions, adding broccoli the last 2 to 3 minutes of cooking. Drain.

2. In the same Dutch oven combine cream cheese, milk, and pepper. Cook and stir over low heat until cream cheese is melted. Add pasta–broccoli mixture and chicken. Heat through. If necessary, stir in additional milk to make desired consistency.

Per serving: 530 cal., 22 g total fat (14 g sat. fat), 90 mg chol., 690 mg sodium, 54 g carbo., 4 g fiber, 24 g pro.

MENU
French baguette slices
Mixed greens salad with vinaigrette dressing
Chocolate cake

65 Smoked Turkey and Tortellini Salad

START TO FINISH:
25 MINUTES

MAKES:
4 SERVINGS

1   7- to 8-ounce package dried cheese-filled tortellini
1   cup chopped cooked smoked turkey, ham, or chicken (5 ounces)
8   cherry tomatoes, quartered
½   cup coarsely chopped green sweet pepper
¼   cup sliced pitted ripe olives (optional)
¼   cup bottled Italian vinaigrette or balsamic vinaigrette salad dressing

1. Cook tortellini according to package directions; drain. Rinse with cold water; drain again.

2. In a large bowl combine tortellini, turkey, tomatoes, sweet pepper, and, if desired, olives. Drizzle salad dressing over mixture; toss to coat. Season to taste with *black pepper.*

Per serving: 330 cal., 15 g total fat (2 g sat. fat), 20 mg chol., 897 mg sodium, 32 g carbo., 1 g fiber, 17 g pro.

TIP: For a vegetarian salad, replace the turkey with
1 cup chopped packaged fresh broccoli or cauliflower.

MENU
Garlic bread
Fresh pear slices and cheese plate

Sausage and Vegetables with Polenta

66

START TO FINISH:
30 MINUTES

MAKES:
4 SERVINGS

1   tablespoon olive oil

1   1-pound tube refrigerated cooked polenta, cut into 12 slices and quartered

8   ounces light smoked turkey sausage, halved lengthwise and cut into ½-inch slices

2   medium red, green, and/or yellow sweet peppers, cut into bite-size pieces

1   medium onion, cut into bite-size pieces

1   cup packaged sliced fresh mushrooms

½   cup bottled pasta sauce

1. In a 12-inch nonstick skillet heat the oil over medium heat. Add polenta in a single layer; cook for 10 to 12 minutes or until light brown, stirring occasionally. Remove polenta from skillet; keep warm.

2. Add sausage, sweet pepper, onion, and mushrooms to skillet. Cook and stir until sausage is brown and vegetables are crisp-tender. Stir in pasta sauce. Add polenta; toss gently to combine ingredients. Heat through.

Per serving: 260 cal., 9 g total fat (2 g sat. fat), 38 mg chol., 1,088 mg sodium, 32 g carbo., 5 g fiber, 14 g pro.

MENU

Whole wheat rolls

Caesar salad

Coffee ice cream with amaretti cookies

67

Sausage and Corn Chowder

START TO FINISH:
20 MINUTES

MAKES:
4 SERVINGS

12 ounces cooked smoked turkey sausage or turkey frankfurters

1   10.75-ounce can condensed cream of potato soup

1⅓ cups milk

1   8.75-ounce can cream-style corn

3   slices American cheese, torn into pieces (3 ounces)

1. Halve the sausage or frankfurters lengthwise; cut into ½-inch slices. Set aside.

2. In a 2-quart saucepan combine soup, milk, and corn. Stir in sausage pieces and American cheese. Cook and stir over medium heat until heated through and cheese is melted.

Per serving: 342 cal., 18 g total fat (8 g sat. fat), 85 mg chol., 1,836 mg sodium, 27 g carbo., 1 g fiber, 23 g pro.

MENU
Texas toast
Vegetable tray with vegetable dip
Pudding (desired flavor)

Sweet Mustard Halibut

68

PREP:
15 MINUTES

BAKE:
6 MINUTES

OVEN:
450°F

MAKES:
4 SERVINGS

1   to 1¼ pounds fresh or frozen halibut steaks, cut ¾ inch thick
½   cup bottled chunky salsa
2   tablespoons honey
2   tablespoons Dijon-style mustard

1. Thaw fish, if frozen. Rinse fish; pat dry with paper towels. Preheat oven to 450°F. Arrange fish steaks in a shallow 2-quart baking dish.

2. Bake, uncovered, about 6 minutes or until fish begins to flake when tested with a fork. Drain liquid from baking dish.

3. Meanwhile, in a small bowl stir together salsa and honey. Spread mustard over fish; spoon salsa mixture on top of mustard. Bake for 2 to 3 minutes more or until salsa mixture is heated through.

Per serving: 176 cal., 4 g total fat (0 g sat. fat), 36 mg chol., 362 mg sodium, 11 g carbo., 0 g fiber, 24 g pro.

MENU
Brown and wild rice pilaf (from a mix)
Roasted Brussels sprouts
Apple crisp

69

Tuna with Tuscan Beans

START TO FINISH:
20 MINUTES

MAKES:
4 SERVINGS

1	pound fresh or frozen tuna or swordfish steaks, cut 1 inch thick
¼	teaspoon salt
¼	teaspoon black pepper
1	tablespoon olive oil
2	teaspoons olive oil
1	teaspoon bottled minced garlic (2 cloves)
1	14.5-ounce can Italian-style stewed tomatoes, undrained
2	teaspoons snipped fresh sage or ¼ teaspoon ground sage
1	15-ounce can navy beans, rinsed and drained
	Lemon wedges (optional)

1. Thaw fish, if frozen. Rinse fish; pat dry with paper towels. Cut fish into 4 serving-size pieces, if necessary. Sprinkle both sides of fish with salt and pepper. In a large skillet heat the 1 tablespoon oil over medium heat. Add the fish. Cook for 10 to 12 minutes or until fish begins to flake when tested with a fork, turning once halfway through cooking. (If using tuna, fish may still be pink in the center.)

2. Meanwhile, in a medium skillet heat the 2 teaspoons olive oil over medium heat. Add garlic; cook and stir for 15 seconds. Stir in undrained tomatoes and sage. Bring to boiling; reduce heat. Simmer, uncovered, for 5 minutes. Stir in beans; heat through.

3. To serve, remove the skin from fish, if present. Divide bean mixture among 4 dinner plates. Place a fish portion on top of bean mixture on each plate. If desired, serve with lemon wedges.

Per serving: 339 cal., 8 g total fat (1 g sat. fat), 51 mg chol., 883 mg sodium, 30 g carbo., 6 g fiber, 36 g pro.

MENU

Wilted spinach salad with crisp-fried bacon

Focaccia

Fresh or dried dates and tangerines

Orange-Onion Glazed Swordfish

70

START TO FINISH:
20 MINUTES

MAKES:
4 SERVINGS

1 pound fresh or frozen swordfish steaks, cut 1 inch thick
¼ teaspoon salt
¼ teaspoon black pepper
    Nonstick cooking spray
1 tablespoon butter or margarine
1 large onion, thinly sliced and separated into rings (1 cup)
½ cup orange juice
1 tablespoon snipped fresh basil or 1 teaspoon dried basil, crushed

1. Thaw fish, if frozen. Rinse fish; pat dry with paper towels. Cut fish into
    4 serving-size pieces, if necessary. Sprinkle fish with salt and pepper.

2. Coat a large skillet with nonstick cooking spray. Heat skillet over medium-high
    heat. Add swordfish to skillet. Cook, covered, about 12 minutes or until fish
    begins to flake when tested with a fork, turning once halfway through cooking.
    Remove fish from skillet; cover to keep warm.

3. Add butter to hot skillet. Cook and stir onion in hot butter until tender.
    Carefully stir in orange juice and basil. Bring to boiling; reduce heat. Simmer,
    uncovered, for 1 to 2 minutes or until most of the liquid has evaporated. Spoon
    onion mixture over fish.

Per serving: 191 cal., 7 g total fat (3 g sat. fat), 51 mg chol., 280 mg sodium, 7 g carbo., 1 g fiber, 23 g pro.

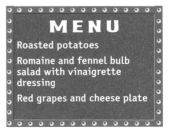

MENU
Roasted potatoes
Romaine and fennel bulb
salad with vinaigrette
dressing
Red grapes and cheese plate

71 Broiled Snapper with Fennel

PREP:
15 MINUTES

BROIL:
4 TO 6 MINUTES
PER ½-INCH
THICKNESS

MAKES:
4 SERVINGS

4	6- to 8-ounce fresh or frozen red snapper fillets
1	tablespoon butter or margarine
1	fennel bulb, trimmed and cut crosswise into thin slices (about 1¼ cups)
1	teaspoon finely shredded lemon peel
4	teaspoons lemon juice
1	teaspoon snipped fresh dill or thyme
	Lemon wedges (optional)

1. Thaw fish, if frozen. Preheat broiler. Rinse fish; pat dry with paper towels. Measure thickness of fish. Place fish on the greased unheated rack of a broiler pan. Sprinkle fish with *salt* and *black pepper*. Broil 4 inches from heat until fish begins to flake when tested with a fork. (Allow 4 to 6 minutes per ½-inch thickness of fish).

2. In a small saucepan melt butter over medium heat. Add fennel; cook for 5 to 8 minutes or just until tender. Stir in lemon peel, lemon juice, and dill. Season to taste with salt and black pepper. Spoon fennel over fish. If desired, garnish with lemon wedges.

Per serving: 237 cal., 6 g total fat (2 g sat. fat), 81 mg chol., 318 mg sodium, 4 g carbo., 2 g fiber, 41 g pro.

MENU
Crusty Italian rolls
Sauteed green beans with toasted walnuts
Mashed butternut squash

Simple Salsa Fish

72

PREP:
15 MINUTES

BROIL:
9 MINUTES

MAKES:
4 SERVINGS

1   pound fresh or frozen skinless orange roughy or red snapper fillets, ½ to 1 inch thick
⅓   cup bottled salsa
½   teaspoon bottled minced garlic (1 clove)
1   14-ounce can vegetable broth
1   cup quick-cooking couscous
¼   cup thinly sliced green onion (2) or coarsely snipped fresh cilantro
    Lime or lemon wedges

1. Thaw fish, if frozen. Rinse fish; pat dry with paper towels. Set fish aside. Preheat broiler. In a small bowl combine salsa and garlic; set aside.

2. In a small saucepan bring vegetable broth to boiling. Stir in couscous; cover and remove from heat. Let stand about 5 minutes or until liquid is absorbed. Stir in green onion.

3. Place fish on the greased unheated rack of a broiler pan. Broil 4 inches from the heat for 8 to 12 minutes or until fish begins to flake when tested with a fork. Turn 1-inch-thick fillets over halfway through broiling.

4. Spoon salsa mixture over fish; broil about 1 minute more or until salsa is heated through. Arrange fish on couscous mixture. Serve with lime wedges.

Per serving: 295 cal., 3 g total fat (0 g sat. fat), 42 mg chol., 549 mg sodium, 39 g carbo., 7 g fiber, 30 g pro.

MENU
Warm flour tortillas
Black beans seasoned with cumin and lime juice
Spinach salad with desired dressing

73

Cajun Catfish with Coleslaw

PREP:
10 MINUTES

BAKE:
15 MINUTES

OVEN:
350°F

MAKES:
4 SERVINGS

1　pound fresh or frozen skinless catfish fillets, ½ inch thick

2½　teaspoons salt-free Cajun seasoning

¼　teaspoon salt

2　cups shredded cabbage with carrot (coleslaw mix)

3　tablespoons mayonnaise or salad dressing

　　Bottled hot pepper sauce (optional)

1. Thaw fish, if frozen. Preheat oven to 350°F. Rinse fish; pat dry with paper towels. Cut fish into 4 serving-size pieces, if necessary. Combine 2 teaspoons of the Cajun seasoning and ¼ teaspoon salt; sprinkle both sides of fish with seasoning mixture. Arrange fish in a greased 3-quart rectangular baking dish, tucking under any thin edges to make fish of uniform thickness.

2. Bake, uncovered, for 15 to 20 minutes or until fish begins to flake when tested with a fork.

3. Meanwhile, in a medium bowl stir together cabbage with carrot, mayonnaise, and the remaining ½ teaspoon Cajun seasoning. If desired, season to taste with *salt* and *black pepper.* Cover and chill until serving time. Serve catfish with coleslaw and, if desired, hot pepper sauce.

Per serving: 241 cal., 17 g total fat (3 g sat. fat), 57 mg chol., 127 mg sodium, 3 g carbo., 1 g fiber, 18 g pro.

MENU
Corn muffins
Oven-fried potatoes
Hot fudge sundaes

Easy Baked Fish

74

PREP:
10 MINUTES

BAKE:
18 MINUTES

OVEN:
425°F

MAKES:
4 SERVINGS

½ cup herb-seasoned stuffing mix, finely crushed

2 tablespoons butter or margarine, melted

2 7.6-ounce packages frozen Caesar Parmesan or grill-flavor fish portions (4 portions)

2 teaspoons lemon juice

1. Preheat oven to 425°F. In a small bowl combine dry stuffing mix and melted butter, tossing until well mixed.

2. Lightly grease a 2-quart rectangular baking dish; place frozen fish portions in prepared baking dish. Sprinkle with lemon juice. Sprinkle stuffing mixture over fish portions.

3. Bake for 18 to 20 minutes or until fish begins to flake when tested with a fork.

Per serving: 183 cal., 9 g total fat (4 g sat. fat), 76 mg chol., 401 mg sodium, 6 g carbo., 1 g fiber, 18 g pro.

MENU
Dinner rolls
Hot cooked noodles
Steamed mixed vegetables

75

Roasted Salmon and Tomatoes

PREP:
15 MINUTES

BAKE:
12 MINUTES

OVEN:
450°F

MAKES:
4 SERVINGS

1   1¼-pound fresh salmon fillet, about 1 inch thick
    Nonstick cooking spray
¼   teaspoon salt
6   roma tomatoes, seeded and chopped (about 1 pound)
1   tablespoon Worcestershire sauce for chicken
¼   teaspoon black pepper
1   tablespoon Dijon-style mustard
1   tablespoon snipped fresh marjoram or oregano

1. Thaw fish, if frozen. Preheat oven to 450°F. Coat a 13x9x2-inch baking pan with nonstick cooking spray. Rinse fish; pat dry with paper towels. Cut fish into 4 serving-size pieces. Sprinkle with ⅛ teaspoon of the salt. Place fillet, skin side up, in pan, tucking under any thin edges to make fish of uniform thickness. Arrange tomatoes around salmon. Sprinkle tomatoes with Worcestershire sauce, pepper, and the remaining ⅛ teaspoon salt.

2. Bake, uncovered, for 12 to 16 minutes or until fish begins to flake when tested with a fork. Remove skin from fish; discard skin. Transfer fish to 4 dinner plates. Stir mustard and marjoram into tomatoes. Serve tomato mixture with fish.

Per serving: 231 cal., 10 g total fat (2 g sat. fat), 75 mg chol., 370 mg sodium, 6 g carbo., 1 g fiber, 30 g pro.

MENU
Steamed broccoli spears
Hot cooked tortellini
Apple pie

Salmon with Tarragon Cream Sauce

76

START TO FINISH:
20 MINUTES

MAKES:
3 SERVINGS

12   ounces fresh or frozen salmon fillets or steaks

1   9-ounce package refrigerated fettuccine

2   cups thinly sliced zucchini, yellow summer squash, and/or red sweet pepper

1   teaspoon cooking oil

⅔   cup milk

3   tablespoons reduced-fat cream cheese (Neufchâtel)

1   tablespoon snipped fresh tarragon, basil, or dill; 1 teaspoon dried tarragon or basil, crushed; or 1 teaspoon dried dill

¼   teaspoon black pepper

1. Thaw fish, if frozen. Skin fish, if necessary. Rinse fish; pat dry with paper towels. Cut fish into 1-inch pieces. Set aside.

2. Cook pasta according to package directions, adding vegetables to pasta for the last minute of cooking. Drain and keep warm.

3. Meanwhile, in a large nonstick skillet heat oil over medium-high heat. Add fish pieces; cook, stirring gently, for 3 to 5 minutes or until fish begins to flake when tested with fork. Remove fish from skillet. Add milk, cream cheese, herb, and pepper to skillet. Cook and whisk until cream cheese is melted and sauce is smooth. Return fish to skillet. Cook and gently stir until heated through. Serve over pasta and vegetables.

Per serving: 535 cal., 21 g total fat (6 g sat. fat), 171 mg chol., 172 mg sodium, 50 g carbo., 3 g fiber, 37 g pro.

MENU
Crusty Italian bread
Rice pudding with raisins

77

Tuna and Pasta Alfredo

START TO FINISH:
25 MINUTES

MAKES:
4 SERVINGS

3 cups dried mini lasagna, broken mafalda, or medium noodles

2 cups packaged fresh broccoli florets

1 medium red sweet pepper, cut into thin strips

1 10-ounce container refrigerated light Alfredo sauce

¾ teaspoon dried dill

2 to 3 tablespoons milk (optional)

1 9.5-ounce can tuna (water pack), drained and broken into chunks

1. In a large saucepan cook pasta according to package directions, adding broccoli and sweet pepper for the last 5 minutes of cooking. Drain well. Return pasta and vegetables to hot pan.

2. Stir Alfredo sauce and dill into pasta mixture in saucepan. If necessary, stir in enough of the milk to make sauce desired consistency. Gently stir tuna into pasta mixture. Heat through.

Per serving: 545 cal., 12 g total fat (7 g sat. fat), 47 mg chol., 821 mg sodium, 78 g carbo., 4 g fiber, 30 g pro.

MENU
Buttermilk biscuits
Steamed peas and carrots
Cheesecake

Hot Tuna Hoagies

78

START TO FINISH:
25 MINUTES

MAKES:
4 OPEN-FACE
SANDWICHES

1½ cups packaged shredded cabbage with carrot (coleslaw mix)
1 9.25-ounce can chunk white tuna (water pack), drained and broken into chunks
2 tablespoons mayonnaise or salad dressing
2 tablespoons bottled buttermilk ranch, creamy cucumber, or creamy
    Parmesan salad dressing
2 hoagie buns, split and toasted
2 ounces cheddar or Swiss cheese, thinly sliced

1. Preheat broiler. In a medium bowl combine shredded cabbage with carrot and
   tuna. In a small bowl stir together mayonnaise and salad dressing. Pour the
   mayonnaise mixture over tuna mixture; toss gently to coat.

2. Spread the tuna mixture on the hoagie bun halves. Place on the unheated rack
   of a broiler pan or on a baking sheet. Broil 4 to 5 inches from the heat for 2 to
   3 minutes or until heated through. Top with cheese. Broil for 30 to 60 seconds
   more or until cheese is melted.

Per open-face sandwich: 406 cal., 19 g total fat (6 g sat. fat), 39 mg chol., 704 mg sodium, 38 g carbo.,
2 g fiber, 20 g pro.

MENU
Corn chips
Three-bean salad
(from a deli)
Brownies

79

Shrimp and Tomatoes with Pasta

START TO FINISH:
25 MINUTES

MAKES:
4 SERVINGS

1   9-ounce package refrigerated fettuccine

12   ounces fresh or frozen uncooked, peeled, and deveined shrimp, thawed

2   tablespoons olive oil or cooking oil

½   cup chopped onion (1 medium)

1   medium green sweet pepper, cut into thin bite-size strips

1   14.5-ounce can diced tomatoes with basil, garlic, and oregano, undrained

¼   teaspoon black pepper

¼   cup finely shredded Parmesan cheese (1 ounce)

1. Using kitchen scissors, cut fettuccine strands in half. In a 4-quart Dutch oven cook the shrimp with the fettuccine according to fettuccine package directions until pasta is tender and shrimp are opaque. Drain. Return pasta and shrimp to the hot pan.

2. Meanwhile, in a large skillet heat oil over medium-high heat. Add onion; cook for 2 minutes. Add sweet pepper strips; cook and stir for 2 to 3 minutes more or until onion is tender. Stir in undrained tomatoes and black pepper. Bring to boiling; reduce heat. Simmer, uncovered, for 2 minutes.

3. Add tomato mixture to fettuccine mixture; toss to combine. Sprinkle individual servings with Parmesan cheese.

Per serving: 406 cal., 12 g total fat (3 g sat. fat), 174 mg chol., 758 mg sodium, 47 g carbo., 3 g fiber, 29 g pro.

MENU
Soft breadsticks
Caesar salad
Baked apples

Curried Shrimp on Rice

80

START TO FINISH:
25 MINUTES

MAKES:
4 SERVINGS

1   10-ounce container refrigerated Alfredo pasta sauce

2   to 3 teaspoons curry powder

12 ounces peeled and deveined, cooked medium shrimp*

2   cups hot cooked rice

¼   cup slivered almonds, toasted

1. In a large saucepan combine Alfredo sauce and curry powder. If necessary, stir in 1 or 2 tablespoons water to make sauce desired consistency. Cook and stir over medium heat just until boiling.

2. Add shrimp. Cook and stir for 2 to 3 minutes more or until heated through. Serve shrimp mixture over rice; sprinkle with almonds.

Per serving: 550 cal., 29 g total fat (1 g sat. fat), 206 mg chol., 426 mg sodium, 41 g carbo., 2 g fiber, 32 g pro.

*NOTE: If tails are present on the shrimp, remove them before using.

MENU
Warm pita bread
Steamed mixed vegetables
Coconut ice cream with
crystallized ginger

81

Spicy Jalapeño Shrimp Pasta

START TO FINISH:
30 MINUTES

MAKES:
4 SERVINGS

12 ounces fresh or frozen large shrimp in shells
8   ounces dried linguine
2   tablespoons olive oil
1   or 2 fresh jalapeño chile peppers, finely chopped*
1   teaspoon bottled minced garlic (2 cloves)
½   teaspoon salt
⅛   teaspoon black pepper
2   cups chopped tomato and/or cherry tomatoes, halved or quartered
    Finely shredded Parmesan cheese (optional)

1. Thaw shrimp, if frozen. Peel and devein shrimp. Rinse shrimp; pat dry with paper towels. Cook linguine according to package directions; drain well. Return to pan. Cover and keep warm.

2. In a large skillet heat oil over medium-high heat. Add chile pepper, garlic, salt, and black pepper; cook and stir for 1 minute. Add shrimp; cook about 3 minutes more or until shrimp are opaque. Stir in tomato; heat through.

3. Toss cooked linguine with shrimp mixture. If desired, sprinkle individual servings with Parmesan cheese.

Per serving: 363 cal., 9 g total fat (1 g sat. fat), 97 mg chol., 396 mg sodium, 48 g carbo., 3 g fiber, 21 g pro.

*NOTE: Because chile peppers contain oils that can burn your skin and eyes, avoid direct contact with them as much as possible. When working with chile peppers, wear plastic or rubber gloves. If your bare hands do touch the peppers, wash your hands and nails well with soap and warm water.

MENU
French baguette slices
Mixed greens salad with desired dressing
Lemon meringue pie

Spanish-Style Rice with Seafood

82

START TO FINISH:
25 MINUTES

MAKES:
4 SERVINGS

1   5.6– to 6.2-ounce package Spanish-style rice mix
1¾ cups water
1   tablespoon butter or margarine
     Several dashes bottled hot pepper sauce
1   12-ounce package frozen peeled, deveined shrimp
1   cup frozen peas
½   cup chopped, seeded tomato (1 medium)

1. In a large skillet stir together rice mix, water, butter, and hot pepper sauce. Bring to boiling; reduce heat. Simmer, covered, for 5 minutes.

2. Stir shrimp into rice mixture. Return to boiling; reduce heat. Simmer, covered, for 2 to 3 minutes more or until shrimp are opaque. Remove from heat. Stir in peas. Cover and let stand for 10 minutes. Sprinkle with tomato before serving.

Per serving: 282 cal., 5 g total fat (2 g sat. fat), 137 mg chol., 897 mg sodium, 36 g carbo., 3 g fiber, 23 g pro.

MENU
Multigrain bread
Steamed cauliflower
Apple and cranberry crisp

83

Sweet and Sour Shrimp

START TO FINISH:
15 MINUTES

MAKES:
4 SERVINGS

1   12-ounce package frozen peeled, deveined shrimp
⅓   cup bottled stir-fry sauce
¼   cup pineapple-orange, orange, or apple juice
    Nonstick cooking spray
3   cups assorted fresh stir-fry vegetables (from produce department)

1. Thaw shrimp. Rinse shrimp; pat dry with paper towels. Set aside. In a small bowl combine stir-fry sauce and juice; set aside.

2. Coat an unheated nonstick wok or large skillet with nonstick cooking spray. (Add oil during cooking, if necessary.) Preheat wok over medium-high heat. Add vegetables; stir-fry for 3 to 5 minutes or until crisp-tender. Remove vegetables from wok. Add shrimp; stir-fry for 2 to 3 minutes or until shrimp are opaque. Push shrimp to side of wok.

3. Add sauce mixture to wok. Return vegetables to wok. Toss gently to coat. Cook and stir about 1 minute more or until heated through.

Per serving: 119 cal., 1 g total fat (0 g sat. fat), 131 mg chol., 666 mg sodium, 11 g carbo., 2 g fiber, 17 g pro.

MENU
Hot cooked rice
Egg rolls
(frozen or takeout)
Fortune cookies

Trattoria-Style Fettuccine

84

START TO FINISH:
18 MINUTES

MAKES:
4 SERVINGS

1   9-ounce package refrigerated spinach or plain fettuccine
1   medium carrot
1   tablespoon olive oil
¼   cup chopped green onion (2)
2   cups chopped red and/or yellow tomato (4 medium)
¼   cup oil-packed dried tomatoes, drained and snipped
½   cup crumbled garlic and herb or peppercorn feta cheese (2 ounces)

1. Using kitchen scissors, cut pasta strands in half. Cook the pasta according to package directions; drain. Return pasta to hot pan.

2. Meanwhile, peel carrot. Using a vegetable peeler, slice carrot lengthwise into wide, flat "ribbons." Set carrot aside.

3. In a large skillet heat oil over medium heat. Add green onion; cook for 30 seconds. Stir in fresh tomato, carrot, and dried tomato. Cook, covered, for 5 minutes, stirring once.

4. Spoon tomato mixture over cooked pasta; toss gently. Sprinkle individual servings with feta cheese.

Per serving: 311 cal., 11 g total fat (4 g sat. fat), 73 mg chol., 250 mg sodium, 44 g carbo., 2 g fiber, 13 g pro.

MENU
Crusty Italian bread
Caesar salad
Tiramisu (frozen)

85

Pasta with Three Cheeses

START TO FINISH:
30 MINUTES

MAKES:
4 SERVINGS

10 ounces packaged dried medium shell macaroni or rotini

2 cups frozen cauliflower, broccoli, and carrots or other vegetable combination

1 cup milk

1 3-ounce package cream cheese, cut up

¼ teaspoon black pepper

¾ cup shredded Gouda, Edam, Havarti, fontina, cheddar, or Swiss cheese (3 ounces)

¼ cup grated Parmesan cheese

Grated Parmesan cheese (optional)

1. In a large saucepan cook pasta according to package directions, adding the frozen vegetables for the last 5 minutes of cooking. Drain.

2. In the same saucepan combine milk, cream cheese, and pepper. Cook and stir over low heat until cheese is melted.

3. Return pasta mixture to saucepan. Toss to coat with cream cheese mixture. Gently stir in the shredded cheese and the ¼ cup Parmesan cheese. If desired, sprinkle individual servings with additional Parmesan cheese.

Per serving: 598 cal., 25 g total fat (14 g sat. fat), 86 mg chol., 596 mg sodium, 66 g carbo., 3 g fiber, 28 g pro.

MENU
Sourdough bread
Apple crisp with
cinnamon ice cream

Veggie Skillet

86

2 tablespoons cooking oil

3 cups frozen loose-pack diced hash brown potatoes with onions and peppers

2 cups meatless pasta sauce with mushrooms*

1 cup frozen peas and carrots

1 cup frozen whole kernel corn

½ cup shredded cheddar or mozzarella cheese (2 ounces)

1. In a large skillet heat oil over medium heat. Add hash brown potatoes; cook for 6 to 8 minutes or until nearly tender, stirring occasionally.

2. Stir pasta sauce, peas and carrots, and corn into the potatoes in the skillet. Bring to boiling; reduce heat. Simmer, covered, for 5 to 7 minutes or until vegetables are tender. Sprinkle with cheese. Let stand, covered, about 1 minute or until cheese starts to melt.

Per serving: 406 cal., 21 g total fat (6 g sat. fat), 20 mg chol., 742 mg sodium, 49 g carbo., 5 g fiber, 10 g pro.

*NOTE: For a zestier flavor, use 1 cup tomato sauce and 1 cup salsa in place of the pasta sauce.

MENU
Buttermilk biscuits
Banana splits

87 Nacho Corn Soup

START TO FINISH:
15 MINUTES

MAKES:
4 SERVINGS

2   cups milk

1   11-ounce can whole kernel corn with sweet peppers, drained

1   11-ounce can condensed nacho cheese soup

½   of a 4-ounce can diced green chile peppers (2 tablespoons)

1   tablespoon dried minced onion

¼   teaspoon ground cumin

¼   teaspoon dried oregano, crushed

Tortilla chips, broken (optional)

1. In a large saucepan stir together milk, corn, soup, chile peppers, dried onion, cumin, and oregano. Cook over medium heat, stirring frequently, until heated through. If desired, top individual servings with tortilla chips.

Per serving: 219 cal., 8 g total fat (4 g sat. fat), 20 mg chol., 898 mg sodium, 29 g carbo., 4 g fiber, 10 g pro.

MENU
Warm flour tortillas
Blonde brownies

Broccoli Chowder

88

½ cup water

1 10-ounce package frozen chopped broccoli

1 tablespoon dried minced onion

1 10.75-ounce can condensed cream of chicken soup

1 cup milk

1 cup shredded cheddar cheese (4 ounces)

⅛ teaspoon cayenne pepper

Croutons (optional)

1. In a medium saucepan bring the water to boiling. Add broccoli and dried onion. Return to boiling. Reduce heat; simmer, covered, about 5 minutes or until broccoli is crisp-tender. Do not drain. Stir in soup, milk, cheese, and cayenne pepper. Cook and stir about 4 minutes or until heated through. If desired, sprinkle individual servings with croutons.

Per serving: 242 cal., 16 g total fat (8 g sat. fat), 40 mg chol., 824 mg sodium, 13 g carbo., 2 g fiber, 13 g pro.

MENU
Ham sandwich
Corn chips
Gingerbread cake

89

Grilled Cheese with Caramelized Onions

START TO FINISH:
30 MINUTES

MAKES:
4 SANDWICHES

6   tablespoons butter or margarine, softened

1   large onion, sliced

1   cup packaged sliced fresh mushrooms

1   teaspoon berry-balsamic vinegar or balsamic vinegar

⅛   teaspoon salt

8   slices sourdough bread

8   slices cheddar cheese, Swiss cheese, Monterey Jack cheese, and/or other cheese

1. For caramelized onions, in a large skillet melt 2 tablespoons of the butter over medium heat. Add onion; cook about 10 minutes or until onion is soft and golden brown, stirring occasionally. Stir in mushrooms. Cook and stir for 2 minutes more. Remove from heat. Sprinkle onion and mushrooms with balsamic vinegar and salt.

2. Butter 1 side of each slice of the bread with the remaining ¼ cup butter. Place 2 slices of the desired cheese on the unbuttered side of each of 4 slices of the bread. Top each with some of the onion-mushroom mixture and another slice of sourdough bread, buttered side up.

3. In a large skillet cook sandwiches over medium heat for 4 to 6 minutes or until cheese is melted, turning once halfway through cooking.

Per sandwich: 552 cal., 39 g total fat (22 g sat. fat), 108 mg chol., 861 mg sodium, 32 g carbo., 2 g fiber, 20 g pro.

MENU
Pasta salad (from a deli)
Relish tray (olives, pickles, raw vegetables)
Pumpkin bars

Black Bean and Corn Quesadillas

90

START TO FINISH:
20 MINUTES

OVEN:
300°F

MAKES:
4 SERVINGS

1   8-ounce package shredded Mexican blend cheese (2 cups)
8   8-inch flour tortillas
1½ cups bottled black bean and corn salsa
1   medium avocado, seeded, peeled, and chopped
     Dairy sour cream

1. Preheat oven to 300°F. Divide cheese evenly among tortillas, sprinkling cheese over half of each tortilla. Top each tortilla with 1 tablespoon of the salsa. Divide avocado among tortillas. Fold tortillas in half, pressing gently.

2. Heat a large nonstick skillet over medium–high heat for 2 minutes; reduce heat to medium. Cook 2 of the quesadillas for 2 to 3 minutes or until light brown and cheese is melted, turning once. Remove quesadillas from skillet; place on a baking sheet. Keep warm in preheated oven. Repeat with remaining quesadillas, cooking 2 at a time.

3. Cut quesadillas into wedges. Serve with sour cream and remaining 1 cup salsa.

Per serving: 512 cal., 33 g total fat (14 g sat. fat), 55 mg chol., 940 mg sodium, 38 g carbo., 4 g fiber, 18 g pro.

MENU
Mexican rice (from a mix)
Marinated vegetable salad (from a deli)
Apple wedges with caramel dip

91

Peasant Pizza with Goat Cheese

PREP:
15 MINUTES

BAKE:
12 MINUTES

OVEN:
400°F

MAKES:
6 SERVINGS

1   16-ounce Italian bread shell (such as Boboli brand)

2   ounces cream cheese

¼   cup crumbled semisoft goat cheese or feta cheese, crumbled (about 2 ounces)

2   tablespoons snipped fresh basil or 2 teaspoons dried basil, crushed

½   teaspoon bottled minced garlic (1 clove)

⅛   teaspoon black pepper

3   plum tomatoes, thinly sliced

1   small yellow, orange, or green sweet pepper, cut into thin bite-size strips

1. Preheat oven to 400°F. Place the Italian bread shell on a baking sheet.

2. In a small bowl stir together cream cheese; goat cheese; dried basil, if using; garlic; and black pepper. Spread mixture over the bread shell. Arrange the tomato slices and sweet pepper strips on top of the cheese mixture.

3. Bake about 12 minutes or until heated through. Sprinkle with fresh basil, if using. To serve, cut into wedges.

Per serving: 284 cal., 11 g total fat (4 g sat. fat), 21 mg chol., 493 mg sodium, 37 g carbo., 2 g fiber, 12 g pro.

MENU
Pasta salad (from a deli)
Fresh pear slices with
dried figs

92 Dijon-Pepper Steak

START TO FINISH:
30 MINUTES

MAKES:
4 SERVINGS

4   beef top sirloin steaks, cut ¾ inch thick (1¼ pounds)
1   teaspoon cracked black pepper
2   tablespoons butter or margarine
1   10.5-ounce can condensed French onion soup
¼   cup water
2   tablespoons Dijon-style mustard
1   tablespoon all-purpose flour
1   4-ounce can (drained weight) sliced mushrooms, drained

1. Trim fat from steaks. Press pepper into both sides of steaks. In a large skillet melt butter over medium heat. Add steaks; cook to desired doneness, turning once halfway through cooking. Allow 10 to 13 minutes for medium rare (145°F) to medium (160°F).

2. Remove steaks from skillet, reserving drippings. Cover steaks to keep warm. Remove skillet from heat and allow to stand for 1 minute.

3. For sauce, in a medium bowl combine soup, water, mustard, and flour; stir into drippings in skillet. Add mushrooms. Cook and stir until slightly thickened and bubbly. Cook and stir for 1 minute more. Serve sauce with steaks.

Per serving: 272 cal., 12 g total fat (6 g sat. fat), 103 mg chol., 935 mg sodium, 7 g carbo., 2 g fiber, 32 g pro.

MENU
Hot buttered noodles
Multigrain rolls
Steamed broccoli spears
Eggnog with gingersnaps

Saucy Strip Steak

93

PREP:
15 MINUTES

BROIL:
12 MINUTES

MAKES:
4 SERVINGS

⅔   cup orange marmalade

2   tablespoons butter or margarine

1   teaspoon snipped fresh rosemary or ¼ teaspoon dried rosemary, crushed

4   beef top loin steaks, cut 1 inch thick (about 2 pounds)

1. Preheat broiler. In a small saucepan combine marmalade, butter, and rosemary. Cook and stir over low heat until butter is melted and mixture is heated through. Set aside.

2. Trim fat from steaks. Season steaks with *salt* and *black pepper.* Place steaks on the unheated rack of a broiler pan. Broil 3 to 4 inches from the heat for 12 to 14 minutes for medium-rare (145°F) or 15 to 18 minutes for medium (160°F), turning once halfway through broiling and brushing with marmalade mixture during the last 5 minutes. Transfer steaks to dinner plates. Spoon any remaining marmalade mixture over steaks.

Per serving: 464 cal., 14 g total fat (7 g sat. fat), 123 mg chol., 357 mg sodium, 35 g carbo., 0 g fiber, 49 g pro.

MENU

Country Italian bread

Roasted butternut squash chunks

Apple crisp with cinnamon ice cream

94

Easy Italian Pepper Steak

START TO FINISH:
25 MINUTES

MAKES:
4 SERVINGS

1   9-ounce package refrigerated fettuccine
12 ounces packaged beef stir-fry strips
¼   teaspoon crushed red pepper
2   tablespoons olive oil
1   16-ounce package frozen sweet pepper and onion stir-fry vegetables,
      thawed and well drained
2   tablespoons balsamic vinegar
1   15-ounce can chunky Italian-style tomato sauce
2   tablespoons pine nuts, toasted (optional)
    Crushed red pepper (optional)

1. Cook pasta according to package directions. Combine beef strips and the
   ¼ teaspoon crushed red pepper; set aside.

2. Meanwhile, in a large skillet heat 1 tablespoon of the oil over medium-high
   heat. Add thawed stir-fry vegetables; stir-fry for 2 to 3 minutes or until crisp-
   tender. Carefully add balsamic vinegar; toss to coat. Remove vegetables from
   skillet; keep warm.

3. Heat the remaining 1 tablespoon oil in the same skillet. Add beef strips;
   stir-fry for 2 to 3 minutes or until meat is slightly pink in center. Add tomato
   sauce; heat through.

4. Drain pasta. Toss the beef mixture with pasta and vegetables. If desired,
   sprinkle with pine nuts and pass additional crushed red pepper.

Per serving: 415 cal., 11 g total fat (2 g sat. fat), 87 mg chol., 648 mg sodium, 50 g carbo., 6 g fiber, 28 g pro.

MENU
Soft breadsticks
Caesar salad
Chocolate cake

Individual Sicilian Meat Loaves

95

START TO FINISH:
30 MINUTES

OVEN:
400°F

MAKES:
4 SERVINGS

1 egg, lightly beaten
1¾ cups bottled garlic and onion pasta sauce
¼ cup seasoned fine dry bread crumbs
¼ teaspoon salt
¼ teaspoon black pepper
12 ounces lean ground beef
2 ounces mozzarella cheese
4 thin slices prosciutto or cooked ham (about 2 ounces)
1 9-ounce package refrigerated fettuccine
Finely shredded Parmesan cheese (optional)

1. Preheat oven to 400°F. In a medium bowl combine egg, ¼ cup of the pasta sauce, the fine dry bread crumbs, salt, and pepper. Add ground beef; mix well.

2. Cut mozzarella cheese into four logs measuring approximately 2¼×¾×½ inches. Wrap a slice of prosciutto around each cheese log. Shape one-fourth of the ground beef mixture around each cheese log to form a loaf. Flatten the meat loaves to 1½ inches thick and place in a shallow baking pan.

3. Bake loaves, uncovered, about 20 minutes or until internal temperature registers 160°F on an instant-read thermometer.

4. Meanwhile, cook pasta according to package directions. Heat remaining pasta sauce in a small saucepan over medium heat until bubbly.

5. To serve, arrange meat loaves on hot cooked pasta. Spoon sauce over top. If desired, sprinkle with Parmesan cheese.

Per serving: 631 cal., 31 g total fat (12 g sat. fat),
173 mg chol., 1,132 mg sodium, 55 g carbo., 3 g fiber, 31 g pro.

MENU
Focaccia bread
Marinated vegetable salad (from a deli)
Spice cupcakes

96

Easy Beef and Noodle Soup

START TO FINISH:
25 MINUTES

MAKES:
4 SERVINGS

1 pound ground beef

2½ cups water

1 10.75-ounce can condensed cream of onion soup

1 10.5-ounce can condensed beef broth

1½ cups dried medium noodles

2 tablespoons dried parsley flakes

Parmesan cheese (optional)

1. In a large saucepan cook ground beef over medium-high heat until brown. Drain off fat. Stir in water, onion soup, broth, uncooked noodles, and parsley flakes.

2. Bring to boiling; reduce heat. Simmer, covered, about 5 minutes or until noodles are tender, stirring occasionally. If desired, sprinkle individual servings with Parmesan cheese.

Per serving: 357 cal., 19 g total fat (7 g sat. fat), 98 mg chol., 1,218 mg sodium, 19 g carbo., 1 g fiber, 27 g pro.

MENU

Sourdough rolls

Mixed greens salad with desired dressing

Oatmeal cookies with spiced apple cider

Tortellini with Meat Sauce

97

START TO FINISH:
25 MINUTES

MAKES:
4 SERVINGS

8   ounces ground beef, ground lamb, or ground pork

1¾ cups bottled tomato and herb pasta sauce

1¼ cups water

¼   cup dry red wine or water

1   9-ounce package refrigerated cheese-filled tortellini or ½ of a 16-ounce package
    frozen cheese-filled tortellini

½   cup shredded mozzarella cheese (2 ounces)

1. In a large saucepan cook ground meat over medium-high heat until brown. Drain off fat.

2. Add pasta sauce, water, and wine to the meat. Bring to boiling. Stir in tortellini. Return to boiling. Simmer, uncovered, for 8 to 10 minutes or until tortellini are tender and sauce is of desired consistency. Sprinkle individual servings with mozzarella cheese. Let stand for 2 to 3 minutes or until cheese is slightly melted.

Per serving: 471 cal., 23 g total fat (9 g sat. fat), 80 mg chol., 784 mg sodium, 40 g carbo., 0 g fiber, 24 g pro.

MENU
Crusty Italian bread
Romaine salad with desired dressing
Brownie sundaes

98 Chili with Polenta

START TO FINISH:
25 MINUTES

MAKES:
4 SERVINGS

12 ounces ground beef
1   15-ounce can hot-style chili beans with chili gravy
1   15-ounce can black beans, rinsed and drained
1   8-ounce can tomato sauce
½   teaspoon ground cumin
1   16-ounce tube refrigerated cooked polenta, crumbled
½   cup shredded taco cheese (2 ounces)
    Sliced green onion (optional)
    Dairy sour cream (optional)

1. In a large skillet cook ground beef over medium-high heat until brown. Drain off fat.

2. Stir undrained chili beans, drained black beans, tomato sauce, and cumin into ground beef in skillet. Bring to boiling.

3. Sprinkle the crumbled polenta over the beef mixture. Simmer, covered, about 5 minutes or until heated through. Sprinkle with cheese. If desired, sprinkle with green onion and serve with sour cream.

Per serving: 497 cal., 15 g total fat (7 g sat. fat), 65 mg chol., 1,464 mg sodium, 58 g carbo., 14 g fiber, 34 g pro.

MENU
Tortilla chips with salsa
Fresh pear slices with
cheese plate

Quick Skillet Lasagna

99

START TO FINISH:
30 MINUTES

MAKES:
6 SERVINGS

3 cups dried mafalda (mini lasagna) noodles (6 ounces)

12 ounces ground beef or bulk pork sausage

1 26- to 27.75-ounce jar red pasta sauce

1½ cups shredded mozzarella cheese (6 ounces)

¼ cup grated Parmesan cheese

1. Cook pasta according to package directions; drain well.

2. Meanwhile, in a 10-inch nonstick skillet cook meat over medium-high heat until brown. Drain off fat. Remove meat from skillet and set aside. Wipe skillet with paper towels.

3. Spread about half of the cooked pasta in the skillet. Cover with about half of the pasta sauce. Spoon cooked meat over sauce. Sprinkle with 1 cup of the mozzarella cheese. Top with remaining pasta and remaining sauce. Sprinkle remaining ½ cup mozzarella cheese and the Parmesan cheese over top.

4. Cook, covered, over medium heat for 5 to 7 minutes or until heated through and cheese is melted. Remove skillet from heat. Let stand, covered, for 1 minute.

Per serving: 375 cal., 17 g total fat (6 g sat. fat), 50 mg chol., 1,046 mg sodium, 30 g carbo., 2 g fiber, 25 g pro.

MENU

Garlic bread

Marinated vegetable salad (from a deli)

Spumoni ice cream with amaretti cookies

100 Zippy Beef, Mac, and Cheese

START TO FINISH:
30 MINUTES

MAKES:
4 SERVINGS

6   ounces dried elbow macaroni or corkscrew macaroni (about 1½ cups)

12   ounces ground beef, ground pork, or uncooked ground turkey

1   15-ounce can tomato sauce

1   14.5-ounce can stewed tomatoes or Mexican-style stewed tomatoes,* undrained

4   ounces American or sharp American cheese, cut into small cubes

2   to 3 teaspoons chili powder*

     Finely shredded or grated Parmesan cheese

1. In a 3-quart saucepan cook pasta according to package directions; drain and return pasta to saucepan.

2. Meanwhile, in a large skillet cook ground meat over medium-high heat until brown. Drain off fat.

3. Stir ground meat, tomato sauce, undrained tomatoes, American cheese, and chili powder into cooked pasta in saucepan. Cook and stir over medium heat until heated through and cheese is melted. Sprinkle individual servings with Parmesan cheese.

*NOTE: If using Mexican-style stewed tomatoes, add only 2 teaspoons chili powder.

Per serving: 587 cal., 25 g total fat (13 g sat. fat), 93 mg chol., 1,665 mg sodium, 49 g carbo., 3 g fiber, 40 g pro.

MENU
Corn bread squares
Vegetable tray with vegetable dip
Pudding (desired flavor)

Sloppy Beef Burgers

101

START TO FINISH:
25 MINUTES

MAKES:
8 BURGERS

1½ pounds ground beef
½ cup chopped onion (1 medium)
⅓ cup chopped green sweet pepper
1 10.75-ounce can reduced-fat and reduced-sodium condensed tomato soup
1 tablespoon Worcestershire sauce
1 tablespoon yellow mustard
8 whole wheat or white hamburger buns, split and toasted
Dill pickle slices (optional)

1. In a large skillet cook ground beef, onion, and sweet pepper over medium-high heat until beef is brown. Drain off fat.

2. Stir soup, Worcestershire sauce, and mustard into meat mixture in skillet. Bring to boiling; reduce heat. Simmer, covered, for 5 minutes. Serve on toasted hamburger buns. If desired, garnish with pickle slices.

Per burger: 289 cal., 11 g total fat (4 g sat. fat), 54 mg chol., 417 mg sodium, 27 g carbo., 2 g fiber, 20 g pro.

MENU
Pasta salad (from a deli)
Carrot and sweet pepper strips with vegetable dip
Oatmeal cookies with eggnog

102 Beefy Calzones

PREP:
20 MINUTES

BAKE:
8 MINUTES

MAKES:
6 CALZONES

8   ounces ground beef

½   cup packaged sliced fresh mushrooms

¼   cup chopped green sweet pepper

½   cup shredded mozzarella cheese (2 ounces)

⅓   cup pizza sauce

1   13.8-ounce package refrigerated pizza dough

1   tablespoon milk

     Grated Parmesan cheese (optional)

     Warmed pizza sauce (optional)

1. Preheat oven to 425°F. In a medium skillet cook ground beef, mushrooms, and sweet pepper over medium-high heat until meat is brown; drain off fat. Stir in mozzarella cheese and the ⅓ cup pizza sauce.

2. Unroll pizza dough. Roll or stretch dough into a 10x15-inch rectangle. Cut dough into six 5-inch squares. Spoon some of the meat mixture onto one half of each square. Brush dough edges with water. Lift a corner and stretch dough over meat mixture to opposite corner. Seal the edges by pressing with the tines of a fork.

3. Place calzones on a greased baking sheet. Prick tops with a fork to allow steam to escape. Brush with the milk. If desired, sprinkle with Parmesan cheese.

4. Bake for 8 to 10 minutes or until golden brown. Let stand for 5 minutes before serving. If desired, serve with warmed pizza sauce.

Per calzone: 235 cal., 8 g total fat (3 g sat. fat), 31 mg chol., 358 mg sodium, 26 g carbo., 1 g fiber, 13 g pro.

MENU
Marinated vegetable salad
(from a deli)
Banana splits

Caliente Pot Roast

103

START TO FINISH:
20 MINUTES

MAKES:
4 TO 6 SERVINGS

1   17-ounce package refrigerated cooked beef pot roast with juices
1½ cups packaged sliced fresh mushrooms
1   8-ounce bottle picante sauce
1   14-ounce can chicken broth
1   cup quick-cooking couscous
2   tablespoons snipped fresh cilantro
    Dairy sour cream (optional)
    Chopped fresh tomato (optional)
    Sliced avocado (optional)

1. Transfer liquid from pot roast package to a large skillet; add mushrooms and picante sauce. Cut pot roast into 1- to 1½-inch cubes; add to skillet. Bring to boiling; reduce heat. Simmer, covered, for 10 minutes.

2. Meanwhile, in a medium saucepan bring chicken broth to boiling; stir in couscous. Remove from heat. Cover and let stand for 5 minutes. Fluff couscous with a fork; stir in cilantro.

3. To serve, spoon pot roast mixture over couscous mixture. If desired, serve with sour cream, tomato, and/or avocado.

Per serving: 379 cal., 10 g total fat (4 g sat. fat), 65 mg chol., 1,314 mg sodium, 44 g carbo., 3 g fiber, 31 g pro.

MENU
Corn bread sticks
Mixed greens salad
with desired dressing
Fudge brownies

104 Quick Honey-Garlic Pot Roast

START TO FINISH:
30 MINUTES

MAKES:
4 SERVINGS

1   17-ounce package refrigerated cooked beef roast au jus or beef pot roast with juices
2   tablespoons honey
1   tablespoon Worcestershire sauce
1   to 1½ teaspoons bottled roasted minced garlic
¼   teaspoon black pepper
2   cups packaged peeled baby carrots, halved lengthwise
12 ounces tiny new potatoes, halved
1   medium red onion, cut into thin wedges

1. Remove meat from package, reserving juices. In a medium bowl combine reserved juices, honey, Worcestershire sauce, roasted garlic, and pepper. Place meat in a large nonstick skillet. Arrange carrots, potatoes, and onion around meat. Pour honey mixture over meat and vegetables.

2. Bring mixture to boiling; reduce heat. Simmer, covered, for 20 to 25 minutes or until vegetables are tender and meat is heated through. Transfer meat and vegetables to a serving platter. Spoon sauce over meat and vegetables.

Per serving: 305 cal., 9 g total fat (4 g sat. fat), 64 mg chol., 502 mg sodium, 35 g carbo., 4 g fiber, 26 g pro.

MENU
Whole wheat rolls
Three-bean salad
(from a deli)
Pear crisp

Roast Beef and Mashed Potato Stacks

105

START TO FINISH:
15 MINUTES

MAKES:
4 SERVINGS

1   17-ounce package refrigerated cooked beef tips with gravy
½   cup onion-seasoned beef broth
1   20-ounce package refrigerated mashed potatoes
2   tablespoons butter or margarine
⅛   teaspoon black pepper
4   thick slices white bread

1. In a large skillet combine beef tips with gravy and beef broth. Cook and stir over medium heat until heated through.

2. Meanwhile, prepare mashed potatoes according to package directions, adding the butter and pepper.

3. To serve, place bread slices on 4 dinner plates. Divide mashed potatoes among bread slices. Ladle beef mixture over potatoes and bread.

Per serving: 372 cal., 15 g total fat (6 g sat. fat), 64 mg chol., 1,174 mg sodium, 36 g carbo., 2 g fiber, 23 g pro.

MENU
Multigrain chips
Steamed mixed vegetables
Peppermint ice cream

106

Stroganoff-Sauced Beef Roast

START TO FINISH:
30 MINUTES

MAKES:
3 TO 4 SERVINGS

1   16-ounce package refrigerated cooked beef pot roast with gravy

2   cups fresh shiitake, cremini, or button mushrooms

½   cup dairy sour cream French onion dip

2   cups hot cooked noodles

1. Transfer beef with gravy to a large skillet (leave meat whole). Remove stems from shiitake mushrooms; halve or quarter mushrooms. Add mushrooms to skillet. Cook, covered, over medium-low heat about 15 minutes or until heated through, stirring mushrooms once and turning roast over halfway through cooking time.

2. Use a wooden spoon to break meat into bite-size pieces. Stir onion dip into meat mixture; heat through (do not boil). Stir in hot cooked noodles.

Per serving: 542 cal., 7 g total fat (11 g sat. fat), 99 mg chol., 787 mg sodium, 46 g carbo., 4 g fiber, 8 g pro.

MENU
Whole wheat rolls
Steamed green beans
Carrot cake

Easy Beef Stew

107

PREP:
15 MINUTES

COOK:
10 MINUTES

MAKES:
4 SERVINGS

1   17-ounce package refrigerated cooked beef roast au jus

2   10.75-ounce cans condensed beefy mushroom soup

1   16-ounce package frozen mixed vegetables (any combination)

4   teaspoons snipped fresh basil or 1½ teaspoons dried basil, crushed

1½ cups milk

1. Cut beef into bite-size pieces. In a 4-quart Dutch oven combine beef and the juices, soup, vegetables, and dried basil (if using).

2. Bring to boiling; reduce heat. Simmer, covered, for 10 minutes. Stir in milk and fresh basil (if using). Heat through.

Per serving: 386 cal., 15 g total fat (7 g sat. fat), 80 mg chol., 1,688 mg sodium, 33 g carbo., 5 g fiber, 33 g pro.

MENU
Buttermilk biscuits
Blonde brownies

108

French Onion and Beef Soup

START TO FINISH:
25 MINUTES

MAKES:
4 SERVINGS

3   tablespoons butter or margarine

1   medium onion, thinly sliced and separated into rings

2   10.5-ounce cans condensed French onion soup

2½ cups water

1½ cups cubed cooked beef (about 8 ounces)

4   1-inch slices French bread

½   cup shredded Gruyère or Swiss cheese (2 ounces)

1. In a large skillet melt butter over medium heat. Add onion; cook about 5 minutes or until very tender. Stir in onion soup, water, and beef. Bring to boiling, stirring occasionally.

2. Meanwhile, preheat broiler. Place the bread slices on a baking sheet. Broil 4 inches from the heat about 1 minute or until toasted on 1 side. Top the toasted sides of bread slices with shredded cheese; broil about 1 minute more or until cheese is melted.

3. To serve, ladle soup into soup bowls. Top with bread slices, cheese sides up.

Per serving: 465 cal., 21 g total fat (10 g sat. fat), 82 mg chol., 1,701 mg sodium, 40 g carbo., 3 g fiber, 28 g pro.

MENU
French baguette slices
Mixed greens salad with
desired dressing
Clementines and dried dates

Italian Meatball Soup

START TO FINISH:
25 MINUTES

MAKES:
4 SERVINGS

1   14-ounce can beef broth
1   14.5-ounce can diced tomatoes with onion and garlic, undrained
1½ cups water
½   teaspoon dried Italian seasoning, crushed
½   of a 16- to 18-ounce package frozen Italian-style cooked meatballs
½   cup small dried pasta (such as ditalini or orzo)
1   cup frozen mixed vegetables (any combination)
1   tablespoon finely shredded or grated Parmesan cheese

1. In a large saucepan stir together beef broth, undrained tomatoes, water, and Italian seasoning; bring to boiling.

2. Add frozen meatballs, pasta, and frozen vegetables. Return to boiling; reduce heat. Simmer, covered, about 10 minutes or until pasta and vegetables are tender. Sprinkle individual servings with cheese.

Per serving: 290 cal., 14 g total fat (7 g sat. fat), 38 mg chol., 1,302 mg sodium, 26 g carbo., 4 g fiber, 15 g pro.

MENU
Soft breadsticks
Caesar salad
Red and green grapes

110

Hurry-Up Beef and Vegetable Stew

START TO FINISH:
20 MINUTES

MAKES:
5 SERVINGS

2   cups water

1   10.75-ounce can condensed golden mushroom soup

1   10.75-ounce can condensed tomato soup

½   cup dry red wine or beef broth

2   cups chopped cooked roast beef (about 10 ounces)

1   16-ounce package frozen sugar snap stir-fry vegetables or one 16-ounce package frozen cut broccoli

½   teaspoon dried thyme, crushed

1. In a 4-quart Dutch oven combine water, mushroom soup, tomato soup, and wine. Stir in beef, frozen vegetables, and thyme. Cook over medium heat until bubbly, stirring frequently. Cook for 4 to 5 minutes more or until vegetables are crisp-tender, stirring occasionally.

Per serving: 231 cal., 4 g total fat (1 g sat. fat), 42 mg chol., 906 mg sodium, 21 g carbo., 4 g fiber, 20 g pro.

MENU

Dinner rolls

Romaine salad with desired dressing

Pudding (desired flavor)

Reuben Chowder

START TO FINISH:
30 MINUTES

OVEN:
325°F

MAKES:
4 SERVINGS

1 tablespoon butter or margarine, softened

4 slices rye bread

½ teaspoon caraway seeds (optional)

3 cups milk

1 10.75-ounce can condensed cream of celery soup

2 ounces process Swiss cheese slices, torn

1 14- or 16-ounce can sauerkraut, rinsed, drained, and snipped

2 5-ounce packages sliced corned beef, chopped or torn

1. Preheat oven to 325°F. Spread butter over both sides of each slice of the bread. If desired, sprinkle bread with caraway seeds. Cut into triangles; place on a baking sheet. Bake for 10 to 15 minutes or until toasted on both sides.

2. Meanwhile, in a large saucepan combine milk, soup, and cheese. Cook and stir just until bubbly. Stir in sauerkraut and corned beef; heat through. Serve soup with toasted bread.

Per serving: 456 cal., 23 g total fat (11 g sat. fat), 77 mg chol., 2,696 mg sodium, 35 g carbo., 5 g fiber, 27 g pro.

MENU
Corn chips
Marinated vegetable salad
(from a deli)
Lemon cake

112

Pork Medallions with Cranberry and Fig Chutney

START TO FINISH:
20 MINUTES

MAKES:
4 SERVINGS

1   cup fresh cranberries or ½ cup canned whole cranberry sauce

½   cup apple juice

¼   cup snipped dried figs

2   tablespoons packed brown sugar or granulated sugar

1   teaspoon snipped fresh rosemary or ½ teaspoon dried rosemary, crushed

12   ounces pork tenderloin

4   teaspoons cooking oil

1. For chutney, in a small heavy saucepan stir together cranberries, apple juice, figs, brown sugar, and rosemary. Bring to boiling; reduce heat. Simmer, uncovered, for 5 to 8 minutes or until chutney is of desired consistency, stirring occasionally. Season to taste with *salt* and *black pepper.* Set aside.

2. Meanwhile, trim fat from meat. Cut meat crosswise into 12 pieces. Press each piece with palm of hand to make an even thickness. In a large nonstick skillet heat oil over medium-high heat. Add pork; cook the pork for 2 to 3 minutes or until juices run clear, turning once.

3. To serve, spoon some of the warm chutney over the pork medallions and pass remaining chutney.

Per serving: 227 cal., 7 g total fat (1 g sat. fat), 55 mg chol., 185 mg sodium, 23 g carbo., 3 g fiber, 18 g pro.

MENU

Brown and wild rice pilaf
(from a mix)

Steamed carrots and peas

Pumpkin cake

Pork Tenderloin with Sweet Potatoes

113

12 ounces pork tenderloin

1 tablespoon cooking oil

1 large onion, cut into wedges

2 10-ounce packages or one 16-ounce package frozen candied sweet potatoes, thawed

1 tablespoon snipped fresh thyme or ½ teaspoon dried thyme, crushed

1. Trim fat from meat. Cut meat crosswise into ½-inch slices. In a large skillet heat oil over medium-high heat. Add pork and onion; cook for 2 to 3 minutes or until meat juices run clear, turning once. Remove pork from skillet; set aside.

2. Stir sweet potatoes with sauce and dried thyme (if using) into onion in skillet. Bring to boiling; reduce heat. Cook, covered, over medium heat about 10 minutes or until sweet potatoes are tender. Return meat to skillet. Heat through. Stir in fresh thyme, if using.

Per serving: 386 cal., 13 g total fat (2 g sat. fat), 55 mg chol., 484 mg sodium, 44 g carbo., 4 g fiber, 20 g pro.

MENU
Multigrain rolls
Steamed green beans
Pecan tart

114 Pork Chops Dijon

START TO FINISH:
30 MINUTES

MAKES:
4 SERVINGS

3 tablespoons Dijon-style mustard

2 tablespoons bottled reduced-calorie Italian salad dressing

¼ teaspoon black pepper

4 pork loin chops, cut ½ inch thick (about 1½ pounds)
  Nonstick cooking spray

1 medium onion, halved and sliced

1. In a small bowl combine mustard, salad dressing, and pepper; set aside. Trim fat from the chops. Coat an unheated 10-inch skillet with nonstick cooking spray. Preheat the skillet over medium-high heat. Add the chops; cook until brown on both sides, turning once. Remove chops from skillet.

2. Add onion to skillet. Cook and stir over medium heat for 3 minutes. Push onion aside; return chops to skillet. Spread mustard mixture over chops. Cook, covered, over medium-low heat about 15 minutes or until chops are 160°F. Spoon onion over chops.

Per serving: 163 cal., 5 g total fat (2 g sat. fat), 53 mg chol., 403 mg sodium, 2 g carbo., 0 g fiber, 22 g pro.

MENU
Hot cooked noodles
Roasted Brussels sprouts
Sorbet (desired flavor)
with pomegranate seeds

Thyme Pork Chops with Roasted Cauliflower

115

START TO FINISH:
30 MINUTES

MAKES:
4 SERVINGS

4   pork rib chops, cut ¾ inch thick
4   teaspoons snipped fresh thyme or 1 teaspoon dried thyme or Italian seasoning, crushed
¼   teaspoon salt
¼   teaspoon black pepper
    Nonstick cooking spray
6   cups packaged cauliflower florets
2   small onions, cut into wedges
2   tablespoons olive oil

1. Trim fat from chops. In a small bowl stir together thyme, salt, and pepper; sprinkle evenly on both sides of chops. Set chops aside.

2. Coat an unheated very large nonstick skillet with nonstick cooking spray. Preheat over medium-high heat. Add cauliflower and onion; cook and stir about 5 minutes or until almost tender. Remove skillet from heat.

3. Push cauliflower and onion to the edge of the skillet. Add oil to the skillet. Arrange the seasoned chops in a single layer in skillet. Return skillet to heat and cook over medium heat for 10 to 15 minutes or until pork chops are 160°F and vegetables are tender, turning chops to brown evenly and stirring the vegetable mixture often.

Per serving: 296 cal., 14 g total fat (3 g sat. fat), 70 mg chol., 389 mg sodium, 11 g carbo., 4 g fiber, 32 g pro.

MENU
Sourdough bread
Mashed sweet potatoes
Cinnamon ice cream
with shortbread cookies

116

Smoked Pork Chop Skillet

START TO FINISH:
25 MINUTES

MAKES:
4 SERVINGS

4   cooked smoked pork chops, cut ¾ inch thick (about 1¾ pounds)

1   16-ounce package frozen French-style green beans

¼   cup water

1½ teaspoons snipped fresh sage or ½ teaspoon dried leaf sage, crushed

½   cup balsamic vinegar

1. Trim fat from chops. In a large nonstick skillet cook chops over medium heat for 6 to 10 minutes or until light brown, turning once halfway through cooking. Remove chops from skillet; keep warm.

2. Add green beans, water, and sage to skillet; return chops to skillet. Cook, covered, over medium heat for 5 minutes.

3. Meanwhile, in a small saucepan gently boil balsamic vinegar about 5 minutes or until reduced to ¼ cup. Brush chops with vinegar; drizzle remaining vinegar over the bean mixture.

Per serving: 257 cal., 14 g total fat (5 g sat. fat), 47 mg chol., 749 mg sodium, 18 g carbo., 3 g fiber, 17 g pro.

MENU
Buttermilk biscuits
Roasted potatoes
Sweet potato or
pumpkin pie

Broccoli and Ham Soup

117

START TO FINISH:
25 MINUTES

MAKES:
4 SERVINGS

2   14-ounce cans chicken broth
1   16-ounce package fresh broccoli florets
½   cup chopped onion (1 medium)
2   teaspoons bottled roasted minced garlic
1   cup shredded Swiss cheese (4 ounces)
1   cup half-and-half or light cream
½   cup cubed ham

1. In a large saucepan combine chicken broth, broccoli, onion, and garlic. Bring to boiling; reduce heat. Simmer, covered, about 10 minutes or until broccoli is very tender. In a blender or food processor blend the broccoli mixture, in 2 or 3 batches, until smooth.

2. Return all of the broccoli mixture to saucepan. Return to a simmer. Add cheese; cook, stirring constantly, until melted. Stir in half-and-half and ham. Season to taste with *salt* and *black pepper*.

Per serving: 283 cal., 18 g total fat (10 g sat. fat), 58 mg chol., 1,213 mg sodium, 14 g carbo., 4 g fiber, 18 g pro.

MENU
Multigrain chips
Relish tray (olives, pickles, raw vegetables)
Brownie sundaes

118

Macaroni and Cheese Chowder

START TO FINISH:
30 MINUTES

MAKES:
4 TO 6 SERVINGS

1 14-ounce can reduced-sodium chicken broth
1 cup water
1 cup dried elbow macaroni
1 cup frozen whole kernel corn
1 cup chopped sliced cooked ham (5 ounces)
6 ounces American cheese, cubed
1 cup milk
   Shredded cheddar cheese (optional)

1. In a large saucepan bring chicken broth and water to boiling. Add macaroni; reduce heat. Simmer, covered, about 12 minutes or until macaroni is tender, stirring occasionally.

2. Stir in corn, ham, American cheese, and milk. Cook and stir over medium heat until cheese is melted. Ladle into bowls. If desired, top individual servings with cheddar cheese.

Per serving: 393 cal., 18 g total fat (10 g sat. fat), 64 mg chol., 1,338 mg sodium, 35 g carbo., 2 g fiber, 23 g pro.

MENU
Corn chips
Vegetable tray with vegetable dip
Chocolate chip cookies

Tex-Mex Skillet

START TO FINISH:
30 MINUTES

MAKES:
4 SERVINGS

8   ounces ground pork

4   ounces uncooked chorizo sausage

1   10-ounce can diced tomatoes and green chile peppers, undrained

1   cup frozen whole kernel corn

¾   cup water

½   cup chopped red sweet pepper

1   cup uncooked instant rice

½   cup shredded cheddar cheese or Monterey Jack cheese (2 ounces)
     Flour tortillas, warmed* (optional)
     Dairy sour cream (optional)

1. In a large skillet cook pork and sausage over medium-high heat until brown. Drain off fat. Stir undrained tomatoes, corn, water, and sweet pepper into pork mixture in skillet. Bring to boiling.

2. Stir uncooked rice into meat mixture in skillet. Remove from heat. Top with cheese. Cover and let stand about 5 minutes or until rice is tender. If desired, serve in flour tortillas and top with sour cream.

Per serving: 395 cal., 20 g total fat (9 g sat. fat), 66 mg chol., 748 mg sodium, 33 g carbo., 1 g fiber, 21 g pro.

*Note: To warm tortillas, wrap them in white microwave-safe paper towels; microwave on 100% power (high) for 15 to 30 seconds or until tortillas are softened. (Or preheat oven to 350°F. Wrap tortillas in foil. Heat in preheated oven for 10 to 15 minutes or until warmed.)

MENU
Tortilla chips
Refried beans
Apple cake

120

Sausage and Polenta with Balsamic Vinaigrette

START TO FINISH:
30 MINUTES

OVEN:
400°F

MAKES:
4 SERVINGS

3   uncooked sweet (mild) Italian sausage links, each cut into 4 pieces (about 12 ounces)

½   of a 16-ounce tube refrigerated polenta (plain or flavored)

1   tablespoon olive oil

6   cups packaged Mediterranean- or Italian-blend torn mixed greens

½   cup apple juice or apple cider

¼   cup balsamic vinegar

2   tablespoons snipped dried tomato (not oil-packed)

¼   cup pine nuts or slivered almonds, toasted (optional)

1. In a 10-inch skillet cook sausage over medium heat for 5 minutes, turning to brown evenly.

2. Meanwhile, preheat oven to 400°F. Cut polenta into ¼-inch slices; cut each slice crosswise in half. Brush tops of polenta slices with oil. Arrange polenta slices in a single layer on a baking sheet. Bake for 10 to 12 minutes or until golden brown, turning once. Divide greens among 4 dinner plates; set aside.

3. Remove sausage from skillet; drain off fat. Wipe skillet with paper towels. Return sausage to skillet; add apple juice, vinegar, and dried tomato. Bring to boiling; reduce heat. Simmer, covered, for 8 to 10 minutes or until sausage is cooked through (160°F).*

4. Arrange polenta slices over greens on plates. Add sausage pieces to plates; drizzle with balsamic mixture. If desired, sprinkle with nuts.

Per serving: 380 cal., 22 g total fat (8 g sat. fat), 57 mg chol., 741 mg sodium, 23 g carbo., 4 g fiber, 15 g pro.

*NOTE: The internal color of a sausage piece is not a reliable doneness indicator. A sausage piece cooked to 160°F is safe, regardless of color. To measure the doneness of a sausage piece, insert an instant-read thermometer from an end into the center of the sausage piece.

MENU

Crusty Italian bread

Tiramisu (frozen)

24 Pork and Sweet Potato Stir-Fry, page 31

29 Ham and Cheese Quesadillas, page 36

62 Turkey Burgers with Cranberry Sauce, page 69

65 Smoked Turkey and Tortellini Salad, page 72

66 Sausage and Vegetables with Polenta, page 73

75 Roasted Salmon and Tomatoes, page 82

77 Tuna and Pasta Alfredo, page 84

84 Trattoria-Style Fettuccine, page 91

95 Individual Sicilian Meat Loaves, page 103

99 Quick Skillet Lasagna, page 107

100 Zippy Beef, Mac, and Cheese, page 108

109 Italian Meatball Soup, page 117

112 Pork Medallions with Cranberry and Fig Chutney, page 120

115 Thyme Pork Chops with Roasted Cauliflower, page 123

118 Macaroni and Cheese Chowder, page 126

131 Shortcut Chicken Mole, page 155

144 Quick-to-Fix Turkey and Rice Soup, page 168

145 Turkey Ravioli Soup, page 169

146 White Bean and Sausage Rigatoni, page 170

155 Maple-Hoisin Glazed Halibut, page 179

181 Jalapeño Corn Chowder, page 205

184 Chard-Topped Steaks, page 209

191 Beef and Bok Choy, page 216

200 Squirt-of-Orange Chops, page 225

211 Cheesy Grilled Ham Sandwiches, page 236

216 Tuscan Lamb Chop Skillet, page 241

226 Chicken Fingers, page 251

230 Chicken Tortilla Soup, page 255

244 Pineapple-Glazed Fish, page 277

249 Oven-Fried Fish, page 282

273 Peppery Artichoke Pitas, page 306

121

Corn and Sausage Chowder

START TO FINISH:
20 MINUTES

MAKES:
5 SERVINGS

1 20-ounce package refrigerated shredded hash brown potatoes

1 14-ounce can reduced-sodium chicken broth

1 10-ounce package frozen whole kernel corn

2 cups milk

12 ounces cooked link sausage, halved lengthwise and sliced

⅓ cup sliced green onion

¼ teaspoon black pepper

Green or red bottled hot pepper sauce (optional)

2 tablespoons snipped fresh cilantro

1. In a 4-quart Dutch oven combine hash brown potatoes, chicken broth, and corn. Bring to boiling; reduce heat. Simmer, covered, about 10 minutes or just until potatoes are tender, stirring occasionally.

2. Using a potato masher, slightly mash potatoes. Stir in milk, sausage, green onion, and black pepper. Heat through. Season to taste with *salt*, and, if desired, hot pepper sauce. Sprinkle individual servings with cilantro.

Per serving: 439 cal., 22 g total fat (8 g sat. fat), 65 mg chol., 873 mg sodium, 41 g carbo., 3 g fiber, 22 g pro.

MENU
Corn bread squares
Mixed greens salad with desired dressing
Chocolate silk pie

122 Quick Sausage and Noodle Soup

START TO FINISH:
20 MINUTES

MAKES:
4 SERVINGS

4 cups water

1 14.5-ounce can diced tomatoes with green pepper and onion, undrained

8 ounces cooked smoked sausage, halved lengthwise and thinly sliced

1 medium green or red sweet pepper, cut into bite-size strips

2 3-ounce packages chicken-flavor ramen noodles

1. In a large saucepan combine water, undrained tomatoes, sausage, sweet pepper, and one of the seasoning packets from the noodles (set noodles aside and discard remaining seasoning packet or save for another use). Bring to boiling.

2. Break noodles into quarters; add to saucepan. Return to boiling; cook for 2 to 3 minutes or until noodles are tender.

Per serving: 435 cal., 25 g total fat (9 g sat. fat), 39 mg chol., 1,940 mg sodium, 35 g carbo., 3 g fiber, 18 g pro.

MENU
Crusty Italian bread
Caesar salad
Spice cake

Lamb with Herbed Mushrooms

123

START TO FINISH:
25 MINUTES

MAKES:
4 SERVINGS

8 lamb loin chops, cut 1 inch thick (about 1½ pounds)
2 teaspoons olive oil
1 small onion, thinly sliced
2 cups packaged sliced fresh mushrooms
1 tablespoon balsamic vinegar
1 teaspoon bottled minced garlic (2 cloves)
1 teaspoon snipped fresh tarragon or basil or ¼ teaspoon dried tarragon or basil, crushed
¼ teaspoon salt
¼ teaspoon black pepper

1. Trim fat from chops. In a large nonstick skillet heat oil over medium-high heat. Add chops; reduce heat to medium. Cook chops for 9 to 11 minutes for medium (160°F), turning once halfway through cooking. Remove chops from skillet, reserving drippings. Cover chops to keep warm.

2. Stir onion into drippings in skillet. Cook and stir for 2 minutes. Stir in mushrooms, balsamic vinegar, garlic, dried tarragon (if using), salt, and pepper. Cook and stir for 3 to 4 minutes or until mushrooms are tender. Stir in fresh tarragon, if using. Serve mushroom mixture over chops.

Per serving: 165 cal., 9 g total fat (3 g sat. fat), 48 mg chol., 280 mg sodium, 4 g carbo., 1 g fiber, 16 g pro.

MENU
Warm pita bread
Hot cooked orzo
Steamed green beans

124

Lamb Chops
with Cranberry Relish

PREP:
15 MINUTES

BROIL:
11 MINUTES

MAKES:
4 SERVINGS

½ cup frozen cranberry-orange relish, thawed

¼ cup chopped pecans, toasted

2 tablespoons orange juice

2 teaspoons snipped fresh rosemary or ½ teaspoon dried rosemary, crushed

8 lamb loin chops, cut 1 inch thick (about 2½ pounds)

1. Preheat broiler. In a small bowl stir together cranberry-orange relish, pecans, orange juice, and rosemary. Set aside.

2. Trim fat from chops. Place chops on the unheated rack of a broiler pan. Sprinkle chops with *salt* and *black pepper*. Broil chops 3 to 4 inches from the heat for 10 to 15 minutes for medium (160°F), turning once halfway through broiling. Spread relish mixture over chops. Broil for 1 minute more.

Per serving: 324 cal., 13 g total fat (3 g sat. fat), 100 mg chol., 172 mg sodium, 18 g carbo., 1 g fiber, 33 g pro.

MENU

Candied sweet potatoes

Brown and wild rice pilaf
(from a mix)

Pecan sandies with eggnog

Greek-Style Sloppy Joes

125

START TO FINISH:
20 MINUTES

MAKES:
6 SANDWICHES

1   pound ground lamb or beef

½   cup chopped onion (1 medium)

1   15-ounce can tomato sauce

⅓   cup bulgur

1   teaspoon dried oregano, crushed

½   teaspoon salt

¼   teaspoon black pepper

2   cups shredded romaine lettuce (optional)

6   kaiser rolls, split and toasted

1   cup crumbled feta cheese with tomato and basil or plain feta cheese (4 ounces)

1. In a large skillet cook ground meat and onion over medium-high heat until meat is brown and onion is tender. Drain off fat. Stir in tomato sauce, bulgur, oregano, salt, and pepper. Bring to boiling; reduce heat. Simmer, uncovered, about 5 minutes or until desired consistency, stirring occasionally.

2. To assemble, if desired, arrange romaine on bottom halves of rolls. Spoon meat mixture onto bottom halves of rolls. Top with feta cheese; replace roll tops.

Per sandwich: 418 cal., 17 g total fat (7 g sat. fat), 67 mg chol., 1,083 mg sodium, 42 g carbo., 4 g fiber, 23 g pro.

MENU
Relish tray (olives, pickles, raw vegetables)
Chunky applesauce
Assorted cookies

126 Hungarian-Style Chicken

START TO FINISH:
30 MINUTES

MAKES:
6 SERVINGS

6   skinless, boneless chicken breast halves (about 2 pounds)
2   teaspoons Hungarian paprika
3   tablespoons cooking oil
1   cup chopped onion (1 large)
1   10.75-ounce can condensed cream of chicken soup
1   8-ounce carton dairy sour cream
¼   cup milk

1. Sprinkle chicken with 1 teaspoon of the paprika. In a large skillet heat 2 tablespoons of the oil over medium-high heat. Add chicken; reduce heat to medium. Cook for 8 to 12 minutes or until chicken is no longer pink (170°F), turning occasionally to brown evenly. Remove chicken from skillet; cover to keep warm.

2. In the same skillet heat remaining 1 tablespoon oil over medium heat. Add onion; cook for 5 to 6 minutes or until tender.

3. Meanwhile, in a small bowl combine soup, sour cream, milk, and the remaining 1 teaspoon paprika. Add to cooked onion; cook and stir until heated through. Serve soup mixture over chicken.

Per serving: 375 cal., 20 g total fat (7 g sat. fat), 109 mg chol., 472 mg sodium, 10 g carbo., 1 g fiber, 38 g pro.

MENU
Hot cooked noodles
Dinner rolls
Steamed green beans
Apple pie

Molasses-Orange Glazed Chicken

127

PREP:
5 MINUTES

BROIL:
12 MINUTES

MAKES:
4 SERVINGS

2   tablespoons frozen orange juice concentrate, thawed

2   tablespoons molasses

¼   teaspoon onion powder

4   skinless, boneless chicken breast halves or 8 skinless, boneless chicken thighs

Orange peel strips* (optional)

1. Preheat broiler. For glaze, in a small bowl stir together orange juice concentrate, molasses, and onion powder; set aside.

2. Sprinkle chicken with *salt* and *black pepper*. Place chicken on the unheated rack of a broiler pan. Broil 4 to 5 inches from the heat for 6 minutes. Brush with some of the glaze. Turn chicken; brush with remaining glaze. Broil for 6 to 9 minutes more or until chicken is no longer pink (170°F for breasts or 180°F for thighs). If desired, garnish with orange peel strips.

Per serving: 204 cal., 2 g total fat (1 g sat. fat), 82 mg chol., 168 mg sodium, 11 g carbo., 0 g fiber, 33 g pro.

---

*NOTE: For orange peel strips, use a vegetable peeler to cut thin strips of peel from the surface of an orange. Make sure to remove only the orange part of the peel.

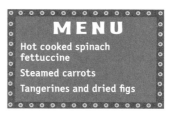

MENU

Hot cooked spinach fettuccine

Steamed carrots

Tangerines and dried figs

128 Chicken Nuggets

PREP:
20 MINUTES

BAKE:
7 MINUTES

OVEN:
450°F

MAKES:
4 SERVINGS

⅔ cup crushed cornflakes

1 teaspoon paprika

½ teaspoon garlic powder

½ teaspoon dried oregano, crushed

⅛ teaspoon cayenne pepper (optional)

1 egg white, lightly beaten

1 pound skinless, boneless chicken breast halves, cut into 1-inch pieces

1. Preheat oven to 450°F. In a plastic bag combine crushed cornflakes, paprika, garlic powder, oregano, and, if desired, cayenne pepper. Place egg white in a small bowl.

2. Dip chicken pieces into egg white, allowing excess to drip off. Add chicken pieces, a few at a time, to cornflake mixture; shake to coat well. Place chicken pieces in a single layer in a shallow baking pan.

3. Bake for 7 to 9 minutes or until chicken is no longer pink.

Per serving: 191 cal., 2 g total fat (0 g sat. fat), 66 mg chol., 228 mg sodium, 13 g carbo., 0 g fiber, 29 g pro.

MENU

Applesauce

Vegetable tray
with vegetable dip

Peppermint ice cream

Orange Chicken and Fried Rice

129

START TO FINISH:
25 MINUTES

MAKES:
4 SERVINGS

1   6-ounce package Oriental-flavor fried rice mix

2   tablespoons butter or margarine

1   pound packaged chicken breast stir-fry strips

8   green onions, bias-cut into 1-inch pieces

1   teaspoon bottled minced garlic (2 cloves) or ¼ teaspoon garlic powder

1   teaspoon ground ginger

1   tablespoon frozen orange juice concentrate, thawed

¼   cup chopped cashews (optional)

1. Cook rice according to package directions.

2. Meanwhile, in a large skillet melt butter over medium-high heat. Add chicken strips, green onion, garlic, and ginger; cook and stir for 3 to 5 minutes or until chicken is no longer pink.

3. Stir orange juice concentrate into cooked rice. Stir rice mixture into chicken mixture in skillet. Cook and stir until heated through. If desired, sprinkle individual servings with cashews.

Per serving: 396 cal., 13 g total fat (5 g sat. fat), 82 mg chol., 985 mg sodium, 38 g carbo., 2 g fiber, 32 g pro.

MENU

Spring rolls
(frozen or takeout)

Steamed broccoli spears

Coconut ice cream with
crystallized ginger

130 Gingered Chicken Stir-Fry

START TO FINISH:
20 MINUTES

MAKES:
4 SERVINGS

12 ounces skinless, boneless chicken breast halves or skinless, boneless chicken thighs

2 tablespoons cooking oil

2 cups frozen mixed vegetables (any combination)

½ cup bottled stir-fry sauce with ginger

2 cups hot cooked rice

1. Cut chicken into 1-inch pieces; set aside. In a wok or large skillet heat oil over medium-high heat. Add vegetables; stir-fry about 3 minutes or until crisp-tender. Remove vegetables from wok.

2. Add chicken to hot wok. (Add more oil if necessary.) Stir-fry for 3 to 4 minutes or until chicken is no longer pink. Push chicken from center of the wok. Add sauce to center of the wok. Cook and stir until bubbly. Return cooked vegetables to wok. Stir to coat. Cook and stir about 1 minute more or until heated through. Serve over hot cooked rice.

Per serving: 382 cal., 9 g total fat (1 g sat. fat), 49 mg chol., 879 mg sodium, 50 g carbo., 3 g fiber, 24 g pro.

MENU
Egg rolls (frozen or takeout)
Lemon cake

Shortcut Chicken Mole

131

1½ cups uncooked instant white rice
1   tablespoon cooking oil
12 ounces packaged chicken breast stir-fry strips
1   tablespoon unsweetened cocoa powder
1   teaspoon ground cumin
1   16-ounce jar thick and chunky salsa
½   of a 16-ounce package frozen sweet pepper and onion stir-fry vegetables (2 cups)
     Fresh herb sprigs (optional)

1. Cook rice according to package directions.

2. Meanwhile, in a large skillet heat oil over medium-high heat. Add chicken strips; cook and stir until no longer pink. Drain off fat.

3. Sprinkle chicken with cocoa powder and cumin; stir to combine. Stir in salsa and frozen stir-fry vegetables. Bring to boiling; reduce heat. Simmer, covered, about 5 minutes or just until vegetables are tender.

4. Serve chicken mixture with the hot cooked rice. If desired, garnish with fresh herb sprigs.

Per serving: 334 cal., 5 g total fat (1 g sat. fat), 49 mg chol., 549 mg sodium, 44 g carbo., 3 g fiber, 26 g pro.

MENU
Corn muffins
Spinach salad with desired dressing
Chocolate ice cream

132 Easy Oriental Chicken Soup

START TO FINISH:
20 MINUTES

MAKES:
3 SERVINGS

1 tablespoon cooking oil

8 ounces packaged chicken breast stir-fry strips

3 cups water

½ of a 16-ounce package frozen broccoli, carrots, and water chestnuts (2 cups)

1 3-ounce package chicken-flavor ramen noodles

2 tablespoons reduced-sodium soy sauce

1. In a large saucepan heat oil over medium-high heat. Add chicken; cook and stir for 2 to 3 minutes or until no longer pink. Remove from heat. Drain off fat.

2. Carefully add water, vegetables, and seasoning packet from ramen noodles to chicken in saucepan. Bring to boiling. Break up noodles; stir noodles into soup. Reduce heat. Simmer, covered, for 3 minutes. Stir in soy sauce.

Per serving: 254 cal., 8 g total fat (1 g sat. fat), 63 mg chol., 829 mg sodium, 22 g carbo., 5 g fiber, 22 g pro.

MENU
Spring rolls
(frozen or takeout)
Fresh pineapple chunks
drizzled with honey

Chicken and Rice Soup

START TO FINISH:
25 MINUTES

MAKES:
4 SERVINGS

1 10.75-ounce can condensed cream of chicken or cream of mushroom soup

1 6- to 6.75-ounce package quick-cooking long grain and wild rice mix

4½ cups water

8 ounces ground uncooked chicken or turkey

1. In a 3-quart saucepan combine soup and package of rice mix with seasoning packet. Gradually stir in the water. Bring to boiling.

2. Drop the ground chicken by small spoonfuls into the boiling mixture (about 36 pieces). Reduce heat. Simmer, covered, about 5 minutes or until no pink remains in chicken. Season to taste with *black pepper.*

Per serving: 334 cal., 13 g total fat (1 g sat. fat), 6 mg chol., 1,253 mg sodium, 39 g carbo., 1 g fiber, 16 g pro.

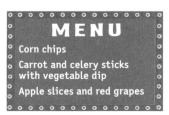

MENU
Corn chips
Carrot and celery sticks
with vegetable dip
Apple slices and red grapes

134 Creamy Chicken and Noodles

START TO FINISH:
25 MINUTES

MAKES:
4 SERVINGS

2 cups frozen stir-fry vegetables (such as broccoli, carrots, onion, red peppers, celery, water chestnuts, and mushrooms)

1 10.75-ounce can condensed cheddar cheese soup

¾ cup milk

½ teaspoon dried thyme, crushed
Several dashes bottled hot pepper sauce

2 cups cubed cooked chicken (10 ounces)

2 cups hot cooked noodles

1. In a large skillet or saucepan cook frozen vegetables according to package directions. Drain, if necessary; set aside.

2. In the same skillet or saucepan stir together soup, milk, thyme, and hot pepper sauce. Add chicken and cooked vegetables. Cook and stir over medium heat about 10 minutes or until heated through. Serve over hot cooked noodles.

Per serving: 352 cal., 12 g total fat (4 g sat. fat), 102 mg chol., 702 mg sodium, 35 g carbo., 2 g fiber, 29 g pro.

MENU
Buttermilk biscuits
Applesauce
Pudding (desired flavor) with oatmeal cookies

Chicken-Biscuit Pie

135

PREP:
15 MINUTES

BAKE:
12 MINUTES

OVEN:
450°F

MAKES:
4 SERVINGS

1   10.75-ounce can condensed cream of chicken soup

½   cup milk

¼   cup dairy sour cream

1   cup cubed cooked chicken or turkey (5 ounces)

1½ cups frozen mixed vegetables

½   teaspoon dried basil, crushed

⅛   teaspoon black pepper

1   package (5 or 6) refrigerated biscuits, quartered

1. **Preheat oven to 425°F. In a medium saucepan stir together soup, milk, and sour cream. Stir in chicken, frozen vegetables, basil, and pepper. Cook and stir over medium heat until boiling.**

2. **Spoon chicken mixture into a lightly greased 1½-quart casserole. Top with quartered biscuits.**

3. **Bake, uncovered, for 10 to 12 minutes or until biscuits are light brown.**

Per serving: 335 cal., 14 g total fat (5 g sat. fat), 49 mg chol., 1,049 mg sodium, 33 g carbo., 3 g fiber, 20 g pro.

MENU

Mixed greens salad
with desired dressing

Fudge brownies

136

Chicken and Dumpling Soup

START TO FINISH:
30 MINUTES

MAKES:
6 SERVINGS

5 cups reduced-sodium chicken broth

1 cup sliced carrot (2 medium)

1 cup chopped celery (2 stalks)

⅛ teaspoon black pepper

1½ cups chopped cooked chicken (8 ounces)

1½ cups packaged biscuit mix

½ cup milk

1. In a medium saucepan combine chicken broth, carrot, celery, and pepper. Bring to boiling; reduce heat. Simmer, covered, for 10 minutes. Stir in chicken.

2. Meanwhile, for dumplings, in a medium bowl combine biscuit mix and milk. Stir just until combined.

3. Spoon dough in 12 mounds on top of hot chicken mixture. Cook, covered, about 10 minutes or until a toothpick inserted into dumplings comes out clean.

Per serving: 222 cal., 8 g total fat (2 g sat. fat), 33 mg chol., 916 mg sodium, 23 g carbo., 1 g fiber, 15 g pro.

MENU
Multigrain chips
Fresh pear slices
Shortbread cookies
with eggnog

Minestrone in Minutes

137

START TO FINISH:
10 MINUTES

MAKES:
4 SERVINGS

2   18- to 19-ounce cans ready-to-serve minestrone soup

2   cups chopped cooked chicken breast (10 ounces)

1   teaspoon bottled roasted minced garlic

2   cups packaged fresh baby spinach leaves

¼   cup shredded Parmesan cheese (1 ounce)

1. **In a large saucepan combine minestrone soup, chicken, and garlic. Cook over medium heat until heated through.**

2. **Add spinach; stir just until wilted. Heat through. Sprinkle individual servings with Parmesan cheese.**

Per serving: 357 cal., 13 g total fat (7 g sat. fat), 82 mg chol., 1,623 mg sodium, 23 g carbo., 5 g fiber, 37 g pro.

MENU
Garlic bread
Caesar salad
Carrot cake

138 Curried Chicken and Corn Chowder

START TO FINISH:
15 MINUTES

MAKES:
4 SERVINGS

1   17-ounce can cream-style corn

2   cups milk

1   10.75-ounce can condensed cream of chicken soup

¾   cup chopped green or red sweet pepper (1 medium)

1   tablespoon dried minced onion

2   to 3 teaspoons curry powder

1   9.75- or 10-ounce can chunk-style chicken or 1½ cups frozen diced cooked chicken
    Coarsely chopped peanuts (optional)

1. In a large saucepan stir together undrained corn, milk, soup, sweet pepper, dried minced onion, and curry powder. Bring to boiling, stirring frequently.

2. Stir in undrained canned chicken or frozen chicken; cook about 2 minutes or until heated through. If desired, sprinkle individual servings with peanuts.

Per serving: 324 cal., 11 g total fat (4 g sat. fat), 49 mg chol., 1,201 mg sodium, 39 g carbo., 3 g fiber, 24 g pro.

MENU

Warm pita bread

Spinach salad with
desired dressing

Coconut ice cream with
fresh pineapple chunks

Broccoli and Chicken Fettuccine Alfredo

139

START TO FINISH:
15 MINUTES

MAKES:
4 SERVINGS

1 9-ounce package refrigerated fettuccine

1 10-ounce package frozen cut broccoli

1 10-ounce container refrigerated Alfredo pasta sauce

6 ounces smoked chicken or turkey breast, chopped

1 teaspoon dried basil, crushed

Finely shredded Parmesan or Romano cheese (optional)

1. In a large saucepan cook pasta and broccoli in a large amount of boiling water for 3 minutes. Drain pasta and broccoli; return to saucepan. Cover; keep warm.

2. Meanwhile, in a medium saucepan combine Alfredo sauce, chicken, and basil. Cook and stir just until heated through (do not boil).

3. Add chicken mixture to cooked pasta mixture; toss gently to coat. If desired, sprinkle individual servings with Parmesan cheese.

Per serving: 480 cal., 25 g total fat (13 g sat. fat), 133 mg chol., 781 mg sodium, 43 g carbo., 4 g fiber, 22 g pro.

MENU
Crusty Italian bread
Mixed greens salad with desired dressing
Apple crisp

140 Turkey Parmigiana

START TO FINISH:
30 MINUTES

MAKES:
4 SERVINGS

8   ounces dried spaghetti

2   turkey breast tenderloins (about 1¼ pounds)

1   tablespoon butter or margarine

2   tablespoons grated Parmesan cheese

1   14-ounce jar tomato and herb pasta sauce (1¾ cups)

¾   cup shredded mozzarella cheese (3 ounces)

1. Cook spaghetti according to package directions; drain. Cover and keep warm.

2. Meanwhile, split each turkey breast tenderloin in half horizontally to make 4 turkey steaks. Sprinkle turkey with *salt* and *black pepper.* In a large skillet melt butter over medium-high heat. Add turkey; reduce heat to medium. Cook for 15 to 18 minutes or until no longer pink (170°F), turning occasionally to brown evenly. Sprinkle turkey with Parmesan cheese. Spoon pasta sauce over turkey. Cover and cook for 1 to 2 minutes or until heated through.

3. Sprinkle turkey with mozzarella cheese. Cover and let stand for 1 to 2 minutes or until cheese is melted. Serve with the cooked spaghetti.

Per serving: 480 cal., 12 g total fat (6 g sat. fat), 95 mg chol., 632 mg sodium, 50 g carbo., 3 g fiber, 41 g pro.

MENU
Focaccia
Steamed green beans
Gingerbread

Quick Turkey Tetrazzini

141

PREP:
15 MINUTES

BAKE:
12 MINUTES

OVEN:
425°F

MAKES:
4 SERVINGS

Nonstick cooking spray

6   ounces dried spaghetti

1   18.75-ounce can ready-to-serve chunky creamy chicken with mushroom soup

1   cup chopped cooked turkey (5 ounces)

½   cup finely shredded Parmesan cheese (2 ounces)

2   tablespoons sliced almonds

1. Preheat oven to 425°F. Lightly coat a 2-quart square baking dish with nonstick cooking spray; set aside.

2. Cook spaghetti according to package directions. Drain spaghetti; return to pan. Add soup, turkey, and ¼ cup of the Parmesan cheese to cooked spaghetti; heat through. Transfer spaghetti mixture to baking dish. Sprinkle with the remaining ¼ cup Parmesan cheese and the almonds.

3. Bake, uncovered, for 12 to 15 minutes or until top is golden.

Per serving: 413 cal., 13 g total fat (5 g sat. fat), 59 mg chol., 752 mg sodium, 43 g carbo., 2 g fiber, 28 g pro.

MENU
Crusty bread
Steamed mixed vegetables
Hot fudge sundaes

142 Easy Turkey-Pesto Mock Pot Pie

PREP:
15 MINUTES

BAKE:
ACCORDING
TO PACKAGE
DIRECTIONS

MAKES:
6 SERVINGS

1   11-ounce package (12) refrigerated breadsticks
1   12-ounce jar turkey gravy
½   cup dairy sour cream
⅓   cup purchased basil or dried tomato pesto
3   cups cubed, cooked turkey (about 1 pound)
1   16-ounce package frozen peas and carrots

1. Bake the breadsticks according to package directions.

2. Meanwhile, in a large saucepan combine turkey gravy, sour cream, and pesto. Stir in turkey and peas and carrots. Bring to boiling, stirring frequently.

3. Spoon turkey mixture into 6 serving bowls. Top with baked breadsticks.

Per serving: 365 cal., 16 g total fat (5 g sat. fat), 52 mg chol., 964 mg sodium, 36 g carbo., 4 g fiber, 20 g pro.

MENU
Relish tray (olives, pickles, raw vegetables)
Carrot cake

Spicy Turkey and Beans

143

START TO FINISH:
30 MINUTES

BAKE:
ACCORDING
TO PACKAGE
DIRECTIONS

MAKES:
6 SERVINGS

1   7- to 8.5-ounce package corn muffin mix

1   to 2 teaspoons chili powder

2   15.5-ounce cans pinto and/or small red beans, rinsed and drained

1   15-ounce can tomato sauce

1   10-ounce can chopped tomatoes and green chile peppers, undrained

1   cup chopped cooked turkey (5 ounces)

½   cup shredded cheddar or Monterey Jack cheese (2 ounces)

1. In a medium bowl combine corn muffin mix and ½ teaspoon of the chili powder. Prepare and bake muffins according to package directions, making 6 muffins.

2. Meanwhile, in a medium saucepan combine remaining ½ to 1½ teaspoons chili powder, beans, tomato sauce, undrained tomatoes, and turkey. Cook and stir for 8 to 10 minutes or until heated through.

3. Split corn muffins; spoon bean mixture over muffins. Sprinkle with cheese.

Per serving: 385 cal., 9 g total fat (2 g sat. fat), 28 mg chol., 1,328 mg sodium, 57 g carbo., 8 g fiber, 22 g pro.

MENU

Corn chips
Coleslaw (from a deli)
Fudge brownies

144 Quick-to-Fix Turkey and Rice Soup

START TO FINISH:
25 MINUTES

MAKES:
6 SERVINGS

4 cups chicken broth

1 cup water

¼ teaspoon dried Italian seasoning, crushed

¼ teaspoon black pepper

2 cups frozen mixed vegetables

1 cup uncooked instant rice

2 cups chopped cooked turkey or chicken (10 ounces)

1 14.5-ounce can diced tomatoes, undrained

1. **In a large saucepan or Dutch oven combine chicken broth, water, Italian seasoning, and pepper. Bring to boiling.**

2. **Stir mixed vegetables and rice into broth mixture in saucepan. Return to boiling; reduce heat. Simmer, covered, for 8 to 10 minutes or until vegetables are tender. Stir in turkey and undrained tomatoes; heat through.**

Per serving: 213 cal., 4 g total fat (1 g sat. fat), 35 mg chol., 687 mg sodium, 24 g carbo., 2 g fiber, 20 g pro.

MENU
Soft breadsticks
Fresh apple and pear slices
Cookies and spiced apple cider

Turkey Ravioli Soup

145

START TO FINISH:
25 MINUTES

MAKES:
6 SERVINGS

6 cups reduced-sodium chicken broth

¾ cup chopped red sweet pepper (1 medium)

½ cup chopped onion (1 medium)

1½ teaspoons dried Italian seasoning, crushed

1½ cups chopped cooked turkey (8 ounces)

1 9-ounce package refrigerated light cheese ravioli

2 cups shredded packaged prewashed fresh spinach

Shaved or finely shredded Parmesan cheese (optional)

1. In a Dutch oven combine chicken broth, sweet pepper, onion, and Italian seasoning. Bring to boiling; reduce heat. Simmer, covered, for 5 minutes.

2. Add turkey and ravioli to broth mixture. Return to boiling; reduce heat. Simmer, uncovered, about 6 minutes or just until ravioli is tender. Stir in spinach. If desired, top individual servings with Parmesan cheese.

Per serving: 246 cal., 7 g total fat (3 g sat. fat), 48 mg chol., 879 mg sodium, 24 g carbo., 2 g fiber, 22 g pro.

MENU
Garlic bread
Marinated vegetable salad
(from a deli)
Clementines and dried dates

146

White Bean and Sausage Rigatoni

START TO FINISH:
20 MINUTES

MAKES:
4 SERVINGS

8   ounces dried rigatoni pasta or medium shell pasta

1   15- to 19-ounce can white kidney (cannellini) beans, Great Northern beans, or navy
    beans, rinsed and drained

1   14.5-ounce can Italian-style stewed tomatoes, undrained

6   ounces cooked smoked turkey sausage, halved lengthwise and cut into ½-inch slices

⅓   cup snipped fresh basil

1   ounce Asiago or Parmesan cheese, shaved or finely shredded (optional)

1. Cook pasta according to package directions. Drain. Return pasta to hot
   saucepan; cover to keep warm.

2. Meanwhile, in a large saucepan combine beans, undrained tomatoes, and
   sausage; heat through. Add pasta and basil; toss gently to combine. If desired,
   sprinkle individual servings with Asiago cheese.

Per serving: 378 cal., 6 g total fat (1 g sat. fat), 29 mg chol., 760 mg sodium, 65 g carbo., 7 g fiber, 21 g pro.

MENU
Crusty Italian bread
Caesar salad
Peppermint ice cream

Spicy Turkey Sauce with Pasta

147

START TO FINISH:
25 MINUTES

MAKES:
4 SERVINGS

1   9-ounce package refrigerated fettuccine or linguine

8   ounces uncooked Italian turkey sausage (remove casings, if present)

1   cup cut-up yellow summer squash or zucchini

1   small red sweet pepper, cut into thin strips

¼   cup chopped red onion

1   14-ounce jar pasta sauce

2   tablespoons shredded Parmesan cheese (optional)

1. Cook pasta according to package directions; drain.

2. Meanwhile, for sauce, in a large skillet cook sausage, squash, sweet pepper, and onion over medium heat until sausage is brown; drain off fat. Stir in pasta sauce; heat through. Serve sauce over pasta. If desired, sprinkle individual servings with Parmesan cheese.

Per serving: 350 cal., 10 g total fat (3 g sat. fat), 115 mg chol., 866 mg sodium, 49 g carbo., 5 g fiber, 20 g pro.

MENU

Country Italian bread

Romaine salad with vinaigrette dressing

Sorbet (desired flavor) with pomegranate seeds

148 Polenta with Turkey Sausage Florentine

START TO FINISH:
25 MINUTES

MAKES:
4 SERVINGS

2　9- or 10-ounce packages frozen creamed spinach

1　pound bulk turkey sausage

2　tablespoons olive oil

1　16-ounce tube refrigerated cooked polenta with wild mushrooms or plain polenta, cut into ¾-inch slices

¼　cup sliced almonds or pine nuts, toasted

1. Cook the spinach according to package directions.

2. Meanwhile, in a large skillet cook sausage over medium heat until brown. Remove sausage from skillet; drain well.

3. In the same skillet heat oil over medium heat. Add polenta slices; cook about 6 minutes or until golden, turning once halfway through cooking. Keep warm.

4. Stir cooked sausage into hot creamed spinach; heat through. Divide polenta among 4 dinner plates. Spoon sausage mixture on top of the polenta. Sprinkle with toasted nuts.

Per serving: 607 cal., 41 g total fat (8 g sat. fat), 119 mg chol., 1,586 mg sodium, 33 g carbo., 6 g fiber, 28 g pro.

MENU
Multigrain rolls
Pasta salad (from a deli)
Spice cake

Turkey Sausage and Bean Soup

149

START TO FINISH:
30 MINUTES

MAKES:
4 SERVINGS

2   15-ounce cans Great Northern or white kidney (cannellini) beans, rinsed and drained

1   10.75-ounce can condensed cream of celery soup

8   ounces cooked smoked turkey sausage, halved lengthwise and sliced

1½ cups milk

1   teaspoon dried minced onion

1   teaspoon bottled minced garlic (2 cloves) or ¼ teaspoon garlic powder

½   teaspoon dried thyme, crushed

⅛   to ¼ teaspoon black pepper

1. In a large saucepan combine beans, soup, sausage, milk, onion, garlic, thyme, and pepper.

2. Bring to boiling over medium-high heat, stirring occasionally; reduce heat. Simmer, covered, for 10 minutes, stirring occasionally.

Per serving: 434 cal., 11 g total fat (3 g sat. fat), 54 mg chol., 1,129 mg sodium, 57 g carbo., 11 g fiber, 29 g pro.

MENU
Buttermilk biscuits
Fresh apple slices and red grapes
Pecan pie

150

Turkey Chili with Hominy

START TO FINISH:
20 MINUTES

MAKES:
4 TO 5 SERVINGS

12 ounces uncooked Italian turkey sausage (remove casings, if present) or uncooked ground turkey

2 15-ounce cans chili beans with chili gravy

1 15-ounce can golden hominy, drained

1 cup bottled salsa with lime

⅔ cup water

⅓ cup sliced green onion

1. In a large saucepan cook the turkey sausage over medium heat until brown.

2. Stir in undrained chili beans, hominy, salsa, and water. Heat through. Ladle chili into bowls. Sprinkle individual servings with green onion.

Per serving: 470 cal., 11 g total fat (3 g sat. fat), 45 mg chol., 1,897 mg sodium, 64 g carbo., 16 g fiber, 28 g pro.

MENU
Corn bread sticks
Coleslaw (from a deli)
Brownie sundaes

Zesty Black Bean Chili

151

PREP:
10 MINUTES

COOK:
20 MINUTES

MAKES:
4 SERVINGS

1   16-ounce jar thick and chunky salsa

1   15- to 16-ounce can black beans, rinsed and drained

1½ cups vegetable juice or hot-style vegetable juice

8   ounces fully cooked turkey kielbasa (Polish sausage), halved lengthwise and sliced

¼   cup water

2   teaspoons chili powder

1   teaspoon bottled minced garlic (2 cloves) or ¼ teaspoon garlic powder

    Dairy sour cream, sliced green onion, and/or chopped, peeled avocado (optional)

1. **In a large saucepan stir together salsa, beans, vegetable juice, turkey kielbasa, water, chili powder, and garlic. Bring to boiling; reduce heat. Simmer, covered, for 20 minutes, stirring occasionally.**

2. **Ladle chili into bowls. If desired, top with sour cream, onion, and/or avocado.**

Per serving: 210 cal., 5 g total fat (2 g sat. fat), 35 mg chol., 1,878 mg sodium, 28 g carbo., 6 g fiber, 16 g pro.

MENU
Tortilla chips
Vegetable tray with
vegetable dip
Banana splits

152

Easy Citrus Salmon Steaks

PREP:
10 MINUTES

BROIL:
8 MINUTES

MAKES:
4 SERVINGS

2   fresh or frozen salmon steaks, cut 1 inch thick (about 1 pound)

2   teaspoons finely shredded lemon peel or orange peel

2   tablespoons lemon juice or orange juice

¼   teaspoon black pepper

1   teaspoon bottled minced garlic (2 cloves)

2   tablespoons sliced green onion (1)

2   medium oranges, peeled and sliced crosswise

1. Thaw fish, if frozen. Rinse fish; pat dry with paper towels. Preheat broiler. In a small bowl stir together lemon peel, lemon juice, pepper, and garlic.

2. Place fish on the greased unheated rack of a broiler pan. Brush with half of the juice mixture. Broil 4 inches from the heat for 8 to 12 minutes or until fish begins to flake when tested with a fork, turning once and brushing with remaining juice mixture halfway through broiling.

3. To serve, cut each fish steak into 2 portions and transfer to dinner plates. Sprinkle with green onion. Serve with orange slices.

Per serving: 226 cal., 10 g total fat (2 g sat. fat), 70 mg chol., 54 mg sodium, 9 g carbo., 2 g fiber, 25 g pro.

MENU
French baguette slices
Rice pilaf (from a mix)
Roasted Brussels sprouts

Broiled Halibut with Dijon Cream

153

START TO FINISH:
15 MINUTES

MAKES:
4 SERVINGS

4   fresh or frozen halibut steaks, cut 1 inch thick (1 to 1½ pounds)
1   teaspoon Greek-style or Mediterranean seasoning blend
¼   teaspoon coarsely ground black pepper
¼   cup dairy sour cream
¼   cup creamy Dijon-style mustard blend
1   tablespoon milk
½   teaspoon dried oregano, crushed

1. Thaw fish, if frozen. Preheat broiler. Rinse fish; pat dry with paper towels. Place fish on the greased unheated rack of a broiler pan. Sprinkle fish with seasoning blend and pepper.

2. Broil fish 4 inches from the heat for 8 to 12 minutes or until fish begins to flake when tested with a fork, turning once halfway through broiling. Invert fish onto 4 dinner plates so seasoning is on top.

3. Meanwhile, for sauce, in a small bowl combine sour cream, mustard blend, milk, and oregano. Serve sauce over fish.

Per serving: 168 cal., 5 g total fat (2 g sat. fat), 42 mg chol., 300 mg sodium, 4 g carbo., 0 g fiber, 24 g pro.

MENU
Warm pita bread
Caesar salad
Candied sweet potatoes

154

Herb-Buttered Fish Steaks

PREP:
10 MINUTES

BROIL:
8 MINUTES

MAKES:
4 SERVINGS

4   fresh or frozen halibut, salmon, shark, or swordfish steaks,
        cut 1 inch thick (1 to 1½ pounds)
2   tablespoons butter or margarine, softened
1   teaspoon finely shredded lime or lemon peel
1   teaspoon lime or lemon juice
1   teaspoon snipped fresh tarragon or rosemary or ¼ teaspoon dried tarragon
        or rosemary, crushed
1   teaspoon butter or margarine, melted

1. Thaw fish, if frozen. Rinse fish; pat dry with paper towels. Preheat broiler.
   For the herb butter, in a small bowl stir together the 2 tablespoons softened
   butter, the lime peel, lime juice, and tarragon. Set aside.

2. Place the fish steaks on the greased unheated rack of a broiler pan. Brush with
   the 1 teaspoon melted butter. Broil 4 inches form the heat for 8 to 12 minutes
   or until fish begins to flake when tested with a fork, turning once halfway
   through broiling. Transfer fish steaks to dinner plates; top with herb butter.

Per serving: 184 cal., 9 g total fat (2 g sat. fat), 36 mg chol., 140 mg sodium, 0 g carbo., 0 g fiber, 24 g pro.

MENU
Hot cooked basmati rice
Steamed broccoli spears
Cheesecake with hot
fudge sauce

Maple-Hoisin Glazed Halibut

155

PREP:
10 MINUTES

BROIL:
8 MINUTES

MAKES:
4 SERVINGS

4   5- to 6-ounce fresh or frozen halibut steaks, 1 inch thick
3   tablespoons hoisin sauce
2   tablespoons seasoned rice vinegar
2   tablespoons maple syrup
1   teaspoon grated fresh ginger
½   teaspoon bottled minced garlic (1 clove)
¼   teaspoon crushed red pepper
¼   teaspoon black pepper
     Shredded leaf lettuce or napa cabbage (optional)

Thaw fish, if frozen. Preheat broiler. Rinse fish; pat dry with paper towels. In a small bowl stir together hoisin sauce, vinegar, maple syrup, ginger, garlic, and crushed red pepper. Set aside.

Sprinkle fish with black pepper. Place fish on the greased unheated rack of a broiler pan. Broil 4 inches from the heat for 5 minutes. Brush with glaze; turn fish. Brush with remaining glaze. Broil for 3 to 7 minutes more or until fish begins to flake when tested with a fork. If desired, serve on a bed of lettuce.

Per serving: 210 cal., 4 g total fat (1 g sat. fat), 45 mg chol., 285 mg sodium, 13 g carbo., 0 g fiber, 30 g pro.

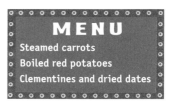

MENU
Steamed carrots
Boiled red potatoes
Clementines and dried dates

156 Italian-Style Fish

START TO FINISH:
20 MINUTES

MAKES:
6 SERVINGS

1½ pounds fresh or frozen fish fillets, ½ to 1 inch thick
¼ teaspoon salt
¼ teaspoon black pepper
1 tablespoon cooking oil
2 cups packaged sliced fresh mushrooms
1 14.5-ounce can Italian-style stewed tomatoes, undrained
1 10.75-ounce can condensed tomato bisque soup
⅓ cup finely shredded Parmesan cheese
3 cups hot cooked pasta

1. Thaw fish, if frozen. Rinse fish; pat dry with paper towels. Cut fish into 6 serving-size pieces, if necessary. Measure thickness of fish. Preheat broiler. Place fish on the greased unheated rack of a broiler pan, tucking under any thin portions to make fish of uniform thickness. Sprinkle with salt and ⅛ teaspoon of the pepper.

2. Broil 4 inches from the heat for 4 to 6 minutes per ½-inch thickness or until fish begins to flake when tested with a fork. (If fillets are 1 inch thick, carefully turn once halfway through broiling.)

3. Meanwhile, for sauce, in a medium saucepan heat oil over medium-high heat. Add mushrooms; cook until tender, stirring occasionally. Stir in undrained tomatoes, soup, and the remaining ⅛ teaspoon pepper. Cook and stir over medium heat until heated through.

4. Spoon the sauce over fish fillets. Sprinkle with Parmesan cheese. Serve with hot cooked pasta.

Per serving: 415 cal., 14 g total fat (6 g sat. fat), 71 mg chol., 1,218 mg sodium, 35 g carbo., 2 g fiber, 37 g pro.

MENU
Soft breadsticks
Hot whole wheat couscous
Steamed mixed vegetables

Fish with Sherry-Mushroom Sauce

157

START TO FINISH:
25 MINUTES

MAKES:
6 SERVINGS

1½ pounds fresh or frozen fish fillets, about 1 inch thick
1 10.75-ounce can condensed cream of shrimp soup
½ cup shredded Swiss cheese (2 ounces)
¼ cup milk
2 tablespoons dry sherry
½ teaspoon dried thyme, crushed
1 4-ounce can (drained weight) sliced mushrooms, drained
Sliced green onion (optional)

1. Thaw fish, if frozen. Preheat broiler. Rinse fish; pat dry with paper towels. Cut fish into 6 serving-size pieces, if necessary. Place fish on the greased unheated rack of a broiler pan, tucking under any thin edges to make fish of uniform thickness. Sprinkle with *salt* and *black pepper.*

2. Broil fish 4 inches from the heat for 8 to 12 minutes or until fish begins to flake when tested with a fork, carefully turning once halfway through broiling.

3. Meanwhile, for sauce, in a small saucepan stir together soup, Swiss cheese, milk, sherry, and thyme. Cook and stir over low heat until cheese is melted. Stir in drained mushrooms; heat through. Spoon sauce over fish. If desired, sprinkle with green onion.

Per serving: 187 cal., 6 g total fat (3 g sat. fat), 66 mg chol., 584 mg sodium, 6 g carbo., 1 g fiber, 24 g pro.

MENU
Steamed green beans
Brown and wild rice pilaf (from a mix)
Apple crisp

158 Fish with Black Bean Sauce

START TO FINISH:
30 MINUTES

MAKES:
6 SERVINGS

1½ pounds fresh or frozen skinless sea bass or orange roughy fillets
1   15-ounce can black beans, rinsed and drained
3   tablespoons bottled teriyaki sauce
2   tablespoons bottled hoisin sauce
     Nonstick cooking spray
6   cups hot cooked rice

1. Thaw fish, if frozen. Rinse fish; pat dry with paper towels. Cut fish into 6 serving-size pieces, if necessary. Set fish aside.

2. For black bean sauce, in a blender or food processor combine drained beans, teriyaki sauce, and hoisin sauce. Cover and blend or process until nearly smooth. Set aside.

3. Coat an unheated 12-inch nonstick skillet with nonstick cooking spray. Preheat skillet over medium-high heat. Carefully place fish fillets in skillet; cook about 4 minutes or until brown on both sides, turning once. Add black bean sauce to fish. Bring to boiling; reduce heat to medium. Simmer, covered, about 8 minutes or until fish begins to flake when tested with a fork. Serve fish with hot cooked rice.

Per serving: 276 cal., 3 g total fat (1 g sat. fat), 46 mg chol., 617 mg sodium, 35 g carbo., 4 g fiber, 28 g pro.

MENU
Spring rolls
(frozen or takeout)
Steamed stir-fry vegetables
Coconut ice cream with
fresh pineapple chunks

Seafood Chowder

159

START TO FINISH:
25 MINUTES

MAKES:
4 SERVINGS

12 ounces fresh or frozen fish fillets (such as salmon, orange roughy, or cod)

3 cups loose-pack frozen diced hash brown potatoes with onions and peppers

1 cup water

1 12-ounce can evaporated milk

1 10.75-ounce can condensed cream of shrimp or cream of potato soup

⅓ of a 3-ounce can cooked bacon pieces (⅓ cup)

2 teaspoons snipped fresh dill or ¾ teaspoon dried dill

¼ teaspoon black pepper

1 2-ounce jar diced pimiento, drained

1. Thaw fish, if frozen. Rinse fish; pat dry with paper towels. Cut fish into 1-inch pieces. Set aside.

2. Meanwhile, in a large saucepan combine hash brown potatoes and water. Bring to boiling; reduce heat. Simmer, covered, about 5 minutes or until tender.

3. Stir in evaporated milk, soup, bacon, dill, and pepper. Return to boiling. Add fish and pimiento; reduce heat. Simmer, covered, for 3 to 5 minutes or until fish begins to flake when tested with a fork.

Per serving: 366 cal., 15 g total fat (7 g sat. fat), 86 mg chol., 1,045 mg sodium, 27 g carbo., 2 g fiber, 30 g pro.

MENU
Sourdough rolls
Mixed greens salad
with desired dressing
Fudge brownies

160 Smoked Salmon Pasta

START TO FINISH:
25 MINUTES

MAKES:
4 TO 6 SERVINGS

8 ounces dried farfalle (bow ties) or mafalda (mini lasagna)

1 cup whipping cream

½ teaspoon seafood seasoning blend

8 ounces smoked salmon, flaked, with skin and bones removed if present

½ cup bottled roasted red sweet peppers, drained and cut into bite-size strips

1. In a large saucepan cook the pasta according to package directions.

2. Meanwhile, in a medium saucepan combine whipping cream and seasoning blend; cook over medium heat until bubbly. Continue to cook, uncovered, about 5 minutes or until thickened, stirring occasionally.

3. Stir in salmon and red pepper strips; heat through. Drain pasta; return to pan. Add salmon mixture to pasta. Toss to coat.

Per serving: 489 cal., 26 g total fat (14 g sat. fat), 95 mg chol., 552 mg sodium, 45 g carbo., 2 g fiber, 19 g pro.

MENU
Focaccia
Spinach salad with desired dressing
Tropical fruit plate

Tuna and Pasta Alfredo Casserole 161

PREP:
20 MINUTES

BAKE:
10 MINUTES

OVEN:
425°F

MAKES:
6 SERVINGS

3   cups dried rigatoni or penne pasta

1   cup fresh or frozen pea pods

1   10-ounce container refrigerated Alfredo pasta sauce or four-cheese pasta sauce

3   tablespoons milk

2   tablespoons purchased dried tomato pesto

1   12-ounce can solid white tuna (water pack), drained and broken into chunks

¼   cup finely shredded Parmesan cheese (1 ounce)

1. Preheat oven to 425°F. In a Dutch oven cook pasta according to package directions, adding the pea pods during the last minute of cooking. Drain well; return to Dutch oven.

2. Meanwhile, in a medium bowl combine Alfredo sauce, milk, and pesto. Add to pasta, stirring gently to coat. Gently fold in tuna. Transfer pasta mixture to a 2-quart oval baking dish. Sprinkle with Parmesan cheese.

3. Bake for 10 to 15 minutes or until heated through and cheese is just melted.

Per serving: 414 cal., 20 g total fat (2 g sat. fat), 51 mg chol., 516 mg sodium, 33 g carbo., 1 g fiber, 23 g pro.

MENU

Multigrain rolls

Marinated vegetable salad (from a deli)

Gingerbread

162 Tuna Chowder

START TO FINISH:
25 MINUTES

MAKES:
4 SERVINGS

4   slices bacon

¾   cup chopped green sweet pepper (1 medium)

⅓   cup chopped onion (1 small)

3   cups milk

2   10.75-ounce cans condensed cream of potato soup

½   teaspoon dried thyme, crushed

2   6-ounce cans tuna, drained and flaked

1. In a large skillet cook bacon over medium heat until crisp. Remove bacon, reserving drippings in skillet. Drain bacon on paper towels. Crumble bacon and set aside.

2. Cook sweet pepper and onion in reserved drippings over medium heat until tender. Stir in milk, soup, and thyme; bring just to boiling. Gently stir in tuna; heat through. Sprinkle individual servings with crumbled bacon.

Per serving: 435 cal., 18 g total fat (7 g sat. fat), 49 mg chol., 1,651 mg sodium, 30 g carbo., 2 g fiber, 36 g pro.

MENU
Soft breadsticks
Mixed greens salad with desired dressing
Banana splits

Tuna Tortellini Soup

163

START TO FINISH:
20 MINUTES

MAKES:
6 SERVINGS

3   cups milk

2   10.75-ounce cans condensed cream of potato soup

1   cup frozen peas

1   teaspoon dried basil, crushed

1   9-ounce package refrigerated cheese tortellini

1   12-ounce can tuna (water pack), drained and flaked

⅓   cup dry white wine or milk

1. **In a large saucepan combine milk, soup, peas, and basil; bring just to boiling. Add tortellini. Simmer, uncovered, for 6 to 8 minutes or until tortellini is tender, stirring frequently to prevent sticking. Stir in tuna and white wine; heat through.**

Per serving: 351 cal., 9 g total fat (4 g sat. fat), 59 mg chol., 1,267 mg sodium, 38 g carbo., 2 g fiber, 27 g pro.

MENU
Country Italian bread
Caesar salad
Fresh pear slices
and dried figs

164 Tuna and Noodles

START TO FINISH:
25 MINUTES

MAKES:
4 TO 6 SERVINGS

1 12-ounce package dried egg noodles (6 cups)

1 10.75-ounce can condensed cream of celery soup

6 ounces American cheese, cubed, or process Swiss cheese slices, torn

½ cup milk

1 12-ounce can solid white tuna (water pack), drained and broken into chunks

1. **In a 4-quart Dutch oven cook noodles according to package directions; drain.**

2. **In the same Dutch oven combine soup, cheese, and milk. Cook and stir over medium heat until bubbly. Stir tuna into soup mixture. Gently stir in cooked noodles; cook for 2 to 3 minutes more or until heated through.**

Per serving: 645 cal., 23 g total fat (11 g sat. fat), 162 mg chol., 1,476 mg sodium, 68 g carbo., 3 g fiber, 40 g pro.

MENU
Buttermilk biscuits
Vegetable tray with
vegetable dip
Chocolate chip cookies

Salmon and Broccoli Chowder

165

2½ cups milk

1   10.75-ounce can condensed broccoli-cheese soup or condensed cream of chicken soup

¾   cup shredded sharp cheddar cheese or process American cheese (3 ounces)

1   cup frozen cut broccoli

½   cup frozen whole kernel corn

1   15-ounce can salmon, drained, flaked, and skin and bones removed

1. **In a medium saucepan stir together milk and soup. Stir in cheese, broccoli, and corn. Cook and stir just until mixture boils. Stir in salmon. Heat through.**

Per serving: 401 cal., 22 g total fat (10 g sat. fat), 65 mg chol., 1,257 mg sodium, 19 g carbo., 2 g fiber, 31 g pro.

MENU
Multigrain chips
Relish tray (carrot and celery sticks, olives, pickles)
Hot caramel sundaes

166 Broccoli and Clam Chowder

START TO FINISH:
20 MINUTES

MAKES:
4 SERVINGS

⅓   cup water

1   10-ounce package frozen chopped broccoli or spinach

⅓   cup chopped onion (1 small)

½   teaspoon dried thyme, crushed

1½ cups milk

1   10.75-ounce can condensed cream of shrimp soup

1   6.5-ounce can minced clams, drained

1   teaspoon Worcestershire sauce

1. **In a medium saucepan bring the water to boiling; add broccoli, onion, and thyme. Cook, covered, about 8 minutes or just until broccoli is tender. Do not drain. Stir in milk, soup, drained clams, and Worcestershire sauce. Heat through.**

Per serving: 181 cal., 7 g total fat (2 g sat. fat), 41 mg chol., 676 mg sodium, 16 g carbo., 3 g fiber, 15 g pro.

MENU
Whole wheat bread
Marinated vegetable salad
(from a deli)
Pumpkin pie

Crab Bisque

167

START TO FINISH:
20 MINUTES

MAKES:
6 SERVINGS

1   10.75-ounce can condensed cream of asparagus soup

1   10.75-ounce can condensed cream of mushroom soup

2¾ cups milk

1   cup half-and-half or light cream

1   6- to 7-ounce can crabmeat, drained, flaked, and cartilage removed

3   tablespoons dry sherry or milk

1. In a large saucepan combine cream of asparagus soup, cream of mushroom soup, milk, and half-and-half. Cook over medium heat just until boiling, stirring frequently. Stir in crabmeat and dry sherry; heat through.

Per serving: 227 cal., 12 g total fat (6 g sat. fat), 63 mg chol., 921 mg sodium, 16 g carbo., 1 g fiber, 12 g pro.

MENU

Fresh baguette slices

Spinach salad with
desired dressing

Tiramisu (frozen)

168 Ravioli with Red Clam Sauce

START TO FINISH:
20 MINUTES

MAKES:
4 SERVINGS

1 9-ounce package refrigerated cheese-filled ravioli or tortellini

1 6.5-ounce can minced clams

1 14.5-ounce can stewed tomatoes, undrained

1 medium zucchini, halved lengthwise and thinly sliced (about 1½ cups)

2 teaspoons dried Italian seasoning, crushed

1 8-ounce can tomato sauce

1 tablespoon cornstarch

Grated Parmesan cheese (optional)

1. Cook ravioli according to package directions. Drain; keep warm.

2. Meanwhile, drain clams, reserving liquid; set clams aside. In a large saucepan combine the clam liquid, the undrained stewed tomatoes, zucchini, and Italian seasoning. Bring to boiling; reduce heat. Simmer, uncovered, for 2 minutes.

3. In a small bowl stir together the tomato sauce and cornstarch until well mixed. Stir cornstarch mixture into hot mixture in saucepan. Cook and stir over medium heat until thickened and bubbly. Cook and stir for 2 minutes more. Stir in clams and ravioli. Heat through. If desired, sprinkle individual servings with Parmesan cheese.

Per serving: 271 cal., 4 g total fat (2 g sat. fat), 46 mg chol., 960 mg sodium, 42 g carbo., 4 g fiber, 18 g pro.

MENU
Crusty dinner rolls
Mixed greens salad
with desired vinaigrette
Cappuccino with biscotti

Ravioli Skillet Lasagna

START TO FINISH:
25 MINUTES

MAKES:
4 SERVINGS

2 cups bottled light chunky-style pasta sauce

⅓ cup water

1 9-ounce package refrigerated or frozen cheese- or meat-filled ravioli

1 egg, lightly beaten

1 15-ounce carton ricotta cheese

¼ cup grated Romano or Parmesan cheese

1 10-ounce package frozen chopped spinach, thawed and well drained

Grated Romano or Parmesan cheese

1. In a 10-inch skillet combine pasta sauce and water. Bring to boiling. Stir in the ravioli. Cook, covered, over medium heat about 5 minutes or until ravioli are nearly tender, stirring once to prevent sticking.

2. Meanwhile, in a medium bowl stir together egg, ricotta cheese, and the ¼ cup Romano cheese. Dot ravioli with spinach. Spoon ricotta mixture on top of spinach. Cook, covered, over low heat about 10 minutes or until ricotta layer is set and pasta is just tender. Sprinkle individual servings with additional Romano cheese.

Per serving: 433 cal., 14 g total fat (3 g sat. fat), 131 mg chol., 501 mg sodium, 49 g carbo., 3 g fiber, 36 g pro.

MENU
Focaccia
Mixed greens salad with vinaigrette dressing
Tiramisu (frozen)

170

Cheesy Tortellini and Vegetables

START TO FINISH:
20 MINUTES

MAKES:
4 SERVINGS

1 6-ounce package dried cheese-filled tortellini
1 16-ounce package frozen broccoli, cauliflower, and carrots
1¼ cups milk
½ of a 1.8-ounce envelope white sauce mix (about 3 tablespoons)
6 ounces Havarti cheese with dill, cubed

1. Cook tortellini according to package directions, adding the frozen vegetables for the last 5 minutes of cooking; drain.

2. Meanwhile, for sauce, in a small saucepan whisk together milk and white sauce mix. Bring to boiling; reduce heat. Cook and stir for 1 minute. Remove from heat. Add cheese, stirring until melted. Pour sauce over vegetable mixture. Toss lightly to coat.

Per serving: 453 cal., 24 g total fat (1 g sat. fat), 59 mg chol., 1,004 mg sodium, 38 g carbo., 4 g fiber, 22 g pro.

MENU
Crusty Italian bread
Fresh apple slices
and red grapes

Pasta with Pepper-Cheese Sauce

171

START TO FINISH:
25 MINUTES

MAKES:
4 TO 6 SERVINGS

8   ounces dried medium shell, mostaccioli, or cut ziti pasta

1   0.9- to 1.25-ounce package hollandaise sauce mix

2   tablespoons butter or margarine

1   cup bottled roasted red sweet peppers, drained and chopped

½   cup shredded Monterey Jack cheese with jalapeño chile peppers (2 ounces)

1. **Cook pasta according to package directions; drain well. Return pasta to pan. Cover to keep warm.**

2. **Meanwhile, prepare hollandaise sauce according to package directions, except use only 2 tablespoons butter. Stir in drained roasted sweet peppers. Remove pan from heat. Add cheese to sauce, stirring until cheese melts. Add sauce to pasta in pan; toss to coat.**

Per serving: 384 cal., 13 g total fat (8 g sat. fat), 36 mg chol., 407 mg sodium, 53 g carbo., 2 g fiber, 13 g pro.

MENU
Corn bread sticks
Marinated vegetable salad (from a deli)
Banana splits

172 Easy Cheesy Macaroni

START TO FINISH:
20 MINUTES

MAKES:
4 SERVINGS

8   ounces dried penne, rotini, or gemelli pasta

2   cups frozen cauliflower, broccoli, and carrots

1   10-ounce container refrigerated light Alfredo pasta sauce

¼   cup milk

1   cup shredded cheddar cheese (4 ounces)

½   cup finely shredded Parmesan cheese (2 ounces)

¼   cup chopped walnuts, toasted

1. In a 4-quart Dutch oven cook pasta according to package directions, adding frozen vegetables for the last 4 minutes of cooking; drain well. Return to Dutch oven; cover to keep warm.

2. Meanwhile, in a medium saucepan combine Alfredo sauce and milk; heat and stir just until bubbly. Gradually add cheddar cheese and Parmesan cheese, stirring until melted. Add cheese mixture to pasta mixture in Dutch oven; stir to coat. Heat through. Top individual servings with toasted walnuts.

Per serving: 586 cal., 28 g total fat (15 g sat. fat), 70 mg chol., 1,054 mg sodium, 57 g carbo., 3 g fiber, 26 g pro.

MENU
Garlic bread
Relish tray (olives, pickles, raw vegetables)
Gingersnaps with eggnog

Tortellini and Peas

173

START TO FINISH:
20 MINUTES

MAKES:
4 SERVINGS

1 9-ounce package refrigerated cheese-filled tortellini or ravioli

1 cup frozen peas

2 tablespoons all-purpose flour

⅛ teaspoon black pepper

1 cup half-and-half, light cream, or milk

1 14.5-ounce can diced tomatoes with basil, garlic, and oregano, undrained

2 tablespoons finely shredded Parmesan cheese

1. Cook tortellini according to package directions, adding peas the last minute of cooking. Drain. Return tortellini mixture to pan; cover to keep warm.

2. Meanwhile, for sauce, in a medium saucepan stir together flour and pepper. Gradually stir in half-and-half. Cook and stir over medium heat until thickened and bubbly. Cook and stir for 1 minute more. Gradually stir in the undrained tomatoes. Season to taste with *salt* and additional black pepper.

3. Pour the sauce over the tortellini mixture; toss gently to coat. Sprinkle individual servings with Parmesan cheese.

Per serving: 410 cal., 13 g total fat (7 g sat. fat), 54 mg chol., 998 mg sodium, 57 g carbo., 4 g fiber, 18 g pro.

MENU
Country Italian bread
Caesar salad
Fudge brownies

174

Pinto Beans and Bulgur

START TO FINISH:
25 MINUTES

MAKES:
4 SERVINGS

1   14-ounce can vegetable broth
¾   cup bulgur
1   medium red sweet pepper, cut into thin bite-size strips
⅓   cup refrigerated basil pesto
¼   cup thinly sliced green onion (2)
1   16-ounce can pinto beans, rinsed and drained
4   Boston or Bibb lettuce cups
    Lemon wedges (optional)

1. In a medium saucepan bring vegetable broth to boiling; add bulgur. Return to boiling; reduce heat. Simmer, covered, for 10 minutes. Remove from heat.

2. Stir sweet pepper, pesto, and green onion into bulgur mixture. Stir in drained beans. Season to taste with *black pepper.* Spoon bulgur mixture into lettuce cups. If desired, serve with lemon wedges.

Per serving: 308 cal., 10 g total fat (2 g sat. fat), 7 mg chol., 916 mg sodium, 45 g carbo., 12 g fiber, 12 g pro.

MENU
Warm pita bread
Roasted acorn squash wedges
Tropical fruit plate (star fruit, pineapple, kiwifruit, pomegranate seeds)

Creamy Barley and Broccoli

175

START TO FINISH:
25 MINUTES

MAKES:
4 SERVINGS

1   14-ounce can vegetable broth
1   cup quick-cooking barley
2   cups packaged fresh broccoli florets
1   10.75-ounce can condensed cream of broccoli or cream of celery soup
½   cup milk
½   teaspoon dried basil, crushed
¼   teaspoon black pepper
1   cup shredded Swiss cheese (4 ounces)

1. In a medium saucepan bring vegetable broth to boiling. Stir in barley. Return to boiling; reduce heat. Simmer, covered, for 10 to 12 minutes or until barley is tender and most of the liquid is absorbed, adding broccoli for the last 5 minutes of cooking. Do not drain.

2. Stir in soup, milk, basil, and pepper. Heat through. Add ½ cup of the cheese, stirring until melted.

3. Sprinkle individual servings with the remaining ½ cup cheese.

Per serving: 331 cal., 13 g total fat (7 g sat. fat), 30 mg chol., 1,005 mg sodium, 40 g carbo., 6 g fiber, 16 g pro.

MENU
Buttermilk biscuits
Baked potatoes
Peppermint ice cream

176 Italian Rice Skillet

START TO FINISH:
20 MINUTES

MAKES:
4 SERVINGS

1 19-ounce can ready-to-serve hearty tomato soup

1 15- to 19-ounce can white kidney (cannellini) beans, rinsed and drained

2 cups frozen cut green beans

1 cup uncooked instant white rice

½ cup water

⅓ cup finely shredded Parmesan cheese

1. In a large skillet combine soup, drained white kidney beans, green beans, uncooked rice, and water. Bring to boiling; reduce heat. Simmer, covered, about 10 minutes or until rice and green beans are tender, stirring frequently.

2. Top individual servings with Parmesan cheese.

Per serving: 271 cal., 4 g total fat (2 g sat. fat), 8 mg chol., 685 mg sodium, 51 g carbo., 9 g fiber, 14 g pro.

MENU
Sauteed polenta slices
Romaine salad with
vinaigrette dressing
Carrot cake

Mixed Bean and Portobello Ragout

177

START TO FINISH:
20 MINUTES

MAKES:
4 SERVINGS

1   10-ounce package frozen baby lima beans

1½ cups frozen cut green beans

3   cups packaged sliced fresh portobello mushrooms or sliced button mushrooms

1   tablespoon olive oil or cooking oil

1   15-ounce can garbanzo beans, rinsed and drained

1   14.5-ounce can Italian-style stewed tomatoes, undrained and cut up

1   8-ounce can tomato sauce

1. In a large saucepan cook lima beans and green beans according to package directions; drain and return to the pan.

2. Meanwhile, in a large skillet heat oil over medium-high heat. Add mushrooms; cook about 5 minutes or until tender, stirring occasionally. Stir in drained garbanzo beans, undrained tomatoes, and tomato sauce; heat through. Add mushroom mixture to lima and green beans in saucepan. Stir to combine.

Per serving: 289 cal., 5 g total fat (1 g sat. fat), 0 mg chol., 934 mg sodium, 50 g carbo., 12 g fiber, 14 g pro.

MENU
Multigrain rolls
Hot cooked couscous
Baklava

178 Asian Noodle Bowl

START TO FINISH:
25 MINUTES

MAKES:
4 SERVINGS

8   ounces dried vermicelli

2   cups vegetable broth

½   cup bottled peanut sauce

2   cups frozen Chinese-style stir-fry vegetables with seasonings

½   cup dry-roasted peanuts, chopped

1. Cook the vermicelli according to package directions. Drain noodles but do not rinse. Set aside.

2. In the same saucepan combine vegetable broth and peanut sauce. Bring to boiling. Stir in frozen vegetables. Return to boiling; reduce heat. Simmer for 2 to 3 minutes or until vegetables are heated through. Add cooked noodles. Divide noodles and broth among 4 bowls. Sprinkle with peanuts.

Per serving: 403 cal., 15 g total fat (2 g sat. fat), 0 mg chol., 1,326 mg sodium, 59 g carbo., 4 g fiber, 15 g pro.

MENU
Egg rolls (frozen or takeout)
Fortune cookies

Mashed Potato Soup

179

START TO FINISH:
15 MINUTES

MAKES:
3 SERVINGS

1 20-ounce package refrigerated mashed potatoes
1 14-ounce can chicken broth
¼ cup sliced green onion (2)
½ cup shredded Swiss, cheddar, or smoked Gouda cheese (2 ounces)
Dairy sour cream (optional)

1. In a medium saucepan combine mashed potatoes, chicken broth, and green onion. Bring to boiling over medium-high heat, whisking to make nearly smooth.

2. Add cheese; whisk until cheese is melted. If desired, serve with sour cream.

Per serving: 239 cal., 9 g total fat (4 g sat. fat), 17 mg chol., 917 mg sodium, 27 g carbo., 2 g fiber, 11 g pro.

MENU
Soft breadsticks
Mixed greens salad with desired dressing
Apple and cranberry crisp

180

Split Pea and Vegetable Soup

START TO FINISH:
25 MINUTES

MAKES:
4 SERVINGS

2   tablespoons cooking oil

1   cup chopped celery (2 stalks)

1   cup chopped carrot (2 medium)

½   cup chopped onion (1 medium)

2   11.25-ounce cans condensed green pea soup

2   10-ounce cans condensed vegetarian vegetable soup

2   cups water

½   teaspoon dried thyme, crushed

⅛   teaspoon black pepper

1. In a large saucepan or 4-quart Dutch oven heat oil over medium heat. Add celery, carrot, and onion; cook about 5 minutes or until tender.

2. Stir in green pea soup, vegetable soup, water, thyme, and pepper. Cook until heated through, stirring occasionally.

Per serving: 403 cal., 11 g total fat (2 g sat. fat), 3 mg chol., 2,117 mg sodium, 62 g carbo., 11 g fiber, 15 g pro.

MENU
Sourdough bread
Relish tray (olives, pickles, raw vegetables)
Pumpkin pie

jalapeño Corn Chowder

181

PREP:
15 MINUTES

COOK:
5 MINUTES

MAKES:
4 SERVINGS

3   cups frozen whole kernel corn

1   14-ounce can vegetable broth or chicken broth

⅔   cup dried small pasta (such as ditalini or tiny shell macaroni)

1   cup milk, half-and-half, or light cream

¼   cup bottled roasted red sweet peppers, drained and chopped

1   or 2 fresh jalapeño chile peppers, seeded and finely chopped*

½   cup shredded cheddar cheese (optional)

1. **In a blender or food processor combine half of the corn and the broth. Cover and blend or process until nearly smooth.**

2. **In a large saucepan combine the broth mixture and the remaining corn; bring to a boil. Add pasta. Reduce heat; simmer, uncovered for 5 to 7 minutes or until pasta is tender. Stir in milk, roasted sweet peppers, and jalapeño peppers; heat through. Ladle soup into bowls. If desired, sprinkle with cheese.**

Per serving: 219 cal., 2 g total fat (1 g sat. fat), 5 mg chol., 419 mg sodium, 45 g carbo., 3 g fiber, 8 g pro.

*Note: Because chile peppers contain volatile oils that can burn your skin and eyes, avoid direct contact with them as much as possible. When working with chile peppers, wear plastic or rubber gloves. If your bare hands do touch the peppers, wash your hands and nails well with soap and warm water.

MENU
Corn bread sticks
Sliced avocados
Grapefruit slices with honey

182 Minestrone

START TO FINISH:
30 MINUTES

MAKES:
4 SERVINGS

2   14-ounce cans chicken broth with Italian herbs

1   cup thinly sliced carrot (2 medium)

½   cup ditalini (tiny thimbles) or tiny farfalle (bow ties)

1¼ cups chopped zucchini (1 medium)

1   14.5-ounce can diced tomatoes with onions and garlic, undrained

1   15- to 15.5-ounce can white kidney (cannellini) beans or navy beans, rinsed and drained

¼   cup slivered fresh basil or spinach

    Bottled hot pepper sauce (optional)

1. In a large saucepan combine chicken broth and carrot. Bring to boiling; reduce heat. Simmer, covered, for 5 minutes.

2. Stir in pasta. Simmer, uncovered, about 8 minutes or just until pasta is tender. Add zucchini, undrained tomatoes, and drained beans; heat through. Sprinkle individual servings with basil. If desired, pass bottled hot pepper sauce.

Per serving: 203 cal., 2 g total fat (0 g sat. fat), 0 mg chol., 1,328 mg sodium, 38 g carbo., 7 g fiber, 14 g pro.

MENU
Focaccia
Red grapes
Spice cake

Spring

183 Steak with Mushrooms

START TO FINISH:
20 MINUTES

MAKES:
4 SERVINGS

4   beef tenderloin steaks, cut 1 inch thick (about 1 pound)

1   tablespoon olive oil

8   ounces fresh cremini, shiitake, baby portobello, and/or button mushrooms, sliced

¼   cup onion-flavor beef broth

¼   cup whipping cream

1. Trim fat from steaks. In a large skillet heat oil over medium-high heat. Add steaks; reduce heat to medium. Cook steaks to desired doneness, turning once halfway through broiling. Allow 7 to 9 minutes for medium-rare (145°F) to medium (160°F). Remove steaks from skillet, reserving drippings. Cover steaks to keep warm.

2. In the same skillet cook and stir mushrooms in drippings over medium heat for 4 to 5 minutes or until tender. Stir in beef broth and cream. Cook and stir over medium heat about 2 minutes or until slightly thickened. Spoon mushroom mixture over steaks.

Per serving: 271 cal., 18 g total fat (7 g sat. fat), 90 mg chol., 116 mg sodium, 2 g carbo., 0 g fiber, 26 g pro.

MENU

Steamed asparagus
with capers

Roasted new potatoes

Carrot cake

Chard-Topped Steaks

184

START TO FINISH:
30 MINUTES

MAKES:
4 SERVINGS

1   slice bacon, chopped

4   beef tenderloin steaks, cut 1 inch thick (about 1 pound)

3   cups very thinly sliced fresh Swiss chard leaves (4 ounces)

½   teaspoon dried thyme, crushed

⅛   teaspoon salt

⅛   teaspoon black pepper

1. In a large skillet cook bacon over medium heat until crisp. Remove bacon from skillet, reserving drippings. Crumble bacon; set aside. Remove skillet from heat; set aside.

2. Preheat broiler. Trim fat from steaks. Sprinkle steaks with salt and black pepper. Place steaks on the unheated rack of a broiler pan. Broil 3 to 4 inches from the heat for 12 to 14 minutes for medium-rare (145°F) or 15 to 18 minutes for medium (160°F), turning once halfway through broiling.

3. Meanwhile, cook and stir Swiss chard in drippings in skillet over medium heat for 4 to 6 minutes or just until tender. Stir in the crumbled bacon, thyme, the ⅛ teaspoon salt, and the ⅛ teaspoon pepper. To serve, spoon Swiss chard mixture on top of steaks.

Per serving: 208 cal., 11 g total fat (4 g sat. fat), 60 mg chol., 363 mg sodium, 1 g carbo., 1 g fiber, 25 g pro.

MENU

Rice pilaf (from a mix)

Spring greens salad with desired dressing

Pound cake with fresh blackberries and whipped cream

185

Steaks with Horseradish Sauce

START TO FINISH:
20 MINUTES

OVEN:
400°F

MAKES:
2 TO 4 SERVINGS

2　beef tenderloin steaks, cut 1½ inches thick (about 1 pound)
1　tablespoon olive oil
½　cup whipping cream
3　tablespoons horseradish mustard
　　Cracked black pepper

1. Preheat oven to 400°F. Trim fat from steaks. Sprinkle both sides of steaks with *salt* and *black pepper.* In a large skillet heat oil over medium-high heat. Add steaks to skillet; reduce heat to medium. Cook about 4 minutes or until brown, turning once. Transfer steaks to a 2-quart square baking dish. Bake the steaks, uncovered, for 10 to 13 minutes or until medium-rare (145°F).

2. Meanwhile, for horseradish sauce, in a medium mixing bowl beat whipping cream with an electric mixer on medium speed until soft peaks form. Fold in horseradish mustard.

3. To serve, place steaks on warm dinner plates; spoon horseradish sauce over steaks. Sprinkle with cracked pepper.

Per serving: 641 cal., 47 g total fat (21 g sat. fat), 221 mg chol., 620 mg sodium, 4 g carbo., 0 g fiber, 50 g pro.

MENU
Twice-baked potatoes
Steamed broccoli spears
Amaretti sundaes (espresso or chocolate ice cream with crushed amaretti cookies and chocolate sauce)

Steak with Creamy Onion Sauce

186

START TO FINISH:
30 MINUTES

MAKES:
4 SERVINGS

1   medium sweet onion (such as Vidalia, Maui, or Walla Walla), thinly sliced

4   beef ribeye steaks, cut 1 inch thick (about 1½ pounds)

1   tablespoon Mediterranean seasoning blend or lemon-pepper seasoning

1   8-ounce carton dairy sour cream

2   tablespoons drained capers

1. Preheat broiler. Place onion slices on the rack of an unheated broiler pan. Broil 3 to 4 inches from heat for 5 minutes; turn onion slices. Meanwhile, sprinkle steaks with 1½ teaspoons of the seasoning blend. Place steaks on the broiler pan rack with the onion slices. Broil steaks and onion slices about 5 minutes or until onion slices are brown. Remove onion slices to a cutting board. Continue to broil steaks until desired doneness, turning once. Allow 7 to 9 minutes more for medium-rare (145°F) or 10 to 13 minutes more for medium (160°F).

2. Meanwhile, for sauce, coarsely chop the broiled onion. In a small saucepan combine the onion, the sour cream, capers, and the remaining 1½ teaspoons seasoning blend. Cook over medium-low heat until heated through (do not boil). Spoon sauce over steaks.

Per serving: 398 cal., 22 g total fat (11 g sat. fat), 106 mg chol., 472 mg sodium, 4 g carbo., 0 g fiber, 39 g pro.

MENU
Caesar salad
Oven-roasted potatoes
Crusty French bread
Raspberry sorbet

187 Beef Loin with Tarragon Sauce

START TO FINISH:
30 MINUTES

MAKES:
4 SERVINGS

2   beef top loin steaks, cut 1 inch thick (about 1¼ pounds)
1   cup plain yogurt
¼   cup mayonnaise or salad dressing
¼   cup thinly sliced green onion (2)
¼   cup apple juice or apple cider
1   tablespoon snipped fresh parsley
1½   teaspoons snipped fresh tarragon or ½ teaspoon dried tarragon, crushed
¼   teaspoon salt
⅛   teaspoon black pepper

1. Preheat broiler. Trim fat from steaks. Cut steaks into 4 serving-size portions. Sprinkle steaks with salt and black pepper.

2. Place steaks on the unheated rack of a broiler pan. Broil 3 to 4 inches from the heat for 12 to 14 minutes for medium-rare (145°F) or 15 to 18 minutes for medium (160°F), turning once halfway through broiling.

3. Meanwhile, for sauce, in a small bowl stir together yogurt, mayonnaise, green onion, apple juice, parsley, tarragon, the ¼ teaspoon salt, and the ⅛ teaspoon pepper. Serve sauce with steaks.

Per serving: 356 cal., 21 g total fat (6 g sat. fat), 94 mg chol., 332 mg sodium, 7 g carbo., 0 g fiber, 34 g pro.

MENU

Glazed baby carrots
(steamed carrots
sauteed with butter
and brown sugar)

Wild and brown rice pilaf
(from a mix)

Lemon meringue pie

Sirloin Steak with Mustard and Chives

188

PREP:
10 MINUTES

BROIL:
15 MINUTES

MAKES:
4 SERVINGS

4   boneless beef top sirloin steaks, cut 1 inch thick (about 1½ pounds)

2   teaspoons garlic-pepper seasoning

½   cup dairy sour cream

2   tablespoons Dijon-style mustard

1   tablespoon snipped fresh chives or sliced green onion

1. Preheat broiler. Trim fat from steaks. Sprinkle steaks with 1½ teaspoons of the seasoning. Place steaks on the unheated rack of a broiler pan. Broil 3 to 4 inches from the heat for 15 to 17 minutes for medium-rare (145°F) or 20 to 22 minutes for medium (160°F), turning once halfway through broiling. Transfer steaks to a serving platter.

2. Meanwhile, in a small bowl stir together sour cream, mustard, chives, and the remaining ½ teaspoon seasoning. Spoon sour cream mixture on top of steaks.

Per serving: 277 cal., 12 g total fat (5 g sat. fat), 114 mg chol., 619 mg sodium, 2 g carbo., 0 g fiber, 37 g pro.

MENU
Baked potatoes
Broccoli slaw mix with creamy coleslaw dressing
Whole wheat rolls

189

Greek Beef and Pasta Skillet

START TO FINISH:
25 MINUTES

MAKES:
4 SERVINGS

8   ounces dried rotini pasta

1   tablespoon cooking oil

12 ounces packaged beef stir-fry strips

1   26- to 28-ounce jar mushroom and ripe olive pasta sauce or marinara pasta sauce

¼   teaspoon salt

¼   teaspoon ground cinnamon

½   of a 10-ounce package frozen chopped spinach, thawed* and well drained

⅓   cup crumbled feta cheese

1. Cook pasta according to package directions; drain.

2. In a large skillet heat oil over medium-high heat. Add beef. Cook and stir for 2 to 3 minutes or until desired doneness. Add pasta sauce, salt, and cinnamon. Cook and stir until sauce is bubbly. Add cooked pasta and spinach. Cook and stir until heated through. Sprinkle individual servings with feta cheese.

Per serving: 483 cal., 12 g total fat (3 g sat. fat), 63 mg chol., 1,063 mg sodium, 60 g carbo., 6 g fiber, 32 g pro.

> *NOTE: To cut a package of spinach in half, unwrap the block of spinach and place on a microwave-safe plate. Microwave on 30% power (medium-low) for 2 to 4 minutes or just until soft enough to cut in half with a sharp knife. Put one half in a freezer bag, seal, and return to freezer. Continue to microwave the remaining half on 30% power for 3 to 5 minutes or until thawed.

MENU
Warm pita bread
Baklava with lemon sorbet

Beef and Asparagus Saute

190

START TO FINISH:
20 MINUTES

MAKES:
4 SERVINGS

12 ounces fresh asparagus

2   teaspoons olive oil

1   pound packaged beef stir-fry strips

½   cup packaged shredded carrot (1 medium)

1   teaspoon dried herbes de Provence, crushed

½   cup dry Marsala

¼   teaspoon finely shredded lemon peel

1. Snap off and discard woody bases from asparagus. Bias-slice asparagus into 2-inch pieces; set aside.

2. In a large nonstick skillet heat 1 teaspoon of the oil over medium-high heat. Add half of the meat to hot oil. Sprinkle with *salt* and *black pepper*. Cook and stir for 3 minutes. Remove meat from skillet. Repeat with the remaining 1 teaspoon oil and the remaining meat.

3. Return all of the meat to the skillet. Add asparagus, carrot, and herbes de Provence; cook and stir for 2 minutes more. Add Marsala and lemon peel; reduce heat. Cook for 3 to 5 minutes more or until beef is desired doneness and asparagus is crisp-tender.

Per serving: 327 cal., 7 g total fat (2 g sat. fat), 69 mg chol., 209 mg sodium, 29 g carbo., 2 g fiber, 28 g pro.

MENU

Hot cooked rice

Brown-and-serve rolls

Spinach and tomato salad with desired dressing

Blueberry shortcakes (with purchased shortcakes)

191

Beef and Bok Choy

START TO FINISH:
20 MINUTES

MAKES:
4 SERVINGS

4   teaspoons toasted sesame oil

12 ounces packaged beef stir-fry strips

1   teaspoon red chili pepper paste

6   cups sliced bok choy

1   teaspoon bottled minced garlic (2 cloves)

1   tablespoon reduced-sodium soy sauce

2   teaspoons sesame seeds, toasted

1. In a 12-inch nonstick skillet heat 2 teaspoons of the sesame oil over medium-high heat. Add beef strips and chili paste to hot oil. Stir-fry about 3 minutes or until beef is desired doneness. Remove skillet from heat. Reduce heat to medium. Remove beef from pan with a slotted spoon, reserving liquid in pan; cover beef to keep warm.

2. Add remaining 2 teaspoons sesame oil to the skillet. Add bok choy and garlic; stir-fry for 2 to 3 minutes or until bok choy is crisp-tender. Transfer to serving dish. Top with warm beef mixture. Drizzle with soy sauce and sprinkle with toasted sesame seeds.

Per serving: 179 cal., 9 g total fat (2 g sat. fat), 52 mg chol., 271 mg sodium, 4 g carbo., 1 g fiber, 20 g pro.

MENU

Hot cooked rice

Egg rolls
(frozen or takeout)

Fortune cookies with
pineapple sherbet

Thai Beef Stir-Fry

192

4   ounces dried rice noodles

2   tablespoons cooking oil

1   16-ounce package frozen sweet pepper and onion stir-fry vegetables

12 ounces packaged beef stir-fry strips

½   cup bottled Thai peanut stir-fry sauce

1. Prepare the noodles according to package directions. Drain and set aside.

2. In a large skillet heat 1 tablespoon of the oil over medium-high heat. Add the stir-fry vegetables; cook and stir for 2 to 3 minutes or until tender. Drain; place stir-fry vegetables in a bowl.

3. In the same skillet stir-fry beef strips in remaining 1 tablespoon hot oil for 2 to 3 minutes or until desired doneness. Return stir-fry vegetables to skillet; add stir-fry sauce. Stir to combine; heat through. Serve over rice noodles.

Per serving: 404 cal., 16 g total fat (4 g sat. fat), 50 mg chol., 597 mg sodium, 39 g carbo., 3 g fiber, 23 g pro.

MENU

Spring rolls
(frozen or takeout)

Coconut ice cream
with crystallized ginger
and honey

193

Bistro Beef
with Mushroom Sauce

START TO FINISH:
30 MINUTES

MAKES:
4 SERVINGS

1   medium onion
1¼ pounds ground beef
¾   teaspoon salt
8   ounces assorted fresh mushrooms (such as oyster, cremini, and shiitake), sliced
1½ cups beer or nonalcoholic beer (12 ounces)
1   0.88-ounce package brown gravy mix
2   teaspoons snipped fresh thyme or ½ teaspoon dried thyme, crushed

1. Cut onion in half. Finely chop half of the onion. Thinly slice the remaining half; set aside.

2. In a large bowl combine the chopped onion, the ground beef, and the ¾ teaspoon salt; mix well. Shape beef mixture into four ½-inch-thick oval patties. Sprinkle tops with additional salt and *black pepper.*

3. Preheat a large nonstick skillet over medium-high heat. Add patties; reduce heat to medium. Cook, uncovered, for 10 to 12 minutes or until done (160°F)*, turning patties once halfway through cooking. Remove patties from skillet; cover to keep warm.

4. For mushroom sauce, add the sliced onion, the mushrooms, and ¼ cup of the beer to drippings in skillet. Cook over medium-high heat about 5 minutes or until onion and mushrooms are tender, stirring occasionally. In a small bowl combine dry gravy mix, the remaining 1¼ cups beer, and the thyme, stirring until smooth. Add gravy mixture to mushroom mixture in skillet. Simmer, uncovered, about 1 minute or until thickened, stirring frequently. Spoon mushroom sauce over patties.

Per serving: 309 cal., 14 g total fat (5 g sat. fat), 89 mg chol., 903 mg sodium, 11 g carbo., 1 g fiber, 28 g pro.

MENU
Multigrain rolls
Mashed potatoes
Steamed green beans

*NOTE: The internal color of a meat patty is not a reliable doneness indicator. A patty cooked to 160°F is safe, regardless of color.
To measure the doneness of the patty, insert an instant-read thermometer through the side of the patty to a depth of 2 to 3 inches.

Pizza Burgers

194

PREP:
15 MINUTES

BROIL:
11 MINUTES

MAKES:
4 BURGERS

1   pound ground beef
4   ¾-inch slices sourdough bread
1   cup bottled mushroom pasta sauce
1   cup shredded provolone or mozzarella cheese (4 ounces)
2   tablespoons thinly sliced fresh basil

1. Preheat broiler. Lightly shape ground beef into four ½-inch-thick patties. Place patties on the unheated rack of a broiler pan. Broil 3 to 4 inches from the heat for 10 to 12 minutes or until done (160°F)*, turning once halfway through broiling. Add the bread slices to broiler pan for the last 2 to 3 minutes of broiling, turning once to toast evenly.

2. Meanwhile, in a medium saucepan heat the pasta sauce over medium heat until bubbly, stirring occasionally. Place patties on toasted bread slices. Spoon pasta sauce over patties; sprinkle with cheese. Place on the rack of the broiler pan. Return to broiler; broil for 1 to 2 minutes more or until cheese melts. Sprinkle with basil.

Per burger: 504 cal., 30 g total fat (13 g sat. fat), 96 mg chol., 815 mg sodium, 27 g carbo., 2 g fiber, 30 g pro.

*NOTE: The internal color of a meat patty is not a reliable doneness indicator. A patty cooked to 160°F is safe, regardless of color.
To measure the doneness of the patty, insert an instant-read thermometer through the side of the patty to a depth of 2 to 3 inches.

MENU
Pasta salad (from a deli)
Potato chips
Spumoni ice cream

195 Italian Wedding Salad

START TO FINISH:
25 MINUTES

MAKES:
4 SERVINGS

6   ounces dried orzo pasta

32 frozen cooked meatballs (about 0.5 ounce each), thawed

½   cup bottled Italian salad dressing

1   6-ounce package prewashed baby spinach

1   6-ounce jar marinated artichoke hearts, drained and chopped

¼   cup chopped walnuts, toasted

Finely shredded Parmesan or Romano cheese (optional)

1. Cook pasta according to package directions; drain well.

2. Meanwhile, in a 4-quart Dutch oven combine meatballs and salad dressing. Cook over medium heat until meatballs are heated through, stirring occasionally. Stir in drained pasta, spinach, drained artichoke hearts, and walnuts. Heat and stir just until spinach is wilted. Season to taste with *salt* and *black pepper*. If desired, sprinkle with cheese.

Per serving: 730 cal., 52 g total fat (15 g sat. fat), 40 mg chol., 1,383 mg sodium, 48 g carbo., 8 g fiber, 23 g pro.

MENU

Focaccia

Fresh fruit plate

Amaretti cookies and coffee

Pork Tenderloin with Raspberry Sauce

196

1   pound pork tenderloin

2   tablespoons butter or margarine

⅓   cup seedless raspberry or strawberry jam

2   tablespoons red wine vinegar

2   teaspoons prepared horseradish

½   teaspoon bottled minced garlic (1 clove)

⅛   teaspoon cayenne pepper

    Fresh raspberries or strawberries (optional)

1. Trim fat from meat. Cut meat crosswise into 1-inch slices. Place each slice of meat between 2 pieces of plastic wrap. Press each slice with the palm of your hand until about ½ inch thick. Discard plastic wrap. Sprinkle meat with *salt* and *black pepper.*

2. In a 12-inch skillet heat butter over medium-high heat. Add meat. Cook for 4 to 6 minutes or until slightly pink in center, turning once halfway through cooking. Remove meat from skillet, reserving drippings; cover meat to keep warm. Reduce heat to medium.

3. For sauce, stir jam, vinegar, horseradish, garlic, and cayenne pepper into reserved drippings in skillet. Cook and stir until bubbly. Cook and stir about 1 minute more or until slightly thickened. Serve the sauce over meat. If desired, garnish with fresh berries.

Per serving: 264 cal., 10 g total fat (5 g sat. fat), 89 mg chol., 259 mg sodium, 19 g carbo., 0 g fiber, 24 g pro.

MENU
Baby peas with butter
Blue cheese mashed potatoes
Raspberry and lemon sorbet

197

Oriental Pork and Vegetables

START TO FINISH:
20 MINUTES

MAKES:
4 SERVINGS

6   ounces rice stick noodles or two 3-ounce packages ramen noodles (any flavor), broken, if desired

2   teaspoons sesame oil or olive oil

1   16-ounce package frozen stir-fry vegetables (any combination)

1   12-ounce pork tenderloin, cut into ¼-inch slices

¼   cup teriyaki sauce

2   tablespoons plum sauce

1. If using ramen noodles, discard spice packet or save for another use. Prepare noodles as directed on package. Set aside and keep warm.

2. Heat a 12-inch nonstick skillet over medium-high heat. Add 1 teaspoon of the sesame oil. Add vegetables. Cook and stir vegetables in the hot oil for 4 to 6 minutes or until crisp-tender. Remove from skillet. Set aside and keep warm.

3. Add the remaining 1 teaspoon oil to the skillet. Add meat. Cook over medium-high heat for 4 to 6 minutes or until slightly pink in center, turning once halfway through cooking. Stir in vegetables (drained if necessary), teriyaki sauce, and plum sauce; heat through. Add noodles; toss to mix.

Per serving: 341 cal., 5 g total fat (1 g sat. fat), 55 mg chol., 820 mg sodium, 48 g carbo., 3 g fiber, 22 g pro.

MENU

Pot stickers
(frozen or takeout)

Fresh mango and
papaya slices

Pork Medallions on Green Beans

198

START TO FINISH:
20 MINUTES

MAKES:
4 SERVINGS

1 1- to 1½-pound honey-mustard marinated pork tenderloin

1 tablespoon butter or margarine

1 9-ounce package frozen French-cut green beans, thawed

1 teaspoon dried dill

1 teaspoon lemon juice

1. Trim fat from meat. Cut meat crosswise into ¼-inch slices. In a 12-inch skillet melt butter over medium-high heat. Add pork; reduce heat to medium. Cook pork for 4 to 6 minutes or until slightly pink in center, turning once halfway through cooking. Remove pork from skillet, reserving drippings. Cover pork to keep warm.

2. Add green beans and dill to drippings in skillet. Cook and stir for 3 to 4 minutes or until beans are tender. Stir in lemon juice. Serve pork medallions on top of green beans.

Per serving: 187 cal., 8 g total fat (4 g sat. fat), 53 mg chol., 549 mg sodium, 7 g carbo., 2 g fiber, 21 g pro.

MENU
Oven-roasted potato wedges
French baguette slices
Angel food cake with fresh berries and whipped cream

199 Pork and Gouda Salad

PREP:
10 MINUTES

ROAST:
20 MINUTES

OVEN:
425°F

MAKES:
4 SERVINGS

1 1-pound pork tenderloin

⅔ cup bottled oil and vinegar or vinaigrette salad dressing

8 cups packaged torn mixed salad greens

2 ounces Gouda or white cheddar cheese, cut into bite-size strips

12 cherry tomatoes, quartered

1. Preheat oven to 425°F. Trim fat from meat. Place on a rack in a shallow roasting pan. Sprinkle meat with *salt* and *black pepper.* Brush meat with 2 tablespoons of the salad dressing. Roast for 20 to 30 minutes or until done (160°F).

2. Meanwhile, arrange salad greens on 4 salad plates. Top with cheese and tomatoes. Thinly slice meat; arrange meat on salads. Serve with remaining salad dressing.

Per serving: 336 cal., 24 g total fat (5 g sat. fat), 71 mg chol., 535 mg sodium, 5 g carbo., 2 g fiber, 23 g pro.

MENU
Corn muffins
Rhubarb pie

Squirt-of-Orange Chops 200

PREP:
10 MINUTES

BROIL:
9 MINUTES

MAKES:
4 SERVINGS

4   boneless pork top loin chops, cut 1 inch thick (about 1¼ pounds)

1   large orange

½   teaspoon garlic-pepper seasoning

¼   teaspoon salt

¼   cup orange marmalade

2   teaspoons snipped fresh rosemary or ½ teaspoon dried rosemary, crushed

1. Preheat broiler. Trim fat from chops; set chops aside.

2. Cut orange in half. Cut one half of the orange into 4 wedges; set wedges aside. Squeeze juice from the remaining orange half. Remove 1 tablespoon of the juice and brush on both sides of each chop. Sprinkle chops with garlic-pepper seasoning and salt. In a small bowl combine remaining orange juice, orange marmalade, and rosemary; set aside.

3. Place chops on the unheated rack of a broiler pan. Broil 3 to 4 inches from the heat for 9 to 11 minutes or until chops are 160°F, turning once halfway through broiling. Brush chops with orange marmalade mixture for the last 2 to 3 minutes of broiling.

4. Serve orange wedges with chops. If desired, squeeze juice from orange wedges over chops.

Per serving: 262 cal., 7 g total fat (3 g sat. fat), 83 mg chol., 343 mg sodium, 17 g carbo., 1 g fiber, 31 g pro.

MENU

Bread stuffing (from mix)

Baby greens salad with sliced strawberries, onion, and toasted almond slices

Pound cake spread with lemon curd and topped with fresh berries

201

Greek-style Pork Chops

PREP:
15 MINUTES

BROIL:
9 MINUTES

MAKES:
4 SERVINGS

½   cup chopped, seeded tomato (1 medium)
1   tablespoon bottled red wine vinaigrette salad dressing
4   boneless pork loin chops, cut ¾ inch thick
1   teaspoon lemon-pepper seasoning
¼   cup crumbled feta cheese with garlic and herb
    Snipped fresh oregano (optional)

1. In a small bowl stir together tomato and salad dressing; set aside.

2. Preheat broiler. Trim fat from chops. Rub lemon-pepper seasoning on both sides
   of chops. Place chops on the unheated rack of a broiler pan. Broil 3 to
   4 inches from the heat for 9 to 11 minutes or until chops are 160°F, turning
   once halfway through broiling.

3. Transfer chops to dinner plates. Top each chop with some of the feta cheese
   and some of the tomato mixture. If desired, sprinkle with oregano.

Per serving: 179 cal., 7 g total fat (3 g sat. fat), 80 mg chol., 298 mg sodium, 3 g carbo., 0 g fiber, 25 g pro.

MENU

Hot cooked orzo

Fresh spinach and onion
salad with balsamic
vinaigrette

Toasted pita bread

Pork Diane

202

START TO FINISH:
30 MINUTES

MAKES:
4 SERVINGS

1 tablespoon Worcestershire sauce for chicken

1 tablespoon water

1 teaspoon lemon juice

1 teaspoon Dijon-style mustard

4 boneless pork top loin chops, cut ¾ to 1 inch thick

½ to 1 teaspoon lemon-pepper seasoning

2 tablespoons butter or margarine

1 tablespoon snipped fresh chives or parsley

1. For sauce, in a small bowl stir together Worcestershire sauce, water, lemon juice, and mustard. Set sauce aside.

2. Trim fat from pork chops. Sprinkle both sides of chops with lemon-pepper seasoning. In a large skillet melt butter over medium-high heat. Add chops; reduce heat to medium. Cook for 8 to 12 minutes or until 160°F, turning once halfway through cooking. Remove chops from skillet, reserving drippings. Cover chops to keep warm.

3. Pour sauce into skillet. Cook and stir to loosen any brown bits in bottom of skillet. Spoon sauce over chops. Sprinkle with chives.

Per serving: 178 cal., 11 g total fat (5 g sat. fat), 66 mg chol., 302 mg sodium, 1 g carbo., 0 g fiber, 18 g pro.

MENU
Steamed peas with butter
Potato salad (from a deli)
Red grapes and assorted cheeses

203 Balsamic and Garlic Pork

START TO FINISH:
15 MINUTES

MAKES:
4 SERVINGS

4 boneless pork loin chops, cut ½ inch thick (12 to 16 ounces)
½ teaspoon dried rosemary, crushed
¼ teaspoon salt
1 tablespoon olive oil
2 teaspoons bottled minced roasted garlic
½ cup bottled balsamic salad dressing
1 tablespoon honey mustard

1. Trim fat from chops. Sprinkle chops with rosemary and salt, pressing into surface of meat.

2. In a large nonstick skillet heat oil over medium-high heat. Add chops; reduce heat to medium. Cook for 8 to 12 minutes or until 160°F, turning once halfway through cooking time. Remove chops from skillet, reserving drippings. Cover chops to keep warm.

3. For sauce, add garlic to hot drippings in skillet; cook for 30 seconds. Stir in salad dressing and honey mustard. Bring to boiling. Spoon sauce over chops.

Per serving: 276 cal., 18 g total fat (4 g sat. fat), 54 mg chol., 562 mg sodium, 5 g carbo., 0 g fiber, 22 g pro.

MENU
Hot cooked tortellini with olive oil
Sauteed sugar snap peas
Crusty Italian bread

Peppered Pork with Chive Sauce

204

START TO FINISH:
25 MINUTES

MAKES:
4 SERVINGS

4   boneless pork top loin chops, cut ¾ inch thick

1   teaspoon coarsely cracked black pepper

2   teaspoons olive oil or cooking oil

¼   cup chicken broth

3   tablespoons dry sherry or chicken broth

½   of an 8-ounce package cream cheese, cut up

1   tablespoon snipped fresh chives

1. Trim fat from chops. Sprinkle chops with cracked black pepper, pressing lightly into meat. In a large skillet heat oil over medium-high heat. Add chops; reduce heat to medium. Cook for 8 to 12 minutes or until 160°F, turning once halfway through cooking. Remove chops from skillet, reserving drippings. Cover chops to keep warm.

2. For sauce, carefully add chicken broth and sherry to skillet. Cook until bubbly, stirring to loosen any brown bits in bottom of skillet. Add cream cheese; stir with a wire whisk over medium heat until cream cheese melts. Stir in chives. Spoon sauce over chops.

Per serving: 348 cal., 21 g total fat (10 g sat. fat), 108 mg chol., 204 mg sodium, 2 g carbo., 0 g fiber, 33 g pro.

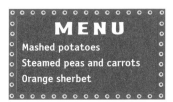

MENU
Mashed potatoes
Steamed peas and carrots
Orange sherbet

205

Pork Chops with Chili-Apricot Glaze

PREP:
15 MINUTES

BROIL:
9 MINUTES

MAKES:
4 SERVINGS

¼ cup apricot jam or preserves

¼ cup chili sauce

1 tablespoon sweet-hot mustard or brown mustard

1 tablespoon water

4 boneless pork loin chops, cut 1 inch thick

1. Preheat broiler. For the glaze, cut up any large pieces of fruit in jam. In a small saucepan combine jam, chili sauce, mustard, and water. Cook and stir over medium-low heat until heated through. Remove from heat.

2. Trim fat from the chops. Place pork chops on the unheated rack of a broiler pan. Broil 3 to 4 inches from heat for 9 to 11 minutes or until 160°F, turning once halfway through broiling and brushing generously with glaze the last 2 to 3 minutes. Spoon any remaining glaze over chops before serving.

Per serving: 307 cal., 8 g total fat (3 g sat. fat), 106 mg chol., 331 mg sodium, 17 g carbo., 1 g fiber, 38 g pro.

MENU
Hot cooked rice
Roasted asparagus
Chocolate cake

Ham Slice with Basil-Cherry Sauce

206

START TO FINISH:
20 MINUTES

MAKES:
4 SERVINGS

2   tablespoons butter or margarine

1   1- to 1¼-pound cooked center-cut ham slice, cut ½ inch thick

1   15- to 17-ounce can pitted dark sweet cherries

2   teaspoons cornstarch

2   teaspoons snipped fresh basil or ½ teaspoon dried basil, crushed

1. In a 12-inch skillet melt 1 tablespoon of the butter over medium heat. Add ham; cook for 8 to 10 minutes or until heated through, turning once. Transfer to a serving platter; cover to keep warm.

2. Meanwhile, for basil-cherry sauce, drain canned cherries, reserving juice. Set cherries aside. In a small saucepan stir reserved cherry juice into cornstarch. Cook and stir over medium heat until thickened and bubbly; cook and stir for 2 minutes more. Add cherries, basil, and the remaining 1 tablespoon butter; cook and stir until butter is melted and cherries are heated through. Serve warm basil-cherry sauce over ham.

Per serving: 338 cal., 18 g total fat (8 g sat. fat), 74 mg chol., 1,285 mg sodium, 20 g carbo., 2 g fiber, 23 g pro.

MENU

Hot cooked spinach fettuccine

Shredded carrot and broccoli salad with honey-Dijon dressing

Multigrain rolls

207

Ham and Asparagus Pasta

START TO FINISH:
20 MINUTES

MAKES:
4 SERVINGS

4 cups dried farfalle (bow ties), rotini (corkscrew), or other medium pasta

1 10-ounce package frozen cut asparagus or broccoli

8 ounces sliced cooked ham, cut into thin strips

1 8-ounce tub soft-style cream cheese spread with chive and onion

⅓ cup milk

1. Cook the pasta according to package directions, adding the frozen asparagus for the last 5 minutes and the ham the last minute of the cooking time. Drain and return to the pan.

2. In a small bowl stir together cream cheese and milk. Add cheese mixture to the pasta mixture in the pan. Stir gently over medium heat until heated through.

Per serving: 505 cal., 24 g total fat (12 g sat. fat), 140 mg chol., 905 mg sodium, 45 g carbo., 1 g fiber, 25 g pro.

MENU
Caesar salad
Whole wheat rolls
Chocolate ice cream
with sliced strawberries

Creamy Ham with Broccoli

208

3½ cups milk

1 10.75-ounce can condensed golden mushroom or cream of mushroom soup

¼ teaspoon dried thyme, crushed

⅛ teaspoon black pepper

2 cups frozen cut broccoli or peas

½ cup packaged instant mashed potatoes

1 5-ounce can chunk-style ham, drained and broken into pieces

1. In a large saucepan combine milk, soup, thyme, and pepper. Bring to boiling over medium heat. Add broccoli; cook, covered, about 5 minutes or just until broccoli is tender.

2. Stir instant potatoes into soup mixture. Stir in ham. Heat through.

Per serving: 349 cal., 13 g total fat (5 g sat. fat), 38 mg chol., 1,208 mg sodium, 40 g carbo., 3 g fiber, 17 g pro.

MENU
Baked potato
Buttermilk biscuits
Blueberry pie

209 Ham and Chutney Pasta Salad

START TO FINISH:
25 MINUTES

MAKES:
4 SERVINGS

8 ounces packaged dried medium shell macaroni
½ cup mango chutney
½ cup mayonnaise or salad dressing
¼ cup sliced green onion (2)
⅛ teaspoon coarsely ground black pepper
1½ cups cubed cooked ham (8 ounces)
Lettuce leaves

1. Cook macaroni according to package directions. Drain. Rinse with cold water. Drain again.

2. Meanwhile, cut up any large pieces of chutney. Stir together the chutney, mayonnaise, green onion, and pepper.

3. In a large bowl combine the macaroni, the chutney mixture, and the ham. Arrange lettuce leaves on 4 salad plates. Serve ham mixture on lettuce.

Per serving: 580 cal., 26 g total fat (4 g sat. fat), 46 mg chol., 850 mg sodium, 66 g carbo., 2 g fiber, 20 g pro.

MENU
Crusty baguette slices
Banana split

Ham and Rye Salad

210

PREP:
10 MINUTES

BAKE:
10 MINUTES

OVEN:
350°F

MAKES:
4 TO 6 SERVINGS

6   slices rye bread

3   tablespoons butter, melted

1   10-ounce package torn mixed salad greens

1½ cups cubed cooked ham (8 ounces)

⅔   cup bottled honey-mustard salad dressing

1. Preheat oven to 350°F. Cut rye bread slices into ¾-inch cubes (should have 4 cups); place in a large bowl. Add the melted butter and toss to coat. Arrange bread cubes in an even layer in a shallow baking pan. Bake for 10 to 15 minutes or until toasted, turning once. Set aside to cool.

2. In a large salad bowl combine salad greens and ham. Drizzle with salad dressing; toss to coat. Add the bread cubes; toss to mix.

Per serving: 503 cal., 36 g total fat (10 g sat. fat), 65 mg chol., 1,602 mg sodium, 29 g carbo., 4 g fiber, 18 g pro.

MENU
Tomato slices
Rhubarb crisp or pie

211

Cheesy Grilled Ham Sandwiches

START TO FINISH:
15 MINUTES

MAKES:
4 SANDWICHES

4　to 6 teaspoons Dijon-style mustard

8　slices firm wheat bread, white bread, or sourdough bread

4　ounces thinly sliced cooked ham

4　slices Swiss cheese (4 ounces)

1　egg, lightly beaten

½　cup milk

　Nonstick cooking spray

1. Spread mustard on 4 of the bread slices. Top with ham and cheese. Place remaining bread slices over ham and cheese. In a shallow bowl or pie plate beat together egg and milk.

2. Coat an unheated nonstick griddle or large skillet with nonstick cooking spray. Preheat griddle or skillet over medium heat. Dip each sandwich in milk mixture, turning to coat. Place on griddle or in skillet; cook for 1 to 2 minutes on each side or until golden and cheese melts.

Per sandwich: 323 cal., 14 g total fat (7 g sat. fat), 98 mg chol., 839 mg sodium, 29 g carbo., 3 g fiber, 20 g pro.

MENU
Kettle-cooked potato chips
Mixed greens with cucumber ranch dressing
Cherry pie

Pasta with Sausage and Sweet Peppers

212

START TO FINISH:
25 MINUTES

MAKES:
4 SERVINGS

8   ounces dried large farfalle (bow ties)

12 ounces spicy Italian sausage links

2   medium red sweet peppers, cut into ¾-inch pieces

½   cup vegetable broth or beef broth

¼   teaspoon coarsely ground black pepper

¼   cup snipped fresh Italian parsley

1. Cook pasta according to package directions; drain. Return pasta to saucepan.

2. Meanwhile, cut the sausage into 1-inch pieces. In a large skillet cook sausage and sweet pepper over medium-high heat until sausage is brown. Drain off fat.

3. Stir broth and black pepper into skillet. Bring to boiling. Reduce heat; simmer, uncovered, for 5 minutes. Remove from heat. Pour over pasta; add parsley. Toss gently to mix.

Per serving: 397 cal., 18 g total fat (6 g sat. fat), 94 mg chol., 713 mg sodium, 38 g carbo., 3 g fiber, 24 g pro.

MENU
Crusty Italian bread
Caesar salad
Fudge brownies

213

Range-Top Sausage Soup

START TO FINISH:
25 MINUTES

MAKES:
3 TO 4 SERVINGS

1 7-ounce package (10 links) frozen maple-flavor brown-and-serve sausage links or original brown-and-serve sausage links
1 15-ounce can Great Northern beans, undrained
1 cup sliced cauliflower florets
½ cup water
1 8-ounce can pizza sauce

1. Cut each sausage link into 3 pieces. In a medium saucepan cook the sausage pieces over medium-high heat about 7 minutes or until brown. Stir in the undrained beans, cauliflower, and water.

2. Bring to boiling; reduce heat. Simmer, covered, for 8 to 10 minutes or just until cauliflower is crisp-tender. Stir in pizza sauce; heat through.

Per serving: 469 cal., 30 g total fat (10 g sat. fat), 58 mg chol., 1,501 mg sodium, 31 g carbo., 8 g fiber, 21 g pro.

MENU
Soft breadsticks
Baby greens salad with desired dressing
Cheesecake with fresh raspberries and chocolate sauce

Pizza Turnovers

PREP:
10 MINUTES

BAKE:
15 MINUTES

OVEN:
400°F

MAKES:
4 TURNOVERS

1   13.8-ounce package refrigerated pizza dough
¼   cup pizza sauce or spaghetti sauce
2   slices mozzarella, American, or provolone cheese, halved diagonally
20 slices pepperoni
1   tablespoon milk
2   tablespoons grated Parmesan cheese

1. Preheat oven to 400°F. Grease a large baking sheet. Unroll pizza dough on the baking sheet. Use a pizza cutter to cut the dough into 4 squares. Spread 1 tablespoon of the pizza sauce over each square, leaving a ¼-inch border around the edges. Place half a cheese slice on half of each square. Top with pepperoni slices.

2. For each turnover, fold one corner of the square down over the opposite corner to make a triangle. Carefully slide triangles apart on the baking sheet, leaving about 2 inches between each. With the tines of a fork or with your fingers, press edges of dough together to seal.

3. Brush tops of turnovers with the milk. Sprinkle with Parmesan cheese. Bake for 15 to 17 minutes or until golden brown.

Per turnover: 377 cal., 17 g total fat (7 g sat. fat), 32 mg chol., 1,110 mg sodium, 35 g carbo., 0 g fiber, 17 g pro.

HAM AND PINEAPPLE TURNOVERS: Prepare as above, except substitute 2 ounces chopped thinly sliced cooked ham or 20 slices pizza-style Canadian-style bacon for pepperoni. Drain an 8-ounce can pineapple tidbits. Place pineapple on top of ham. Continue as directed in Step 2.

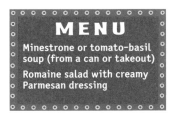

MENU
Minestrone or tomato-basil soup (from a can or takeout)
Romaine salad with creamy Parmesan dressing

215 Lamb Chops with Mint Salad

START TO FINISH:
30 MINUTES

MAKES:
4 SERVINGS

¼ cup snipped fresh mint
¼ cup snipped fresh Italian parsley
¼ cup crumbled feta cheese (1 ounce)
¼ cup chopped pecans, toasted
8 lamb rib or loin chops, cut 1 inch thick (1½ to 2 pounds)
2 teaspoons olive oil
¼ teaspoon salt
⅛ teaspoon black pepper
Olive oil and/or lemon juice (optional)

1. In a small bowl combine mint, parsley, feta cheese, and pecans; set aside.

2. Trim fat from chops. Rub chops with the 2 teaspoons olive oil, the salt, and pepper. Preheat a heavy, large nonstick skillet over medium-high heat. Add chops; reduce heat to medium. Cook for 9 to 11 minutes or until medium doneness (160°F), turning once halfway through cooking.

3. To serve, sprinkle chops with mint mixture. If desired, drizzle additional olive oil and/or lemon juice over mint mixture.

Per serving: 252 cal., 17 g total fat (5 g sat. fat), 72 mg chol., 311 mg sodium, 2 g carbo., 1 g fiber, 22 g pro.

MENU
Baby spinach salad with desired vinaigrette dressing
Hot cooked orzo
Soft pita bread

216

Tuscan Lamb Chop Skillet

START TO FINISH:
20 MINUTES

MAKES:
4 SERVINGS

8   lamb rib or loin chops, cut 1 inch thick (1½ to 2 pounds)

2   teaspoons olive oil

1½ teaspoons bottled minced garlic (3 cloves)

1   19-ounce can cannellini (white kidney) beans, rinsed and drained

1   8-ounce can Italian-style stewed tomatoes, undrained

1   tablespoon balsamic vinegar

2   teaspoons snipped fresh rosemary or ½ teaspoon dried rosemary, crushed

1. Trim fat from chops. In a large skillet heat oil over medium-high heat. Add chops; reduce heat to medium. Cook for 9 to 11 minutes or until medium doneness (160°F), turning once halfway through cooking. Remove chops from skillet, reserving drippings. Cover chops to keep warm.

2. Stir garlic into drippings in skillet. Cook and stir for 1 minute. Stir in drained beans, undrained tomatoes, vinegar, and rosemary. Bring to boiling; reduce heat. Simmer, uncovered, for 3 minutes.

3. Divide bean mixture among 4 dinner plates; arrange 2 chops on top of beans on each plate.

Per serving: 272 cal., 9 g total fat (3 g sat. fat), 67 mg chol., 466 mg sodium, 24 g carbo., 6 g fiber, 30 g pro.

MENU

Romaine salad with balsamic vinaigrette dressing

Country Italian bread

Chocolate ice cream with crushed biscotti

217 Chicken with Asparagus

START TO FINISH:
30 MINUTES

MAKES:
4 SERVINGS

1 pound fresh asparagus spears
Nonstick cooking spray
4 skinless, boneless chicken breast halves
1 cup water
1 10.75-ounce can condensed cream of chicken or cream of asparagus soup
¾ cup chicken broth
1 tablespoon lemon juice
2 cups hot cooked couscous

1. Snap off and discard woody bases from asparagus. Set asparagus aside.

2. Lightly coat a large nonstick skillet with nonstick cooking spray. Preheat skillet over medium-high heat. Add chicken; reduce heat to medium. Cook for 8 to 10 minutes or until no longer pink (170°F), turning occasionally to brown evenly. Remove chicken from skillet; cover to keep warm.

3. In the same skillet combine asparagus and water. Bring to boiling; reduce heat. Simmer, covered, for 3 to 5 minutes or until asparagus is crisp-tender. Drain.

4. Meanwhile, in a small saucepan combine chicken soup, chicken broth, and lemon juice. Cook and stir until heated through. Serve sauce with chicken, asparagus, and hot cooked couscous.

Per serving: 354 cal., 8 g total fat (3 g sat. fat), 88 mg chol., 844 mg sodium, 27 g carbo., 3 g fiber, 40 g pro.

MENU
Mixed greens salad
Whole wheat rolls
Ice cream sandwiches (made with chocolate chip cookies and desired ice cream)

Chicken Breasts with Jalapeño Jelly

218

PREP:
10 MINUTES

COOK:
12 MINUTES

MAKES:
4 SERVINGS

4   skinless, boneless chicken breast halves

2   tablespoons butter or margarine

1   tablespoon water

2   cups bias-sliced celery (4 stalks)

¼   cup red jalapeño jelly

2   tablespoons lemon juice

1   tablespoon Dijon-style mustard

1. Sprinkle chicken with *salt* and *black pepper.* In a 12-inch skillet melt butter over medium-high heat. Add chicken; reduce heat to medium. Cook for 8 to 10 minutes or until chicken is no longer pink (170°F), turning occasionally to brown evenly. Remove chicken from skillet; cover to keep warm.

2. For sauce, carefully stir water into skillet, scraping up any brown bits in bottom of skillet. Add celery; cook and stir for 1 minute. Add jelly, lemon juice, and mustard; cook and stir about 3 minutes more or until slightly thickened. Return chicken to skillet; heat through.

Per serving: 281 cal., 9 g total fat (4 g sat. fat), 99 mg chol., 236 mg sodium, 16 g carbo., 1 g fiber, 34 g pro.

MENU
Mexican rice (from a mix)
Steamed green beans
Vanilla pudding with gingersnaps

219

Chicken Medallions with Mustard Sauce

START TO FINISH:
25 MINUTES

MAKES:
4 SERVINGS

4   skinless, boneless chicken breast halves
2   tablespoons olive oil or cooking oil
¼   cup dry white wine or chicken broth
2   tablespoons crème fraîche
2   tablespoons tarragon mustard or dill mustard

1. Place each chicken breast half between 2 pieces of plastic wrap. Using the flat side of a meat mallet, pound chicken lightly to about ½ inch thick. Discard plastic wrap. Sprinkle chicken with *salt* and *black pepper.*

2. In a 12-inch skillet heat oil over medium-high heat. Cook chicken breasts, two at a time, in hot oil for 2 to 3 minutes or until golden, turning to brown evenly. Remove chicken from skillet; cover to keep warm.

3. For sauce, carefully add wine to hot skillet. Cook until bubbly, stirring to loosen any brown bits in bottom of skillet. Add crème fraîche and mustard to skillet; stir with a wire whisk until combined. Serve sauce over chicken.

Per serving: 255 cal., 11 g total fat (3 g sat. fat), 92 mg chol., 306 mg sodium, 1 g carbo., 0 g fiber, 33 g pro.

MENU
Rice pilaf (from a mix)
Steamed baby peas
French baguette slices
Lemon meringue pie

Chicken with Mushroom Sauce

220

START TO FINISH:
25 MINUTES

MAKES:
4 SERVINGS

4   skinless, boneless chicken breast halves
½   teaspoon salt
⅛   teaspoon black pepper
3   tablespoons butter or margarine
1   8-ounce package sliced fresh mushrooms (3 cups)
1   10.75-ounce can condensed cream of mushroom or golden mushroom soup
¼   cup dry sherry
½   teaspoon dried thyme, crushed

1. Sprinkle chicken with salt and pepper. In a 12-inch skillet melt 2 tablespoons of the butter over medium-high heat. Add chicken; reduce heat to medium. Cook for 8 to 12 minutes or until no longer pink (170°F), turning occasionally to brown evenly. Remove chicken from skillet; cover to keep warm.

2. For mushroom sauce, add the remaining 1 tablespoon butter to the skillet. Add mushrooms; cook and stir about 5 minutes or until mushrooms are tender. Stir in soup, sherry, and thyme. Cook and stir until heated through. Serve mushroom sauce over chicken.

Per serving: 351 cal., 18 g total fat (8 g sat. fat), 107 mg chol., 992 mg sodium, 8 g carbo., 1 g fiber, 37 g pro.

MENU
Hot cooked fettuccine
Steamed broccoli spears
Fresh fruit plate

221 Lemon Chicken

START TO FINISH:
25 MINUTES

MAKES:
4 SERVINGS

⅓ cup all-purpose flour

¼ teaspoon black pepper

4 skinless, boneless chicken breast halves

2 tablespoons butter or margarine

1 cup chicken broth

3 tablespoons lemon juice

1 tablespoon cornstarch

¼ cup sliced green onion (2)

1. In a shallow dish stir together flour and pepper. Lightly coat each chicken breast half with the flour mixture.

2. In a large skillet melt butter over medium-high heat. Add chicken; reduce heat to medium. Cook for 8 to 12 minutes or until chicken is no longer pink (170°F), turning occasionally to brown evenly. Remove chicken from skillet; cover to keep warm.

3. For sauce, in a small bowl stir together chicken broth, lemon juice, and cornstarch. Add to skillet. Cook and stir over medium heat until thickened and bubbly. Cook and stir for 2 minutes more. Stir in green onion. Serve chicken with sauce.

Per serving: 262 cal., 8 g total fat (4 g sat. fat), 98 mg chol., 360 mg sodium, 11 g carbo., 1 g fiber, 34 g pro.

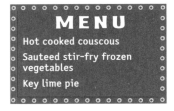

MENU
Hot cooked couscous
Sauteed stir-fry frozen vegetables
Key lime pie

Dijon Chicken and Mushrooms

222

3 tablespoons butter or margarine

2 cups packaged sliced fresh mushrooms

4 skinless, boneless chicken breast halves

1 10.75-ounce can condensed cream of chicken soup

¼ cup dry white wine or water

¼ cup water

2 tablespoons Dijon-style mustard

½ teaspoon dried thyme or tarragon, crushed

1. In a large skillet melt 1 tablespoon of the butter over medium-high heat. Add mushrooms; cook for 3 to 4 minutes or until mushrooms are tender. Remove mushrooms from skillet. In the same skillet cook chicken in remaining 2 tablespoons butter for 8 to 12 minutes or until no longer pink (170°F), turning occasionally to brown evenly.

2. Meanwhile, in a small bowl stir together soup, wine, water, mustard, and thyme.

3. Return the mushrooms to the skillet with the chicken; add soup mixture. Bring to boiling; reduce heat. Simmer, uncovered, for 2 minutes. Serve mushroom mixture over chicken.

Per serving: 346 cal., 17 g total fat (7 g sat. fat), 110 mg chol., 914 mg sodium, 8 g carbo., 0 g fiber, 36 g pro.

MENU
Hot cooked noodles
Steamed sugar snap peas
Crusty French rolls
Blueberries with
lemon sherbet

223

Chicken and Pea Pods

START TO FINISH:
25 MINUTES

MAKES:
4 SERVINGS

4 skinless, boneless chicken breast halves

2 teaspoons lemon-pepper seasoning

3 tablespoons butter or margarine

2 cups fresh sugar snap peas, strings and tips removed, or one 6-ounce package frozen pea pods, thawed

1. Sprinkle both sides of chicken breasts with 1½ teaspoons of the lemon-pepper seasoning. In a large skillet melt 2 tablespoons of the butter over medium-high heat. Add chicken; reduce heat to medium. Cook for 8 to 12 minutes or until no longer pink (170°F), turning occasionally to brown evenly. Remove chicken from skillet; cover to keep warm.

2. Add remaining 1 tablespoon butter to skillet. Stir in pea pods and remaining ½ teaspoon lemon-pepper seasoning. Cook and stir over medium heat about 2 minutes or until pea pods are crisp-tender. Serve pea pods with chicken.

Per serving: 259 cal., 11 g total fat (6 g sat. fat), 107 mg chol., 716 mg sodium, 5 g carbo., 1 g fiber, 34 g pro.

MENU
Egg rolls (frozen or takeout)
Kiwifruit and strawberries

Chicken and Vegetables Alfredo with Rice

224

START TO FINISH:
25 MINUTES

MAKES:
4 SERVINGS

1   tablespoon butter or margarine

4   skinless, boneless chicken breast halves or 8 skinless, boneless chicken thighs

2½ cups frozen stir-fry vegetables (such as broccoli, carrots, onions, and red
    sweet peppers)

1⅓ cups uncooked instant white rice

1   10-ounce container refrigerated light Alfredo pasta sauce

1   cup milk

    Finely shredded or grated Parmesan cheese (optional)

1. In a large skillet melt butter over medium-high heat. Add chicken; reduce
   heat to medium. Cook for 6 to 8 minutes or until chicken is brown, turning
   occasionally. Remove chicken from skillet.

2. Add frozen vegetables, rice, Alfredo sauce, and milk to the skillet. Bring to
   boiling, stirring occasionally; reduce heat. Top with chicken. Cook, covered,
   over medium-low heat for 6 to 8 minutes or until chicken is no longer pink
   (170°F for breasts; 180°F for thighs), stirring once or twice. If desired, sprinkle
   with Parmesan cheese.

Per serving: 433 cal., 13 g total fat (8 g sat. fat), 105 mg chol., 638 mg sodium, 39 g carbo., 2 g fiber, 38 g pro.

MENU
Crusty Italian bread
Red and green grapes
with blue cheese slices

225 Oriental-Style Chicken

START TO FINISH:
25 MINUTES

MAKES:
4 SERVINGS

2 cups frozen stir-fry vegetables (any combination)

1 8-ounce can pineapple tidbits (juice pack)

½ cup bottled teriyaki sauce

2 teaspoons cornstarch

½ teaspoon ground ginger

1 tablespoon cooking oil

12 ounces packaged chicken breast stir-fry strips

Coarsely chopped honey roasted peanuts (optional)

1. In a colander run water over frozen vegetables just until thawed. Drain well. Meanwhile, drain pineapple, reserving ¼ cup of the juice. Set pineapple aside. In a small bowl stir together reserved pineapple juice, teriyaki sauce, cornstarch, and ginger. Set aside.

2. In a large skillet heat oil over medium-high heat. Add chicken; stir-fry for 2 to 3 minutes or until no longer pink. Add vegetables and pineapple; cook for 1 minute more.

3. Push chicken and vegetables to the edge of the skillet. Add teriyaki mixture to the skillet. Cook and stir until thickened and bubbly. Cook and stir for 2 minutes more. If desired, sprinkle with peanuts.

Per serving: 218 cal., 5 g total fat (1 g sat. fat), 49 mg chol., 2,109 mg sodium, 18 g carbo., 2 g fiber, 23 g pro.

MENU
Hot cooked rice
Pot stickers
(frozen or takeout)
Fresh mango and
papaya slices

Chicken Fingers

226

PREP:
15 MINUTES

BAKE:
12 MINUTES

OVEN:
450°F

MAKES:
4 SERVINGS

12 ounces skinless, boneless chicken breast halves
1   egg, lightly beaten
1   tablespoon honey
1   teaspoon prepared mustard
1   cup packaged cornflake crumbs or 2 cups cornflakes, finely crushed
    Dash black pepper
    Purchased dipping sauce (optional)

1. Preheat oven to 450°F. Cut chicken into 3×¾-inch strips. In a shallow dish combine egg, honey, and mustard. In another shallow dish stir together cornflake crumbs and pepper. Dip chicken strips into the egg mixture; roll in crumb mixture to coat. Arrange chicken strips on an ungreased baking sheet.

2. Bake about 12 minutes or until golden and chicken is no longer pink. If desired, serve with your favorite dipping sauce.

Per serving: 212 cal., 3 g total fat (1 g sat. fat), 102 mg chol., 236 mg sodium, 23 g carbo., 0 g fiber, 23 g pro.

MENU
Steamed carrots and peas
Boiled new potatoes
Hot fudge sundaes

227 Mexican Chicken Posole

START TO FINISH:
20 MINUTES

MAKES:
4 SERVINGS

12 ounces skinless, boneless chicken thighs or breast halves

3 to 4 teaspoons chili powder or salt-free Mexican seasoning

1 tablespoon cooking oil or olive oil

1 medium red or yellow sweet pepper, cut into bite-size pieces

2 14-ounce cans reduced-sodium chicken broth

1 15-ounce can hominy or black-eyed peas, rinsed and drained

Salsa, dairy sour cream, and/or lime wedges (optional)

1. Cut chicken into 1-inch pieces; place chicken in a large bowl. Sprinkle chicken with chili powder; toss to coat evenly.

2. In a large saucepan heat oil over medium-high heat. Add chicken; cook and stir for 3 minutes. Add sweet pepper; cook and stir about 1 minute more or until chicken is no longer pink.

3. Carefully add chicken broth and hominy to chicken mixture in saucepan. Bring to boiling; reduce heat. Simmer, covered, for 3 minutes. If desired, serve with salsa, sour cream, and/or lime wedges.

Per serving: 234 cal., 8 g total fat (2 g sat. fat), 71 mg chol., 788 mg sodium, 19 g carbo., 4 g fiber, 21 g pro.

MENU

Spring greens salad with
ranch dressing

Warm flour tortillas

Brownies

Ranch-Style Chicken Salad

228

START TO FINISH:
10 MINUTES

MAKES:
4 SERVINGS

1   10-ounce package torn mixed salad greens
1   6-ounce package refrigerated cooked chicken breast strips
½   cup orange and/or yellow sweet pepper strips
½   cup halved cherry tomatoes
¼   cup sliced red onion
½   cup bottled ranch salad dressing

1. Arrange mixed greens on 4 salad plates. Top with chicken, sweet pepper, tomatoes, and onion. Drizzle with salad dressing or serve dressing on the side.

Per serving: 232 cal., 18 g total fat (3 g sat. fat), 31 mg chol., 618 mg sodium, 8 g carbo., 2 g fiber, 12 g pro.

MENU
Soft breadsticks
Root beer floats

229 Chicken and Mushroom Quesadillas

START TO FINISH:
20 MINUTES

MAKES:
4 QUESADILLAS

2   cups chopped cooked chicken (10 ounces)

4   8- to 10-inch flour tortillas

2   cups packaged prewashed fresh spinach leaves, chopped

1   6-ounce jar (drained weight) sliced mushrooms, drained

2   cups shredded Monterey Jack cheese (8 ounces)

Salsa and/or guacamole (optional)

1. Spoon chicken evenly onto bottom halves of tortillas. Top with spinach and mushrooms. Sprinkle cheese evenly over mushrooms. Fold tortillas in half.

2. Heat quesadillas in a large nonstick skillet or on a griddle over medium heat until brown on both sides and cheese is melted. If desired, serve with salsa and/or guacamole.

Per quesadilla: 447 cal., 25 g total fat (13 g sat. fat), 113 mg chol., 676 mg sodium, 18 g carbo., 2 g fiber, 37 g pro.

MENU
Spanish rice (from a mix)
Fresh fruit salad

Chicken Tortilla Soup

230

START TO FINISH:
20 MINUTES

MAKES:
4 SERVINGS

2   14-ounce cans chicken broth
2   cups frozen sweet pepper and onion stir-fry vegetables
1   14.5-ounce can Mexican-style stewed tomatoes, undrained
2   cups chopped cooked chicken (10 ounces)
1   cup crushed packaged baked tortilla chips (about 2 cups uncrushed)
    Light dairy sour cream, chopped avocado, and/or sprig of fresh cilantro (optional)

1. In a large saucepan combine chicken broth, frozen vegetables, and undrained tomatoes. Bring to boiling; reduce heat. Simmer, covered, for 3 to 5 minutes or until vegetables are tender. Stir in chicken; heat through.

2. Ladle soup into warm soup bowls. Sprinkle with crushed tortilla chips. If desired, top with sour cream, avocado, and/or cilantro.

Per serving: 247 cal., 6 g total fat (1 g sat. fat), 64 mg chol., 1,266 mg sodium, 17 g carbo., 2 g fiber, 24 g pro.

MENU
Crusty rolls
Cheesecake with strawberries and chocolate sauce

231

Chicken Noodle Soup Florentine

START TO FINISH:
25 MINUTES

MAKES:
6 SERVINGS

1 49-ounce can chicken broth

3 cups packaged sliced fresh mushrooms

1 cup sliced green onion (8)

1½ teaspoons dried fines herbes, crushed

¼ teaspoon black pepper

2½ cups dried medium noodles or linguine, broken (5 ounces)

1 9-ounce package frozen diced cooked chicken or 2 cups cubed cooked chicken (10 ounces)

½ of a 10-ounce package frozen chopped spinach, thawed*

1. In a 4½-quart Dutch oven or kettle combine chicken broth, mushrooms, green onion, fines herbes, and pepper. Bring to boiling; add noodles. Cook and stir until mixture returns to boiling; reduce heat.

2. Cover and boil gently for 7 to 9 minutes or until noodles are tender (do not overcook). Stir chicken and spinach into soup; heat through.

Per serving: 222 cal., 6 g total fat (1 g sat. fat), 59 mg chol., 866 mg sodium, 20 g carbo., 1 g fiber, 22 g pro.

*NOTE: To cut a package of spinach in half, unwrap the block of spinach and place on a microwave-safe plate. Microwave on 30% power (medium-low) for 2 to 4 minutes or just until soft enough to cut in half with a sharp knife. Put one half in a freezer bag, seal, and return to the freezer. Continue to microwave the remaining half on 30% power for 3 to 5 minutes or until thawed.

MENU
Crusty Italian bread
Ice cream cake

276 Lemon-Pepper Flank Steak, page 310

290 Jamaican Pork Kabobs, page 324

304 Chicken with Brandied Fruit, page 338

305 20-Minute Chicken Fettuccine, page 339

306 Chicken Soup with Spinach and Orzo, page 340

312 Asian Chicken Salad, page 346

313 Cool-as-a-Cucumber Chicken Salad, page 347

317 Chicken and Prosciutto Sandwiches, page 351

324 Thai Turkey Burgers, page 358

328 Brats with Onion-Pepper Relish, page 362

336 Red Snapper Veracruz, page 370

337 Flounder with Roma Tomatoes, page

342 Sweet Pepper and Salsa Fish, page 376

347 Shrimp Kabobs, page 381

355 Beans, Barley, and Tomatoes, page 389

360 Fresh Tomato Pizza, page 394

Curried Chicken and Noodles

232

START TO FINISH:
15 MINUTES

MAKES:
4 SERVINGS

5   cups water

2   3-ounce packages chicken-flavor ramen noodles

2   cups frozen broccoli, cauliflower, and carrots

½   cup purchased coconut milk

1   to 2 teaspoons curry powder
     Dash cayenne pepper

1   cup cubed cooked chicken breast (5 ounces)

1. In a large saucepan bring water to boiling. Add ramen noodles with seasoning packets and vegetables to saucepan. Cook, uncovered, about 3 minutes or until noodles and vegetables are tender. Drain. Return noodle mixture to saucepan.

2. Stir together coconut milk, curry powder, and cayenne pepper. Stir coconut milk mixture and chicken into saucepan. Heat through.

Per serving: 333 cal., 15 g total fat (10 g sat. fat), 30 mg chol., 934 mg sodium, 32 g carbo., 3 g fiber, 18 g pro.

MENU

Soft pita bread

Baby greens salad with desired dressing

Fresh papaya wedges

233

Mexican Chicken Casserole

PREP:
15 MINUTES

BAKE:
15 MINUTES

OVEN:
350°F

MAKES:
4 SERVINGS

1   15-ounce can black beans, rinsed and drained
½   cup chunky salsa
½   teaspoon ground cumin
1   2- to 2¼-pound deli-roasted chicken
¼   cup shredded Monterey Jack cheese with jalapeño peppers (1 ounce)
    Dairy sour cream (optional)

1. Preheat oven to 350°F. In a small bowl stir together beans, ¼ cup of the salsa, and the cumin. Divide bean mixture among 4 individual au gratin dishes or casseroles. Set aside.

2. Cut chicken into quarters. Place one piece on bean mixture in each dish. Spoon remaining ¼ cup salsa evenly over chicken pieces. Sprinkle with cheese.

3. Bake for 15 to 20 minutes or until heated through. If desired, garnish with sour cream.

Per serving: 468 cal., 23 g total fat (7 g sat. fat), 140 mg chol., 596 mg sodium, 16 g carbo., 5 g fiber, 50 g pro.

MENU
Mexican rice (from a mix)
Avocado and tomato slices
Pound cake with mixed
berries and whipped cream

Pesto Penne with Chicken

234

START TO FINISH:
30 MINUTES

MAKES:
4 SERVINGS

8 ounces dried penne, mostaccioli, or farfalle (bow ties) (4 cups)

2 cups packaged fresh broccoli florets

1 7-ounce container purchased basil pesto (about ¾ cup)

12 ounces cooked chicken, cut into bite-size strips, or purchased refrigerated cooked chicken strips

1 cup bottled roasted red sweet peppers, drained and cut into strips

¼ cup finely shredded Parmesan cheese (1 ounce)

1. Cook pasta according to package directions, adding broccoli the last 2 minutes of cooking. Drain, reserving ½ cup of the pasta water. Return drained pasta and broccoli to saucepan.

2. In a small bowl combine pesto and the reserved pasta water. Add chicken, roasted red peppers, and pesto mixture to pasta in saucepan. Toss gently to coat. Heat through over medium heat. Add Parmesan cheese to pasta mixture and toss to combine. Divide the pasta among 4 warm pasta bowls.

Per serving: 672 cal., 35 g total fat (7 g sat. fat), 93 mg chol., 857 mg sodium, 53 g carbo., 3 g fiber, 37 g pro.

MENU

Baby romaine salad with honey-Dijon dressing

Sourdough rolls

Cheesecake with red raspberries

235 Thai Chicken Pasta

START TO FINISH:
25 MINUTES

MAKES:
4 SERVINGS

6   ounces dried angel hair pasta

3   cups cooked chicken cut into strips (about 1 pound)

1   14-ounce can unsweetened coconut milk

⅓   cup thinly sliced green onion

⅓   cup packaged shredded carrot (1 small)

2   teaspoons Thai seasoning

½   cup chopped dry-roasted peanuts

1. Cook pasta according to package directions; drain well. Return pasta to pan; keep warm.

2. Meanwhile, in a large skillet combine chicken, coconut milk, green onion, carrot, and Thai seasoning. Cook and gently stir over medium heat until heated through. Pour hot chicken mixture over cooked pasta in pan. Toss gently to coat. Sprinkle individual servings with peanuts.

Per serving: 653 cal., 36 g total fat (20 g sat. fat), 93 mg chol., 287 mg sodium, 41 g carbo., 3 g fiber, 42 g pro.

MENU

Deli or frozen egg rolls (heated)

Steamed baby carrots and sliced leek

Pound cake with lemon curd and toasted coconut

Three-Corner Chicken Salad Bowls

236

PREP:
10 MINUTES

BAKE:
15 MINUTES

OVEN:
400°F

MAKES:
4 SERVINGS

1 13.8-ounce package refrigerated pizza dough
1 9- or 10-ounce package frozen cooked chicken strips
6 cups packaged torn mixed salad greens
⅓ cup bottled salad dressing (any flavor)

1. For bread bowls, preheat oven to 400°F. Invert four 10-ounce custard cups in a shallow baking pan; generously grease the outside of each custard cup. Set aside. On a cutting board unroll refrigerated pizza dough. Shape into a 10-inch square. Cut the square diagonally into 4 triangles. Drape each triangle over one of the prepared custard cups. Bake about 15 minutes or until deep golden. Remove bread bowls from custard cups; cool.

2. Meanwhile, prepare frozen chicken strips according to package directions.

3. To serve, divide the mixed salad greens and the chicken among bread bowls. Drizzle with salad dressing.

Per serving: 419 cal., 21 g total fat (4 g sat. fat), 43 mg chol., 1,333 mg sodium, 37 g carbo., 2 g fiber, 21 g pro.

MENU
Relish tray with radishes, baby carrots, and olives
Lemon meringue pie

237 Apricot Turkey Steaks

START TO FINISH:
25 MINUTES

MAKES:
4 SERVINGS

1 6-ounce package chicken-flavor rice and vermicelli mix
2 turkey breast tenderloins (about 1¼ pounds)
1 5.5-ounce can apricot nectar
½ teaspoon salt
⅛ teaspoon ground cinnamon
  Dash black pepper
3 tablespoons apricot preserves
1½ teaspoons cornstarch

1. Prepare rice mix according to package directions. Set aside.

2. Meanwhile, split each turkey breast tenderloin in half horizontally to make 4 turkey steaks. In a large skillet combine apricot nectar, salt, cinnamon, and pepper. Add turkey steaks. Bring to boiling; reduce heat. Cover and simmer about 10 minutes or until turkey is no longer pink (170°F). Remove turkey from skillet, reserving cooking liquid in the skillet. Cover turkey to keep warm.

3. For sauce, in a bowl stir together apricot preserves and cornstarch; stir into cooking liquid in skillet. Cook and stir until thickened and bubbly. Cook and stir for 2 minutes more. Divide rice mixture among 4 dinner plates; place a turkey steak on each plate. Pour some of the sauce over turkey; pass remaining sauce.

Per serving: 374 cal., 2 g total fat (1 g sat. fat), 88 mg chol., 1,054 mg sodium, 48 g carbo., 1 g fiber, 39 g pro.

MENU
Sauteed sugar snap peas
Corn muffins
Rhubarb pie

Turkey with Raspberry Sauce

238

PREP:
10 MINUTES

COOK:
20 MINUTES

MAKES:
4 SERVINGS

½   teaspoon dried thyme, crushed

½   teaspoon dried sage, crushed

¼   teaspoon salt

¼   teaspoon black pepper

1   pound turkey tenderloins

1   tablespoon olive oil or cooking oil

¼   cup seedless raspberry jam

2   tablespoons orange juice

2   tablespoons red wine vinegar

1. In a small bowl combine thyme, sage, salt, and pepper; rub evenly over turkey.

2. In a large skillet heat oil over medium heat. Cook turkey in hot oil for 18 to 20 minutes or until no longer pink (170°F), turning occasionally to brown evenly. Remove turkey from skillet; keep warm.

3. For raspberry sauce, stir together raspberry jam, orange juice, and vinegar; carefully stir into the skillet. Bring to boiling; reduce heat. Boil gently, uncovered, about 2 minutes or until sauce is desired consistency. Bias-cut tenderloins into ½-inch slices. Arrange turkey on 4 dinner plates. Drizzle with the raspberry sauce.

Per serving: 221 cal., 5 g total fat (1 g sat. fat), 68 mg chol., 206 mg sodium, 15 g carbo., 0 g fiber, 27 g pro.

MENU
Bread stuffing (from a mix)
Steamed green beans
Pecan sandies with praline ice cream

239

Grilled Teriyaki Turkey Patties

PREP:
15 MINUTES

GRILL:
5 MINUTES
(COVERED)
OR 14 MINUTES
(UNCOVERED)

MAKES:
4 SERVINGS

1   egg, lightly beaten

½   cup soft bread crumbs

¼   cup chopped water chestnuts

2   tablespoons chopped onion

2   tablespoons teriyaki sauce

1   pound uncooked ground turkey

¼   cup orange marmalade

½   teaspoon sesame seeds (optional)

1. Lightly grease the rack of an indoor electric grill. Preheat grill.

2. In a medium bowl combine egg, bread crumbs, water chestnuts, onion, and 1 tablespoon of the teriyaki sauce. Add ground turkey; mix well. Shape turkey mixture into four ¾-inch-thick patties (mixture will be soft).

3. Place turkey patties on the grill rack. If using a covered grill, close lid. Grill patties until turkey is no longer pink (165°F). For a covered grill, allow 5 to 7 minutes. For an uncovered grill, allow 14 to 18 minutes, turning once halfway through grilling time.

4. For sauce, in a small saucepan combine the remaining 1 tablespoon teriyaki sauce, orange marmalade, and, if desired, sesame seeds. Cook over low heat until marmalade melts, stirring occasionally. To serve, spoon sauce over patties.

Per serving: 266 cal., 11 g total fat (3 g sat. fat), 143 mg chol., 453 mg sodium, 19 g carbo., 0 g fiber, 23 g pro.

MENU

Hot cooked rice

Steamed snow pea pods and red sweet pepper strips

Fresh berries with vanilla yogurt

Turkey Dinner Burgers

PREP:
15 MINUTES

COOK:
14 MINUTES

MAKES:
4 BURGERS

1   egg, lightly beaten
¼   cup fine dry bread crumbs
½   teaspoon salt
¼   teaspoon black pepper
1   pound uncooked ground turkey
1   tablespoon olive oil
¼   cup bottled barbecue sauce
4   potato rolls, kaiser rolls, or hamburger buns; split and toasted
    Lettuce leaves, thinly sliced red onion, and/or thinly sliced tomato (optional)

1. In a medium bowl combine egg, bread crumbs, salt, and pepper. Add turkey; mix well. Shape the turkey mixture into four ¾-inch-thick patties.

2. In a large nonstick skillet heat oil over medium heat. Cook turkey burgers in hot oil for 12 to 14 minutes or until no longer pink (165°F), turning once halfway through cooking. Brush patties on each side with barbecue sauce. Cook 1 minute more on each side to glaze. Serve burgers in rolls. If desired, top burgers with lettuce, onion, and/or tomato.

Per burger: 372 cal., 16 g total fat (4 g sat. fat), 142 mg chol., 900 mg sodium, 29 g carbo., 2 g fiber, 26 g pro.

BROILER METHOD: Preheat broiler. Mix and shape patties as directed. Place patties on the unheated rack of a broiler pan. Broil 4 to 5 inches from the heat for 14 to 18 minutes or until no longer pink (165°F), turning once halfway through broiling. Brush patties on each side with barbecue sauce. Broil for 1 minute more on each side to glaze. Serve as above.

MENU
Pasta salad (from a deli)
Potato chips and dill pickles
Root beer floats made with chocolate ice cream

241

Quick and Crunchy Turkey Salad

START TO FINISH:
10 MINUTES

MAKES:
4 SERVINGS

1 16-ounce package shredded cabbage with carrot (coleslaw mix)
6 ounces sliced cooked turkey breast, cubed
1 3-ounce package ramen noodles (any flavor)
⅔ cup bottled vinaigrette salad dressing
1 11-ounce can mandarin orange sections, drained

1. In a large salad bowl combine shredded cabbage with carrot and turkey. Remove seasoning packet from noodles; reserve for another use. Crumble noodles and add to cabbage mixture. Pour the dressing over the salad; toss to coat. Gently fold in orange sections.

Per serving: 527 cal., 23 g total fat (1 g sat. fat), 15 mg chol., 1,552 mg sodium, 67 g carbo., 3 g fiber, 17 g pro.

MENU
Buttermilk biscuits
Chocolate pudding with
chocolate sandwich cookies

Turkey and Kiwi Salad with Strawberry Vinaigrette

242

START TO FINISH:
25 MINUTES

MAKES:
4 SERVINGS

8 cups packaged torn mixed salad greens

2½ cups cooked turkey or chicken, cut into bite-size strips (12 ounces)

2 cups sliced, peeled kiwifruit (about 6)

1 cup red cherry tomatoes and/or yellow baby pear tomatoes, halved

½ cup butter toffee-glazed flavored sliced almonds or toasted sliced almonds

1 cup cut-up fresh strawberries

2 tablespoons red wine vinegar

⅛ teaspoon black pepper

1. Divide salad greens among 4 salad plates. Top with turkey, kiwifruit, tomatoes, and almonds.

2. For vinaigrette, in a food processor or blender combine strawberries, vinegar, and black pepper. Cover and process or blend until smooth. Drizzle vinaigrette over salads.

Per serving: 318 cal., 11 g total fat (2 g sat. fat), 67 mg chol., 138 mg sodium, 25 g carbo., 7 g fiber, 30 g pro.

MENU
Multigrain bread
Brownie sundaes

243

Salmon with Dijon-Cream Sauce

START TO FINISH:
25 MINUTES

MAKES:
4 SERVINGS

1¼ pounds fresh or frozen skinless salmon fillets
1 tablespoon butter with garlic or plain butter
⅓ cup reduced-sodium chicken broth
⅓ cup half-and-half or light cream
2 tablespoons Dijon-style mustard
¼ teaspoon coarsely ground black pepper

1. Thaw salmon, if frozen. Cut fillets crosswise into ½-inch slices. Rinse fish; pat dry with paper towels.

2. In a large skillet melt butter over medium-high heat. Add half of the fish; cook about 2 minutes or until fish begins to flake when tested with a fork, turning once. Remove from skillet; keep warm. Repeat with remaining fish.

3. For sauce, add chicken broth to skillet. Bring to boiling; reduce heat. Simmer, uncovered, for 1 minute. Whisk together half-and-half and mustard; stir into skillet. Return to boiling; reduce heat. Simmer, uncovered, for 2 to 3 minutes more or until sauce is slightly thickened. Spoon sauce over salmon; sprinkle with pepper.

Per serving: 318 cal., 20 g total fat (6 g sat. fat), 95 mg chol., 343 mg sodium, 1 g carbo., 0 g fiber, 29 g pro.

MENU
Roasted asparagus
Rice pilaf (from a mix)
Fruit sorbet

Pineapple-Glazed Fish   244

PREP:
10 MINUTES

BROIL:
4 TO 6 MINUTES
PER ½-INCH
THICKNESS

MAKES:
4 SERVINGS

1   pound fresh or frozen fish fillets, ¾ to 1 inch thick
3   tablespoons pineapple preserves
2   tablespoons rice vinegar
2   teaspoons snipped fresh thyme or ½ teaspoon dried thyme, crushed
⅛   teaspoon crushed red pepper
½   teaspoon bottled minced garlic (1 clove)
¼   teaspoon black pepper
⅛   teaspoon salt

1. Thaw fish, if frozen. Rinse fish; pat dry with paper towels. Cut fish into
   4 serving-size pieces, if necessary. Measure thickness of fish. Set fish aside.

2. Preheat broiler. For glaze, in a small bowl stir together pineapple preserves,
   vinegar, thyme, crushed red pepper, and garlic; set aside.

3. Sprinkle fish with black pepper and salt. Place fish on the greased unheated rack
   of a broiler pan, tucking under any thin edges to make fish of uniform thickness.
   Broil 4 to 5 inches from the heat until fish begins to flake when tested with
   a fork, brushing occasionally with glaze. (Allow 4 to 6 minutes per ½-inch
   thickness of fish.)

Per serving: 125 cal., 1 g total fat (0 g sat. fat), 22 mg chol., 150 mg sodium, 11 g carbo., 0 g fiber, 17 g pro.

MENU
Cucumber and red onion
salad with ranch dressing

Hot cooked basmati rice
with snipped fresh parsley

Vanilla ice cream with
pineapple topping and
toasted coconut

245 Broiled Fish Steaks with Tarragon Sauce

START TO FINISH:
20 MINUTES

MAKES:
4 SERVINGS

4   5- to 6-ounce fresh or frozen salmon, swordfish, or tuna steaks (about ¾ inch thick)

½   cup plain yogurt or light dairy sour cream

½   cup shredded mozzarella or Monterey Jack cheese (2 ounces)

2   teaspoons snipped fresh tarragon or ½ teaspoon dried tarragon, crushed

1. Thaw fish, if frozen. Preheat broiler. In a small bowl stir together yogurt, cheese, and tarragon. Set aside.

2. Rinse fish; pat dry. Place fish on the unheated rack of broiler pan. Sprinkle fish with *salt* and *black pepper.* Broil 4 inches from the heat for 6 to 9 minutes or until fish begins to flake when tested with a fork. Spoon yogurt mixture over fish steaks. Broil 30 to 60 seconds more or until heated through.

Per serving: 322 cal., 19 g total fat (5 g sat. fat), 97 mg chol., 267 mg sodium, 3 g carbo., 0 g fiber, 33 g pro.

MENU

Hot cooked pasta

Fresh spinach and tomato salad with desired dressing

French baguette slices

Fresh mango and papaya slices

Parmesan Baked Fish

246

PREP:
10 MINUTES

BAKE:
12 MINUTES

OVEN:
450°F

MAKES:
4 SERVINGS

4   4- to 5-ounce fresh or frozen skinless salmon or other firm fish fillets, ¾ to 1 inch thick
¼   cup mayonnaise or salad dressing
2   tablespoons grated Parmesan cheese
1   tablespoon snipped fresh chives or sliced green onion
1   teaspoon Worcestershire sauce for chicken

1. Thaw fish, if frozen. Preheat oven to 450°F. Rinse fish; pat dry with paper towels. Place fish in a greased 2-quart square or rectangular baking dish, tucking under any thin edges to make fish of uniform thickness. Set aside.

2. In a small bowl stir together mayonnaise, Parmesan cheese, chives, and Worcestershire sauce. Spread mayonnaise mixture evenly over fish.

3. Bake, uncovered, for 12 to 15 minutes or until fish begins to flake when tested with a fork.

Per serving: 302 cal., 22 g total fat (4 g sat. fat), 77 mg chol., 185 mg sodium, 0 g carbo., 0 g fiber, 25 g pro.

MENU

Hot cooked tortellini tossed with olive oil, chopped tomato, and snipped fresh basil

Breadsticks

Spumoni ice cream with chocolate sauce and gingersnaps

247

Fish with Green Onion and Ginger

START TO FINISH:
20 MINUTES

MAKES:
4 SERVINGS

4 4- to 5-ounce fresh or frozen skinless sea bass or other
   firm white fish fillets, ¾ to 1 inch thick

⅔ cup thinly sliced green onion

4 teaspoons lemon juice or dry sherry

2 teaspoons grated fresh ginger

1 teaspoon bottled minced garlic (2 cloves)

2 teaspoons fish sauce or reduced-sodium soy sauce

1 small fresh jalapeño chile pepper, seeded and finely chopped*

1. Thaw fish, if frozen. Rinse fish; pat dry with paper towels. In a small bowl stir together green onion, 2 teaspoons of the lemon juice, the ginger, and garlic.

2. Arrange fish fillets in a single layer in a microwave-safe baking dish, tucking under any thin edges to make fish of uniform thickness. Spoon green onion mixture over fish. Cover dish with vented plastic wrap. Microwave on 100% (high) power for 3 to 5 minutes or until fish begins to flake when tested with a fork, giving the dish a half-turn halfway through cooking.

3. Using a slotted spatula, transfer fish to 4 dinner plates. In a small bowl stir together fish sauce, jalapeño pepper, and remaining 2 teaspoons lemon juice; drizzle over fish.

Per serving: 121 cal., 2 g total fat (1 g sat. fat), 46 mg chol., 312 mg sodium, 3 g carbo., 1 g fiber, 22 g pro.

*NOTE: Because chile peppers contain volatile oils that can burn your skin and eyes, avoid direct contact with them as much as possible. When working with chile peppers, wear plastic or rubber gloves. If your bare hands do touch the peppers, wash your hands and nails well with soap and warm water.

MENU

- Hot cooked brown rice
- Steamed broccoli spears
- Angel food cake with fresh berries

Lime-Fish Lettuce Wraps

248

PREP:
5 MINUTES

BROIL:
4 TO 6 MINUTES
PER ½-INCH
THICKNESS

MAKES:
4 SERVINGS
(2 WRAPS EACH)

1   pound fresh or frozen skinless cod, orange roughy, or other fish fillets, ½ to ¾ inch thick
2   teaspoons Mexican seasoning blend
¼   teaspoon salt
½   cup dairy sour cream
½   teaspoon finely shredded lime peel
1   tablespoon lime juice
8   romaine leaves

1. Thaw fish, if frozen. Preheat broiler. Rinse fish; pat dry with paper towels. Measure thickness of fish. In a small bowl combine Mexican seasoning and salt; sprinkle both sides of fish with seasoning mixture.

2. Place fish on the greased unheated rack of a broiler pan, tucking under any thin edges to make fish of uniform thickness. Broil 4 to 5 inches from the heat until fish begins to flake when tested with a fork. (Allow 4 to 6 minutes per ½-inch thickness of fish.)

3. Meanwhile, in a small bowl stir together sour cream, lime peel, and lime juice. Set aside.

4. Using a fork, flake fish into bite-size pieces. Spoon fish on romaine leaves; top with sour cream mixture. Roll up.

Per serving: 154 cal., 6 g total fat (3 g sat. fat), 59 mg chol., 315 mg sodium, 3 g carbo., 0 g fiber, 22 g pro.

> LIME-FISH TACOS: Prepare fish and sour cream mixture as above. Omit romaine. Divide fish among four 8-inch flour or whole wheat tortillas; top with sour cream mixture. Roll up.

MENU
Spanish rice (from a mix)
Refried black beans topped with shredded cheddar cheese and snipped fresh cilantro
Pineapple sorbet

249 Oven-Fried Fish

PREP:
10 MINUTES

BAKE:
4 TO 6 MINUTES
PER ½-INCH
THICKNESS

OVEN:
450°F

MAKES:
4 SERVINGS

1 pound fresh or frozen skinless cod, orange roughy, or catfish fillets

¼ cup milk

⅓ cup all-purpose flour

½ cup fine dry bread crumbs

2 tablespoons grated Parmesan cheese

¼ teaspoon lemon-pepper seasoning

2 tablespoons butter or margarine, melted

Fresh parsley sprigs and/or lemon wedges (optional)

1. Thaw fish, if frozen. Preheat oven to 450°F. Rinse fish; pat dry with paper towels. Cut fish into 4 serving-size pieces, if necessary. Measure thickness of fish. Set fish aside.

2. Place milk in a shallow dish. Place flour in a second shallow dish. In a third shallow dish combine bread crumbs, Parmesan cheese, and lemon-pepper seasoning. Add melted butter to bread crumb mixture; stir until combined.

3. Dip fish in the milk; coat with flour. Dip again in the milk, then dip in the crumb mixture, turning to coat all sides. Place fish on a greased baking sheet.

4. Bake, uncovered, until fish begins to flake when tested with a fork. (Allow 4 to 6 minutes per ½-inch thickness of fish.) If desired, garnish with parsley and/or lemon wedges.

Per serving: 254 cal., 9 g total fat (5 g sat. fat), 75 mg chol., 565 mg sodium, 15 g carbo., 1 g fiber, 26 g pro.

MENU
Steamed green beans
Potato salad (from a deli)
Strawberry shortcakes

Fish Stew with Asparagus

250

START TO FINISH:
20 MINUTES

MAKES:
4 SERVINGS

12 ounces fresh or frozen cod or other firm white fish fillets
1 14-ounce can chicken broth
1 10.75-ounce can condensed cream of onion soup
1 10-ounce package frozen cut asparagus
1 cup water
½ teaspoon dried thyme, crushed
¼ cup grated Parmesan cheese

1. Thaw fish, if frozen. Rinse fish; pat dry with paper towels. Cut fish into ½-inch pieces; set aside.

2. In a large saucepan stir together chicken broth, soup, frozen asparagus, water, and thyme. Bring to boiling, stirring occasionally.

3. Stir in fish. Return to boiling; reduce heat. Simmer, covered, for 5 to 7 minutes or until fish begins to flake when tested with a fork. Sprinkle individual servings with Parmesan cheese.

Per serving: 194 cal., 7 g total fat (2 g sat. fat), 53 mg chol., 1,129 mg sodium, 12 g carbo., 2 g fiber, 22 g pro.

MENU
Crusty Italian bread
Tossed baby greens salad with desired dressing
Cheesecake

251

Shortcut Asian Fish Soup

START TO FINISH:
25 MINUTES

MAKES:
6 SERVINGS

1   pound fresh or frozen monkfish, cusk, or cod fillets

2   10.75-ounce cans condensed chicken with rice soup

3   cups water

¼   cup reduced-sodium soy sauce

⅛   to ¼ teaspoon cayenne pepper

3   cups frozen broccoli, red pepper, onions, and mushrooms

2   tablespoons lemon juice

1. Thaw fish, if frozen. Rinse fish; pat dry with paper towels. Cut fish into ½-inch pieces; set aside.

2. In a large saucepan combine soup, water, soy sauce, and cayenne pepper. Bring to boiling. Stir in frozen vegetables. Return to boiling; reduce heat. Simmer, covered, for 5 minutes.

3. Add fish. Cook, covered, for 3 to 5 minutes more or until fish begins to flake when tested with a fork. Stir in lemon juice.

Per serving: 139 cal., 3 g total fat (1 g sat. fat), 23 mg chol., 1,211 mg sodium, 11 g carbo., 1 g fiber, 15 g pro.

MENU

Spring rolls
(frozen or takeout)

Cucumber and onion salad
with sesame-ginger dressing

Fortune cookies and
ice cream

Sesame-Coated Tilapia Salad

252

START TO FINISH:
20 MINUTES

MAKES:
4 SERVINGS

1   pound fresh or frozen tilapia fillets

¼   cup all-purpose flour

¼   cup sesame seeds

½   teaspoon black pepper

⅔   cup bottled honey-Dijon salad dressing

2   tablespoons cooking oil

1   5-ounce package fresh baby spinach and red leaf lettuce or baby spinach with radicchio

1. Thaw fish, if frozen. Rinse fish; pat dry with paper towels. Cut fish into 4 serving-size pieces, if necessary.

2. In a shallow bowl combine flour, sesame seeds, and pepper. Transfer 2 tablespoons of the salad dressing to a small bowl. Brush all sides of the fish pieces with the 2 tablespoons salad dressing. Firmly press both sides of each fish piece into the sesame seed mixture.

3. In a 12-inch skillet heat oil over medium heat. Add fish; cook about 6 minutes or until fish begins to flake when tested with a fork, turning once.

4. Arrange spinach mixture on 4 salad plates; top each with a fish piece. Drizzle with remaining salad dressing.

Per serving: 418 cal., 30 g total fat (3 g sat. fat), 0 mg chol., 247 mg sodium, 16 g carbo., 4 g fiber, 22 g pro.

MENU
Soft breadsticks
Fresh fruit skewers

253 Easy Salmon Pasta

START TO FINISH:
20 MINUTES

MAKES:
4 SERVINGS

1½ cups dried penne, cut ziti, or gemelli pasta

2 cups frozen broccoli florets

1 10.75-ounce can condensed cheddar cheese soup

½ cup milk

1 tablespoon Dijon-style mustard

½ teaspoon dried dill

⅛ teaspoon black pepper

2 6-ounce cans skinless, boneless salmon or tuna, drained

1. In a large saucepan cook pasta according to package directions, adding broccoli for the last 3 minutes of cooking. Drain well; return to saucepan.

2. Stir soup, milk, mustard, dill, and pepper into pasta mixture. Cook over low heat until heated through, stirring occasionally. Gently fold in salmon; heat through.

Per serving: 315 cal., 10 g total fat (3 g sat. fat), 58 mg chol., 1,049 mg sodium, 34 g carbo., 4 g fiber, 25 g pro.

MENU

Focaccia

Baby romaine salad with cherry tomatoes, green onions, and desired dressing

Cantaloupe and honeydew melon slices

Creamy Tuna Mac

254

START TO FINISH:
25 MINUTES

MAKES:
4 SERVINGS

1   7.25-ounce package macaroni and cheese dinner mix
½   cup frozen peas
¼   cup butter or margarine, softened
¼   cup milk
½   cup dairy sour cream ranch-, onion-, or chive-flavor dip
1   6-ounce can solid white tuna, drained and broken into chunks
½   cup bottled roasted red sweet peppers, drained and chopped

1. Cook macaroni from dinner mix according to package directions, except add the peas the last 2 minutes of cooking. Drain. Continue preparing the dinner mix with the butter and milk according to package directions.

2. Stir sour cream dip into macaroni mixture. Add tuna and roasted red peppers, stirring gently just until combined. Heat through.

Per serving: 474 cal., 21 g total fat (11 g sat. fat), 80 mg chol., 962 mg sodium, 49 g carbo., 2 g fiber, 23 g pro.

MENU

Vegetable skewers (cherry tomatoes, artichoke heart quarters, black olives, and mozzarella chunks)

Buttermilk biscuits

Brownies

255 Mediterranean Shrimp and Couscous

START TO FINISH:
25 MINUTES

MAKES:
4 SERVINGS

1   pound fresh or frozen medium shrimp

1   14.5-ounce can diced tomatoes with garlic and onion, undrained

¾   cup water

1   5.6-ounce package toasted pine nut couscous mix

½   cup golden raisins

1. Thaw shrimp, if frozen. Peel and devein shrimp. Rinse shrimp; pat dry with paper towels. Set aside.

2. In a large skillet combine undrained tomatoes, water, and the seasoning packet from the couscous mix; bring to boiling. Stir in shrimp; cook over high heat for 2 to 3 minutes or until shrimp are opaque. Stir in couscous and raisins. Remove from heat. Cover and let stand about 5 minutes or until liquid is absorbed.

Per serving: 338 cal., 4 g total fat (1 g sat. fat), 129 mg chol., 967 mg sodium, 53 g carbo., 6 g fiber, 25 g pro.

MENU

Spinach salad with feta, onion, tomato, and purchased balsamic vinaigrette dressing

Soft pita bread

Lemon sorbet

Shrimp Piccata

256

START TO FINISH:
25 MINUTES

MAKES:
4 SERVINGS

1 pound fresh or frozen, peeled and deveined large shrimp
2 tablespoons all-purpose flour
⅓ cup dry white wine
2 tablespoons lemon juice
1 tablespoon drained capers (optional)
¼ teaspoon salt
⅛ teaspoon black pepper
1 tablespoon butter or margarine
1 teaspoon bottled minced garlic (2 cloves)
2 cups hot cooked instant brown rice
Lemon slices, halved (optional)

1. Thaw shrimp, if frozen. Rinse shrimp; pat dry with paper towels. In a medium bowl toss shrimp with flour until coated. Set aside.

2. For sauce, in a small bowl stir together wine, lemon juice, capers (if desired), salt, and pepper. Set aside.

3. In a wok or large skillet melt butter over medium-high heat (add more butter if necessary during cooking). Add garlic; cook and stir for 15 seconds.

4. Add half of the shrimp to wok. Stir-fry for 2 to 3 minutes or until shrimp are opaque. Remove from wok. Repeat with the remaining shrimp. Remove all shrimp from wok.

5. Add sauce to wok. Cook and stir until sauce is bubbly and slightly reduced. Return shrimp to wok. Cook and stir about 1 minute more or until heated through. Serve over hot cooked brown rice.
If desired, garnish with lemon slices.

Per serving: 283 cal., 5 g total fat (2 g sat. fat), 180 mg chol., 336 mg sodium, 28 g carbo., 0 g fiber, 26 g pro.

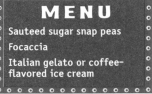

MENU
Sauteed sugar snap peas
Focaccia
Italian gelato or coffee-flavored ice cream

257 Stir-Fry Hoisin and Citrus Shrimp

START TO FINISH:
25 MINUTES

MAKES:
4 SERVINGS

12 ounces peeled and deveined fresh or frozen large shrimp

2 tablespoons cooking oil

1 teaspoon bottled minced garlic (2 cloves)

1 medium red sweet pepper, cut into thin bite-size strips

⅓ cup orange juice

3 tablespoons hoisin sauce

1½ cups shredded packaged prewashed fresh spinach

Crushed red pepper (optional)

1. Thaw shrimp, if frozen. Rinse shrimp; pat dry with paper towels. Remove tails, if present. Set aside.

2. In a large skillet heat 1 tablespoon of the oil over medium-high heat. Add garlic; cook and stir for 15 seconds. Add sweet pepper; cook and stir about 3 minutes or until crisp-tender. Remove sweet pepper with a slotted spoon.

3. Add remaining 1 tablespoon oil to skillet. Add shrimp; stir-fry for 3 to 5 minutes or until shrimp are opaque. Remove shrimp with a slotted spoon. Add orange juice and hoisin sauce to the skillet. Bring to boiling. Simmer, uncovered, about 1 minute or until slightly thickened. Return shrimp and sweet pepper to skillet along with spinach; toss just until combined. If desired, sprinkle with crushed red pepper.

Per serving: 191 cal., 9 g total fat (1 g sat. fat), 129 mg chol., 290 mg sodium, 9 g carbo., 1 g fiber, 19 g pro.

MENU
Hot cooked rice
Potstickers
(frozen or takeout)
Hot green tea
Fresh pineapple wedges

Shrimp Alfredo

258

START TO FINISH:
25 MINUTES

MAKES:
4 SERVINGS

3 cups water

1 cup milk

¼ cup butter or margarine

2 4.4-ounce packages noodles with Alfredo-style sauce

2½ cups thinly sliced zucchini (2 medium)

12 ounces frozen peeled, deveined, cooked shrimp, thawed, or 12 ounces chunk-style imitation crabmeat

1. In a large saucepan combine water, milk, and butter. Bring to boiling. Stir in noodle mix. Return to boiling; reduce heat. Simmer, uncovered, for 5 minutes.

2. Stir in zucchini. Return to a gentle boil; cook, uncovered, about 3 minutes more or until noodles are tender.

3. Gently stir in shrimp. Heat through. Remove from heat; let stand for 3 to 5 minutes or until slightly thickened.

Per serving: 486 cal., 21 g total fat (12 g sat. fat), 264 mg chol., 1,279 mg sodium, 44 g carbo., 2 g fiber, 30 g pro.

MENU

Crusty Italian bread

Baby greens salad with green onions and desired vinaigrette dressing

Blueberries with vanilla yogurt or whipped cream

259 Shrimp over Rice

START TO FINISH:
25 MINUTES

MAKES:
4 SERVINGS

1 cup uncooked instant rice

3 cups water

1 12-ounce package frozen peeled, deveined shrimp

1 15.5-ounce jar chunky-style meatless pasta sauce (about 2 cups)

¼ cup dry red wine

¼ teaspoon Worcestershire sauce

Several dashes bottled hot pepper sauce

1. Prepare rice according to package directions. Set aside.

2. Meanwhile, in a large saucepan bring the water to boiling. Add shrimp. Return to boiling; reduce heat. Simmer, uncovered, for 1 to 3 minutes or until shrimp are opaque. Drain in a colander.

3. In the same saucepan combine pasta sauce, red wine, Worcestershire sauce, and hot pepper sauce. Bring to boiling. Stir in shrimp; heat through. Serve shrimp mixture over rice.

Per serving: 246 cal., 2 g total fat (0 g sat. fat), 129 mg chol., 657 mg sodium, 34 g carbo., 3 g fiber, 21 g pro.

MENU

Marinated vegetable salad from a deli

Breadsticks

Chocolate ice cream with shortbread cookies

Curried Shrimp Soup

260

START TO FINISH:
15 MINUTES

MAKES:
4 SERVINGS

12 ounces fresh or frozen medium shrimp, peeled and deveined
4   cups water
1   3-ounce package chicken-flavor ramen noodles
1   tablespoon curry powder
2   medium stalks bok choy, cut into ¼-inch slices
1   small apple, cored and chopped

1. Thaw shrimp, if frozen. Rinse shrimp; pat dry with paper towels.

2. In a medium saucepan combine water, flavoring packet from noodles, and curry powder. Bring to boiling.

3. Break up noodles. Add noodles, shrimp, and bok choy to mixture in saucepan. Return to boiling. Reduce heat. Simmer, uncovered, about 3 minutes or until shrimp are opaque. Stir in apple; heat through.

Per serving: 237 cal., 3 g total fat (0 g sat. fat), 129 mg chol., 861 mg sodium, 29 g carbo., 5 g fiber, 26 g pro.

MENU
Toasted pita bread
Avocado halves filled with purchased tabbouleh
Coconut ice cream

261

Jerk-Spiced Shrimp with Wilted Spinach

START TO FINISH:
25 MINUTES

MAKES:
4 SERVINGS

12 ounces fresh or frozen peeled, deveined medium shrimp
1½ teaspoons Jamaican jerk seasoning
2 tablespoons olive oil
1½ teaspoons bottled minced garlic (3 cloves)
8 cups torn packaged prewashed fresh spinach

1. Thaw shrimp, if frozen. Rinse shrimp; pat dry with paper towels. In a small bowl toss together shrimp and jerk seasoning; set aside.

2. In a large skillet heat 1 tablespoon of the oil over medium heat. Add garlic; cook and stir for 15 to 30 seconds. Add half of the spinach. Cook and stir about 1 minute or just until spinach wilts; remove from skillet and keep warm. Repeat with remaining spinach.

3. Carefully add remaining oil to skillet. Add shrimp. Cook and stir for 2 to 3 minutes or until shrimp are opaque. Serve shrimp over wilted spinach.

Per serving: 159 cal., 8 g total fat (1 g sat. fat), 129 mg chol., 315 mg sodium, 2 g carbo., 6 g fiber, 19 g pro.

MENU
Hot cooked basmati rice
Fresh mango slices
Vanilla ice cream with caramel sauce and chopped crystallized ginger

Pan-Seared Scallops

262

START TO FINISH:
20 MINUTES

MAKES:
4 SERVINGS

1   pound fresh or frozen sea scallops
2   tablespoons all-purpose flour
1   to 2 teaspoons blackened steak seasoning or Cajun seasoning
1   tablespoon olive oil or cooking oil
1   10-ounce package torn fresh spinach or baby spinach (8 cups)
1   tablespoon water
2   tablespoons balsamic vinegar
¼   cup cooked bacon pieces

1. Thaw scallops, if frozen. Rinse scallops; pat dry with paper towels. In a medium bowl combine flour and steak seasoning. Add scallops; toss to coat.

2. In a large skillet heat oil over medium-high heat. Add scallops; cook about 3 minutes or until coating is brown and scallops are opaque inside, turning once halfway through cooking. Remove scallops from skillet.

3. Add spinach to hot skillet; sprinkle with water. Cover and cook over medium-high heat for 1 to 2 minutes or until spinach is wilted. Add vinegar, tossing to coat spinach evenly. Return scallops to skillet; heat through. Sprinkle with bacon pieces.

Per serving: 207 cal., 8 g total fat (2 g sat. fat), 44 mg chol., 434 mg sodium, 8 g carbo., 6 g fiber, 24 g pro.

MENU

Hot cooked orzo with chopped tomatoes and sliced ripe or kalamata olives

Focaccia

Cheesecake drizzled with chocolate sauce

263 Crab-Tomato Bisque

START TO FINISH:
15 MINUTES

MAKES:
4 SERVINGS

1   19-ounce can ready-to-eat tomato basil soup
1   10.75-ounce can condensed cream of shrimp soup
1   cup vegetable broth
1   cup half-and-half, light cream, or milk
1   tablespoon dried minced onion
1   teaspoon dried parsley flakes
1   6.5-ounce can crabmeat, drained, flaked, and cartilage removed

1. In a large saucepan combine tomato basil soup, cream of shrimp soup, vegetable broth, half-and-half, dried onion, and parsley flakes.

2. Cook over medium heat until bubbly, stirring occasionally. Stir in crabmeat; heat through.

Per serving: 242 cal., 12 g total fat (6 g sat. fat), 73 mg chol., 1,447 mg sodium, 20 g carbo., 1 g fiber, 15 g pro.

MENU
Crusty Italian bread
Tortellini salad (from a deli)
Mixed fresh berries
with whipped cream

Tortellini Alfredo with Roasted Peppers

264

1   16-ounce package frozen meat- or cheese-filled tortellini (4 cups)
1   10-ounce container refrigerated light Alfredo pasta sauce
1   cup bottled roasted red sweet peppers, drained and cut into ½-inch strips
¼   cup snipped fresh basil
    Coarsely ground black pepper

1. Cook tortellini according to package directions; drain well. Return tortellini to hot pan.

2. Gently stir Alfredo sauce and roasted sweet peppers into the hot tortellini in pan. Cook over medium heat until hot and bubbly. Stir in basil. Season to taste with black pepper.

Per serving: 495 cal., 15 g total fat (6 g sat. fat), 98 mg chol., 1,150 mg sodium, 65 g carbo., 1 g fiber, 24 g pro.

MENU
Country Italian bread
Roasted asparagus
Italian ice or gelato

265

Sweet Beans and Noodles

START TO FINISH:
30 MINUTES

MAKES:
4 SERVINGS

8   ounces dried linguine

1½ cups frozen green soybeans (shelled edamane)

1   cup packaged shredded carrot (2 medium)

1   10-ounce container refrigerated Alfredo pasta sauce

2   teaspoons snipped fresh rosemary or ½ teaspoon dried rosemary, crushed

1. Cook linguine according to package directions, adding the soybeans and carrot for the last 10 minutes of cooking. Drain and return to pan.

2. Add Alfredo sauce and rosemary to linguine mixture in pan; toss to combine. Heat through.

Per serving: 544 cal., 27 g total fat (1 g sat. fat), 35 mg chol., 280 mg sodium, 57 g carbo., 5 g fiber, 20 g pro.

MENU

Multigrain bread

Spinach and tomato salad with desired dressing

Strawberry and blueberry shortcakes (with purchased shortcakes)

Saucy Pizza Skillet Dinner

266

START TO FINISH:
30 MINUTES

MAKES:
4 SERVINGS

1   6.4-ounce package lasagna dinner mix
3   cups water
1   4-ounce can (drained weight) mushroom stems and pieces, undrained
½   cup chopped green sweet pepper
½   cup sliced pitted ripe olives (optional)
½   cup shredded mozzarella cheese (2 ounces)

1. If the noodles in the dinner mix are large, break them into bite-size pieces. In a large skillet combine noodles and seasoning from dinner mix, the water, undrained mushrooms, and sweet pepper.

2. Bring to boiling, stirring occasionally; reduce heat. Simmer, covered, about 13 minutes or until pasta is tender. Uncover and cook for 2 to 3 minutes more or until sauce is of desired consistency.

3. If desired, sprinkle with olives. Top with cheese. Remove from heat; let stand for 1 to 2 minutes or until cheese melts.

Per serving: 318 cal., 14 g total fat (5 g sat. fat), 28 mg chol., 1,774 mg sodium, 37 g carbo., 3 g fiber, 14 g pro.

MENU
Mixed spring greens salad with shredded radishes
Purchased garlic bread
Hot caramel sundaes

267

Linguine with Gorgonzola Sauce

START TO FINISH:
20 MINUTES

MAKES:
4 SERVINGS

1 9-ounce package refrigerated linguine

1 pound fresh asparagus, trimmed and cut into 1-inch pieces, or one 10-ounce package frozen cut asparagus

1 cup half-and-half or light cream

1 cup crumbled Gorgonzola or other blue cheese (4 ounces)

¼ teaspoon salt

2 tablespoons chopped walnuts, toasted

1. Cook pasta and asparagus according to package directions for the pasta; drain well. Return pasta and asparagus to pan. Cover and keep warm.

2. Meanwhile, for sauce, in a medium saucepan combine half-and-half, ¾ cup of the cheese, and the salt. Bring to boiling over medium heat; reduce heat. Simmer, uncovered, for 3 minutes, stirring frequently.

3. Pour sauce over pasta mixture; toss gently to coat. Transfer to 4 dinner plates. Sprinkle with remaining ¼ cup cheese and the walnuts.

Per serving: 399 cal., 20 g total fat (11 g sat. fat), 111 mg chol., 590 mg sodium, 39 g carbo., 3 g fiber, 18 g pro.

MENU

Butterhead lettuce salad with sliced oranges, slivered fennel bulb, and vinaigrette dressing

Coffee ice cream with chocolate sauce

Lemony Alfredo-style Fettuccine

268

START TO FINISH:
20 MINUTES

MAKES:
4 SERVINGS

8   ounces dried spinach fettuccine or plain fettuccine

2   cups frozen California blend, Oriental blend, or Italian blend mixed vegetables

1   5-ounce can evaporated milk

2   ounces cream cheese, cut up

¼   cup grated Parmesan cheese

½   teaspoon finely shredded lemon peel

¼   teaspoon black pepper

    Dash ground nutmeg

1. In a Dutch oven cook pasta according to package directions, adding frozen vegetables for the last 6 minutes of cooking. When the pasta is nearly done, carefully remove ¼ cup of the cooking water with a ladle. Set aside. Drain pasta and vegetables; return to pan.

2. Add evaporated milk, cream cheese, Parmesan cheese, lemon peel, pepper, and nutmeg to pasta mixture. Cook, tossing constantly, over low heat until cheese is melted. If necessary, stir in some of the reserved pasta liquid to make desired consistency. Serve immediately.

Per serving: 349 cal., 10 g total fat (6 g sat. fat), 30 mg chol., 189 mg sodium, 50 g carbo., 8 g fiber, 14 g pro.

MENU
Focaccia
Strawberry pie
with whipped cream

269

Penne Salad with Italian Beans and Gorgonzola

START TO FINISH:
25 MINUTES

MAKES:
4 SERVINGS

6   ounces dried penne, ziti, or elbow macaroni

1   9-ounce package frozen Italian green beans, thawed

⅓   cup bottled nonfat Italian salad dressing

1   tablespoon snipped fresh tarragon or ½ teaspoon dried tarragon, crushed

½   teaspoon black pepper

2   cups torn radicchio or 1 cup finely shredded red cabbage

4   cups packaged prewashed fresh spinach leaves

½   cup crumbled Gorgonzola or other blue cheese (2 ounces)

1. Cook pasta according to package directions, adding green beans the last 3 to 4 minutes of cooking; drain. Rinse pasta and beans with cold water; drain again.

2. In a large bowl combine salad dressing, tarragon, and pepper. Add pasta mixture and radicchio; toss gently to coat.

3. To serve, arrange spinach on 4 salad plates. Top with pasta mixture. Sprinkle each serving with cheese.

Per serving: 269 cal., 6 g total fat (3 g sat. fat), 13 mg chol., 566 mg sodium, 42 g carbo., 3 g fiber, 12 g pro.

MENU

Crusty Italian bread

Berry parfaits (chocolate and/or vanilla ice cream layered with fresh berries and whipped cream)

Tortellini and Tomato Soup

270

START TO FINISH:
20 MINUTES

MAKES:
4 SERVINGS

1   9-ounce package refrigerated cheese tortellini
1   14-ounce can reduced-sodium chicken broth
1   14.5-ounce can diced tomatoes with basil, garlic, and oregano, undrained
1   cup water
2   tablespoons tomato paste
1   cup finely chopped zucchini (1 small)
1   tablespoon snipped fresh sage or 1 teaspoon dried sage, crushed
¼   cup shredded Asiago or Parmesan cheese (1 ounce)

1. Prepare tortellini according to package directions; drain.

2. Meanwhile, in a large saucepan combine broth, undrained diced tomatoes, water, and tomato paste. Bring to boiling. Stir in zucchini, sage, and drained tortellini; heat through.

3. Ladle soup into soup bowls and top each serving with cheese.

Per serving: 287 cal., 7 g total fat (3 g sat. fat), 38 mg chol., 1,113 mg sodium, 41 g carbo., 1 g fiber, 15 g pro.

MENU
Baby greens salad with balsamic vinaigrette dressing
Soft breadsticks
Brownie sundaes

271

Alfredo and Sweet Pepper Pizza

PREP:
15 MINUTES

BAKE:
10 MINUTES

OVEN:
425°F

MAKES:
4 SERVINGS

1   16-ounce Italian bread shell
½   of a 10-ounce container refrigerated Alfredo pasta sauce (about ⅔ cup)
½   teaspoon dried Italian seasoning, crushed
1   8-ounce package shredded 4-cheese pizza cheese (2 cups)
1   16-ounce package frozen sweet pepper and onion stir-fry vegetables, thawed and
       well drained

1. Preheat oven to 425°F. Place bread shell on an ungreased baking sheet or pizza pan. In a small bowl stir together Alfredo sauce and Italian seasoning. Spread Alfredo sauce mixture over bread shell.

2. Sprinkle bread shell with 1 cup of the cheese. Top with stir-fry vegetables. Sprinkle with remaining 1 cup cheese.

3. Bake about 10 minutes or until heated through.

Per serving: 626 cal., 30 g total fat (8 g sat. fat), 63 mg chol., 1,136 mg sodium, 60 g carbo., 3 g fiber, 30 g pro.

MENU
Marinated vegetable salad (from a deli)
Cheesecake with caramel sauce

Sicilian-Style Pizza

272

PREP:
15 MINUTES

BAKE:
10 MINUTES

OVEN:
425°F

MAKES:
4 SERVINGS

1 16-ounce Italian bread shell
3 medium tomatoes, thinly sliced
4 ounces mozzarella cheese, thinly sliced
⅓ cup halved, pitted kalamata olives
1 tablespoon olive oil
1 cup coarsely chopped escarole or curly endive
¼ cup finely shredded Romano or Parmesan cheese (1 ounce)
Black pepper

1. Preheat oven to 425°F. Place bread shell on an ungreased baking sheet or pizza pan. Top with tomato slices, mozzarella cheese, and olives. Drizzle with oil.

2. Bake for 8 minutes. Carefully sprinkle with escarole. Bake for 2 minutes more. Before serving, sprinkle with Romano cheese and pepper.

Per serving: 460 cal., 20 g total fat (5 g sat. fat), 31 mg chol., 936 mg sodium, 53 g carbo., 3 g fiber, 21 g pro.

MENU
Spinach and sweet pepper salad with desired dressing
Biscotti and cappuccino

273 Peppery Artichoke Pitas

START TO FINISH:
20 MINUTES

MAKES:
6 SANDWICHES

1   15-ounce can black-eyed peas, rinsed and drained
1   13.75- to 14-ounce can artichoke hearts, drained and cut up
½   cup packaged torn mixed salad greens
¼   cup bottled creamy Italian salad dressing or creamy garlic salad dressing
¼   teaspoon black pepper
1   small tomato, sliced
3   pita bread rounds, halved crosswise*

1. In a medium bowl combine black-eyed peas, artichoke hearts, salad greens, salad dressing, and pepper. Place tomato slices inside pita bread halves. Spoon artichoke mixture into pita bread halves.

Per sandwich: 211 cal., 5 g total fat (1 g sat. fat), 0 mg chol., 746 mg sodium, 34 g carbo., 6 g fiber, 8 g pro.

> *NOTE: For softer pita breads, wrap the pita bread rounds in foil and warm in a 350°F oven for 10 minutes. Soft pita bread rounds are easier to split.

MENU
Fresh fruit salad
Baklava

Summer

274 Pepper of a Steak

PREP:
10 MINUTES

BROIL:
12 MINUTES

MAKES:
4 SERVINGS

2   boneless beef top loin steaks, cut 1 inch thick (1 to 1¼ pounds)

½   teaspoon salt

½   teaspoon cracked black pepper

2   teaspoons olive oil

1   cup red, green, and/or yellow sweet pepper strips

½   teaspoon bottled minced garlic (1 clove)

1   to 1½ teaspoons snipped fresh oregano or ¼ teaspoon dried oregano, crushed

1. **Preheat broiler. Trim fat from steak. Cut each steak in half. Sprinkle meat with salt. Press cracked pepper onto meat.**

2. **Place meat on the unheated rack of a broiler pan. Broil 3 to 4 inches from the heat for 12 to 14 minutes for medium rare (145°F) or 15 to 18 minutes for medium (160°F), turning once halfway through broiling.**

3. **Meanwhile, in a large skillet heat oil over medium-high heat. Add sweet pepper strips and garlic; cook until tender. Stir in oregano. Spoon sweet pepper mixture over meat.**

Per serving: 189 cal., 8 g total fat (2 g sat. fat), 66 mg chol., 349 mg sodium, 3 g carbo., 1 g fiber, 25 g pro.

MENU
- Boiled new potatoes with butter
- Steamed broccoli spears
- Chocolate cake

Beef with Cucumber Raita

275

PREP:
10 MINUTES

BROIL:
15 MINUTES

MAKES:
4 SERVINGS

1 boneless beef sirloin steak, cut 1 inch thick
1 8-ounce carton dairy sour cream
¼ cup coarsely shredded, seeded cucumber
2 tablespoons sliced green onion (1)
1 tablespoon snipped fresh mint
   Fresh mint sprigs (optional)

1. Preheat broiler. Trim fat from steaks. Sprinkle meat with *salt* and *black pepper.* Place meat on the unheated rack of a broiler pan. Broil 3 to 4 inches from the heat for 15 to 17 minutes for medium rare (145°F) or 20 to 22 minutes for medium (160°F).

2. Meanwhile, for raita, in a small bowl stir together sour cream, cucumber, green onion, and snipped mint. Season to taste with salt and black pepper.

3. Thinly slice meat across the grain. Serve with raita. If desired, garnish with fresh mint sprigs.

Per serving: 268 cal., 16 g total fat (9 g sat. fat), 94 mg chol., 232 mg sodium, 3 g carbo., 26 g pro.

MENU
Hot cooked basmati rice
Corn on the cob
Fresh mango and papaya slices

276

Lemon-Pepper Flank Steak

PREP:
10 MINUTES

BROIL:
15 MINUTES

MAKES:
4 SERVINGS

2   tablespoons snipped fresh oregano or 2 teaspoons dried oregano, crushed

2   teaspoons bottled minced garlic (4 cloves)

2   teaspoons finely shredded lemon peel

2   teaspoons olive oil or cooking oil

½   teaspoon coarsely ground black pepper

1½ pounds beef flank steak
     Lemon slices (optional)

1. Preheat broiler. In a small bowl stir together oregano, garlic, lemon peel, oil, and pepper; set aside. Trim fat from meat. Using your fingers, rub oregano mixture onto both sides of meat.

2. Place meat on the unheated rack of a broiler pan. Broil 3 to 4 inches from heat for 15 to 18 minutes or until medium doneness (160°F), turning once halfway through broiling.

3. To serve, thinly slice steak diagonally across the grain. If desired, garnish with lemon slices.

Per serving: 287 cal., 14 g total fat (5 g sat. fat), 68 mg chol., 90 mg sodium, 1 g carbo., 0 g fiber, 39 g pro.

MENU

Grilled or broiled yellow squash

Hot cooked spinach fettuccine

Multigrain bread

277

Flank Steak with Spanish Rice

START TO FINISH:
30 MINUTES

MAKES:
4 TO 6 SERVINGS

1   14.5-ounce can Mexican-style stewed tomatoes, undrained
1¾ cups water
    Several dashes bottled hot pepper sauce
1¼ cups uncooked long grain rice
1   teaspoon chili powder
½   teaspoon salt
¼   teaspoon ground cumin
¼   teaspoon black pepper
    Dash ground cinnamon
1   to 1¼ pounds beef flank steak

1. In a 2-quart saucepan combine undrained tomatoes, water, and hot pepper sauce. Bring to boiling. Stir in rice. Return to boiling; reduce heat. Simmer, covered, about 20 minutes or until rice is tender. Remove from heat; let stand for 5 minutes.

2. Meanwhile, preheat broiler. In a small bowl combine chili powder, salt, cumin, pepper, and cinnamon. Rub spice mixture onto both sides of steak. Place steak on the unheated rack of broiler pan. Broil 4 to 5 inches from the heat for 15 to 18 minutes or until medium doneness (160°F), turning once halfway through broiling.

3. To serve, thinly slice flank steak diagonally across the grain. Fluff rice with a fork. Serve steak slices with rice.

Per serving: 409 cal., 7 g total fat (3 g sat. fat), 47 mg chol., 709 mg sodium, 54 g carbo., 1 g fiber, 30 g pro.

M E N U
Roasted zucchini and sweet pepper strips
Crusty rolls
Cheesecake with fresh berries

278 Beef Steak with Red Onion Relish

START TO FINISH:
25 MINUTES

MAKES:
4 SERVINGS

1   pound boneless beef top sirloin steak, cut ¾ inch thick

¼   to 1 teaspoon coarsely ground black pepper

2   teaspoons cooking oil

1   large red onion, sliced and separated into rings

½   of a 14.5-ounce can diced tomatoes with basil, garlic, and oregano, undrained (about 1 cup)

¼   cup dry red wine

½   teaspoon dried sage, crushed

⅛   teaspoon salt

1. Trim fat from steak. Cut into 4 serving-size pieces. Rub both sides of meat with pepper. In a large nonstick skillet heat oil over medium-high heat. Add steaks. Reduce heat to medium. Cook to desired doneness, turning once halfway through cooking. Allow 10 to 13 minutes for medium rare (145°F) to medium (160°F). If steaks brown too quickly, reduce heat to medium-low. Remove steaks from skillet, reserving drippings. Cover meat to keep warm.

2. For red onion relish, add onion to drippings in skillet. Cook, covered, over medium heat for 5 to 7 minutes or until crisp-tender, stirring occasionally. Remove skillet from heat. Carefully add undrained tomatoes, wine, sage, and salt. Return skillet to heat. Bring to boiling. Cook, uncovered, for 4 to 5 minutes or until most of the liquid evaporates, stirring occasionally. Serve red onion relish over steaks.

Per serving: 236 cal., 6 g total fat (2 g sat. fat), 69 mg chol., 660 mg sodium, 15 g carbo., 1 g fiber, 26 g pro.

MENU

Wild and brown rice pilaf (from a mix)

Spinach and tomato salad with desired dressing

Sourdough rolls

Blackened Beef Stir-Fry

279

START TO FINISH:
25 MINUTES

MAKES:
4 SERVINGS

12 ounces packaged beef stir-fry strips

2¼ teaspoons blackened steak seasoning

⅔ cup water

2 tablespoons tomato paste

2 teaspoons cornstarch

½ teaspoon instant beef bouillon granules

1 tablespoon cooking oil

1 16-ounce package frozen stir-fry vegetables (any combination)

1. Sprinkle steak strips with 2 teaspoons of the steak seasoning; toss to coat well. Set beef strips aside.

2. For sauce, in a small bowl stir together remaining ¼ teaspoon steak seasoning, the water, tomato paste, cornstarch, and bouillon granules. Set aside.

3. In a wok or large skillet heat oil over medium-high heat. Add stir-fry vegetables. Cook and stir for 2 to 3 minutes or until crisp-tender. Remove vegetables from wok. Add beef strips to hot wok. (Add more oil as necessary during cooking.) Cook and stir for 2 to 3 minutes or until meat is slightly pink in center.

4. Push meat from center of wok. Stir sauce; add to center of wok. Cook and stir until thickened and bubbly. Return vegetables to wok. Stir together to coat all ingredients with sauce. Heat through.

Per serving: 190 cal., 6 g total fat (2 g sat. fat), 40 mg chol., 373 mg sodium, 10 g carbo., 3 g fiber, 21 g pro.

MENU

Hot cooked rice

Spring rolls
(frozen or takeout)

Coconut ice cream with
fresh pineapple

280

Tomato, Beef, and Basil Salad

PREP:
15 MINUTES

BROIL:
12 MINUTES

MAKES:
4 SERVINGS

12 ounces boneless beef top loin steak, cut 1 inch thick

¼ teaspoon salt

¼ teaspoon black pepper

⅔ cup bottled oil and vinegar salad dressing

6 cups packaged torn mixed salad greens

2 cups red and/or yellow cherry tomatoes, halved

1 cup fresh basil leaves, cut into long, thin strips

1. Preheat broiler. Trim fat from steaks. Sprinkle meat with salt and pepper; brush with 2 tablespoons of the salad dressing. Place meat on the unheated rack of a broiler pan. Broil 3 to 4 inches from the heat for 12 to 14 minutes for medium rare (145°F) or 15 to 18 minutes for medium (160°F), turning once halfway through broiling.

2. Meanwhile, in a large bowl combine salad greens, tomatoes, and basil. Add remaining salad dressing; toss to coat. Arrange greens mixture on 4 salad plates. Thinly slice steak across the grain; arrange steak on greens mixture.

Per serving: 326 cal., 25 g total fat (5 g sat. fat), 40 mg chol., 210 mg sodium, 8 g carbo., 2 g fiber, 20 g pro.

MENU
Whole wheat rolls
Peach pie

Hot Italian Beef Salad

START TO FINISH:
20 MINUTES

MAKES:
4 SERVINGS

2 teaspoons olive oil or cooking oil

12 ounces packaged beef stir-fry strips

1 medium red or green sweet pepper, cut into bite-size strips

½ cup bottled Italian salad dressing

6 cups packaged torn mixed salad greens

¼ cup finely shredded Parmesan cheese (1 ounce)

Coarsely ground black pepper

1. In a large nonstick skillet heat oil over medium-high heat. Add steak and sweet pepper strips. Cook and stir for 3 to 5 minutes or until steak is desired doneness and pepper is crisp-tender; drain. Add salad dressing to skillet. Cook and stir until heated through.

2. Arrange greens on 4 salad plates. Top with the beef mixture. Sprinkle with Parmesan cheese and black pepper.

Per serving: 272 cal., 18 g total fat (5 g sat. fat), 39 mg chol., 628 mg sodium, 8 g carbo., 2 g fiber, 22 g pro.

MENU
Garlic bread
Chocolate gelato

282

Steak, Mango, and Pear Salad

PREP:
15 MINUTES

BROIL:
12 MINUTES

MAKES:
4 SERVINGS

12 ounces boneless beef top loin steak, cut 1 inch thick

1   tablespoon olive oil or cooking oil

½   teaspoon salt

¼   teaspoon black pepper

1   10-ounce package torn mixed salad greens (about 8 cups)

1   24-ounce jar refrigerated sliced mango, drained

1   medium pear, peeled, cored, and chopped

¾   cup refrigerated or bottled blue cheese salad dressing
    Cracked black pepper

1. Preheat broiler. Trim fat from steak. Brush steak with oil; sprinkle both sides of meat with salt and the ¼ teaspoon pepper.

2. Place meat on the unheated rack of a broiler pan. Broil 3 to 4 inches from the heat for 12 to 14 minutes for medium rare (145°F) or 15 to 18 minutes for medium (160°F), turning once halfway through broiling.

3. To serve, thinly slice meat across the grain. Arrange greens on 4 salad plates; top with meat, mango, and pear. Drizzle salad dressing over meat and fruit. Sprinkle with cracked black pepper.

Per serving: 492 cal., 31 g total fat (6 g sat. fat), 48 mg chol., 869 mg sodium, 36 g carbo., 2 g fiber, 22 g pro.

MENU
Sourdough bread
Praline ice cream with pecan sandies

Steak Salad with Ranch Dressing

283

START TO FINISH:
20 MINUTES

MAKES:
4 SERVINGS

1 tablespoon olive oil

12 ounces packaged beef stir-fry strips

¼ cup finely shredded fresh basil

1 10-ounce package torn mixed salad greens (about 8 cups)

1 medium yellow sweet pepper, cut into thin bite-size strips

1 cup yellow and/or red pear-shape tomatoes or cherry tomatoes, halved

½ to ¾ cup bottled buttermilk ranch salad dressing

1. In a large skillet heat oil over medium-high heat. Add beef; cook and stir for 2 to 3 minutes or until desired doneness. Remove skillet from heat. Stir in basil. Season to taste with *salt* and *black pepper.*

2. Arrange greens on 4 salad plates. Top with the meat, the sweet pepper, and tomatoes. Drizzle with salad dressing.

Per serving: 317 cal., 23 g total fat (4 g sat. fat), 57 mg chol., 375 mg sodium, 9 g carbo., 2 g fiber, 20 g pro.

MENU
Multigrain chips
Ice cream sandwiches made with chocolate chip cookies

284 Bacon Cheeseburgers

PREP:
15 MINUTES

BROIL:
10 MINUTES

MAKES:
4 SERVINGS

1¼ pounds lean ground beef

4 thin slices Colby and Monterey Jack cheese or cheddar cheese (2 ounces)

4 slices bacon, crisp-cooked and cut in half crosswise

4 hamburger buns, split and toasted

¼ cup dairy sour cream onion dip

Lettuce leaves (optional)

1. Shape the ground beef into four ½-inch-thick patties.

2. Place patties on the unheated rack of a broiler pan. Broil 3 to 4 inches from the heat for 10 to 12 minutes or until done (160°F)*, turning once halfway through broiling. Place cheese slices on top of the patties. Broil for 1 minute more.

3. Meanwhile, spread cut sides of toasted buns with the onion dip. Top burgers with bacon; place burgers on prepared buns. If desired, add lettuce leaves.

Per serving: 598 cal., 36 g total fat (17 g sat. fat), 119 mg chol., 778 mg sodium, 23 g carbo., 1 g fiber, 41 g pro.

*NOTE: The internal color of a beef patty is not a reliable doneness indicator. A patty cooked to 160°F is safe, regardless of color. To measure doneness of patty, insert an instant-read thermometer through the side of the patty to a depth of 2 to 3 inches.

MENU
Baked beans
Coleslaw (from a deli)
Dill pickles
Watermelon wedges

Beef and Cabbage Wraps

285

START TO FINISH:
20 MINUTES

OVEN:
350°F

MAKES:
4 SERVINGS

8   8-inch flour tortillas
12 ounces ground beef
½   cup chopped onion (1 medium)
2   cups packaged shredded cabbage with carrot (coleslaw mix)
1   cup frozen whole kernel corn
¼   cup bottled barbecue or hoisin sauce
1   teaspoon toasted sesame oil
    Bottled barbecue sauce or hoisin sauce (optional)

1. Stack tortillas and wrap in foil. Heat in a 350°F oven about 10 minutes or until softened. (Or wrap tortillas in white, microwave-safe paper towels; microwave on high [100%] power for 15 to 30 seconds or until tortillas are softened.)

2. Meanwhile, for filling, in a large skillet cook ground beef and onion until meat is brown and onion is tender. Drain off fat. Stir coleslaw mix and corn into meat mixture in skillet. Cook, covered, about 4 minutes or until vegetables are tender, stirring once. Stir in the ¼ cup barbecue sauce and the sesame oil. Cook and stir until heated through.

3. Spoon about ½ cup of the filling below center of each tortilla. Fold bottom edge up and over filling. Fold opposite sides in, just until they meet. Roll up from bottom. If desired, serve with additional barbecue sauce.

Per serving: 388 cal., 14 g total fat (5 g sat. fat), 54 mg chol., 409 mg sodium, 44 g carbo., 4 g fiber, 21 g pro.

MENU
Corn chips
Ice cream with sliced peaches

286 Deli-Style Submarines

START TO FINISH:
20 MINUTES

MAKES:
8 SANDWICHES

1   16-ounce loaf French bread

½   of an 8-ounce carton dairy sour cream ranch dip

¾   cup packaged shredded carrot (1 large)

1   cup shredded lettuce

½   of a medium cucumber, seeded and shredded

8   ounces thinly sliced cooked roast beef, ham, or turkey

4   ounces thinly sliced mozzarella or provolone cheese

1. **Cut French bread in half lengthwise. Spread cut sides of bread with sour cream dip. On the bottom portion of the bread, layer carrot, lettuce, cucumber, meat, and cheese. Top with top portion of bread. Cut into 8 pieces. Secure pieces with decorative toothpicks.**

Per sandwich: 286 cal., 10 g total fat (5 g sat. fat), 41 mg chol., 551 mg sodium, 33 g carbo., 2 g fiber, 17 g pro.

MAKE-AHEAD DIRECTIONS: Prepare as directed, except do not cut into pieces. Wrap sandwich in plastic wrap and chill for up to 4 hours. Cut and serve as directed.

MENU

Potato chips

Green and red sweet pepper
strips with veggie dip

Blonde brownies

Middle Eastern-Style Pitas

287

START TO FINISH:
10 MINUTES

MAKES:
4 SERVINGS

1   7- or 8-ounce container roasted-garlic-flavor hummus
4   pita rounds, halved crosswise
12 ounces thinly sliced deli roast beef
½   cup plain yogurt
½   cup chopped cucumber

1. Spread hummus into the pita halves. Add beef to pita halves. In a small bowl stir together yogurt and cucumber; spoon over beef in pita halves. Serve immediately.

Per serving: 463 cal., 18 g total fat (5 g sat. fat), 70 mg chol., 735 mg sodium, 44 g carbo., 3 g fiber, 34 g pro.

MENU
Kettle-cooked potato chips
Greek olives
Baklava

288 Italian Steak and Cheese Sandwiches

START TO FINISH:
25 MINUTES

MAKES:
6 SANDWICHES

10 tablespoons bottled zesty-style clear Italian salad dressing

2 medium green sweet peppers, cut into thin strips

1 medium onion, sliced

12 ounces thinly sliced cooked roast beef

6 French-style rolls, split and toasted

½ cup shredded mozzarella cheese (2 ounces)

1. In a large skillet heat 2 tablespoons of the salad dressing over medium heat. Add sweet pepper and onion; cook and stir about 5 minutes or until vegetables are tender. Remove vegetable mixture from skillet; keep warm.

2. Add another 2 tablespoons salad dressing to same skillet. Add beef; cook over medium heat for 2 to 3 minutes or until heated through. Fill rolls with meat and vegetable mixture. Drizzle meat and vegetables in each sandwich with 1 tablespoon salad dressing. Top with cheese.

Per sandwich: 311 cal., 13 g total fat (3 g sat. fat), 45 mg chol., 732 mg sodium, 26 g carbo., 2 g fiber, 23 g pro.

MENU
Tomato soup
Cantaloupe or honeydew
melon wedges

Roasted Vegetable and Pastrami Panini

289

START TO FINISH:
30 MINUTES

MAKES:
4 SERVINGS

4   thin slices provolone cheese (2 ounces)
8   ½-inch slices sourdough or Vienna bread
1   cup roasted or grilled vegetables from the deli or deli-marinated vegetables,
      coarsely chopped
4   thin slices pastrami (3 ounces)
1   tablespoon olive oil or basil-flavored olive oil

1. Place a cheese slice on each of 4 of the bread slices. Spread vegetables evenly over cheese. Top with pastrami and remaining 4 bread slices. Brush the outsides of the sandwiches with oil.

2. If desired, wrap a brick completely in foil. Heat a nonstick griddle or large skillet over medium heat. Place a sandwich on heated pan; place brick on top to flatten slightly*. Cook for 4 to 6 minutes or until sandwich is golden and cheese is melted, turning once. Repeat for remaining sandwiches.

Per serving: 314 cal., 16 g total fat (6 g sat. fat), 29 mg chol., 689 mg sodium, 30 g carbo., 2 g fiber, 12 g pro.

*NOTE: Or place sandwich on a covered indoor grill or panini grill.
Close lid; grill for 4 to 5 minutes or until golden and cheese is melted.

MENU
Pasta salad (from a deli)
Multigrain chips
Spumoni ice cream
with chocolate sauce

290 Jamaican Pork Kabobs

PREP:
15 MINUTES

BROIL:
12 MINUTES

MAKES:
4 SERVINGS

2 ears corn, husked and cleaned, or 2 medium red or yellow sweet peppers, cut into 1-inch pieces

1 12- to 14-ounce pork tenderloin

16 baby pattypan squash (each about 1 inch in diameter) or 2 small zucchini or yellow summer squash, halved lengthwise and cut into 1-inch slices

1 small red onion, cut into ½-inch wedges

¼ cup mango chutney, finely chopped

3 tablespoons Pickapeppa sauce*

1 tablespoon cooking oil

1 tablespoon water

1. Cut ears of corn (if using) crosswise into 1-inch pieces. In a medium saucepan cook corn pieces in a small amount of boiling water for 3 minutes; drain and rinse with cold water. Meanwhile, cut tenderloin into 1-inch slices.

2. Preheat broiler. For kabobs, on 8 long metal skewers, alternately thread corn or sweet pepper pieces, pork slices, squash, and onion wedges, leaving a ¼-inch space between pieces. In a small bowl combine chutney, Pickapeppa sauce, oil, and water; set aside.

3. Place kabobs on the unheated rack of a broiler pan. Broil 3 to 4 inches from the heat for 12 to 14 minutes or until no pink remains in meat and the vegetables are tender, turning once halfway through broiling and brushing with the chutney mixture for the last 5 minutes of broiling.

Per serving: 254 cal., 6 g total fat (1 g sat. fat), 50 mg chol., 264 mg sodium, 26 g carbo., 3 g fiber, 23 g pro.

*NOTE: If you can't find Pickapeppa sauce, substitute 3 tablespoons Worcestershire sauce mixed with a dash of bottled hot pepper sauce.

MENU

Hot cooked rice

Sourdough bread

Mango sorbet with shortbread cookies

Pork Medallions with Cherry Sauce

291

START TO FINISH:
20 MINUTES

MAKES:
4 SERVINGS

1   pound pork tenderloin

1   tablespoon olive oil or cooking oil

¾   cup cranberry juice or apple juice

2   teaspoons spicy brown mustard

1   teaspoon cornstarch

1   cup fresh sweet cherries (such as Rainier or Bing), halved and pitted, or 1 cup frozen unsweetened pitted dark sweet cherries, thawed

1. Trim fat from meat. Cut meat crosswise into 1-inch slices. Place each slice between 2 pieces of plastic wrap. Pound lightly with the flat side of a meat mallet to ½-inch thickness. Discard plastic wrap. Sprinkle meat with *salt* and *black pepper.*

2. In a large skillet heat oil over medium-high heat. Add meat; cook about 6 minutes or until juices run clear, turning once. Remove meat from skillet, reserving drippings. Cover meat to keep warm.

3. For cherry sauce, combine cranberry juice, mustard, and cornstarch; add to skillet. Cook and stir until thickened and bubbly. Cook and stir for 2 minutes more. Add cherries to skillet; heat through. Serve sauce over pork.

Per serving: 220 cal., 7 g total fat (2 g sat. fat), 73 mg chol., 158 mg sodium, 14 g carbo., 1 g fiber, 24 g pro.

MENU
Roasted potatoes
Steamed mixed vegetables
Root beer floats

292

Jamaican Pork with Melon Salsa

PREP:
15 MINUTES

GRILL:
6 MINUTES
(COVERED) OR
12 MINUTES
(UNCOVERED)

MAKES:
4 SERVINGS

1 cup chopped honeydew melon

1 cup chopped cantaloupe melon

1 tablespoon snipped fresh mint

1 tablespoon honey

4 boneless pork loin chops, cut ¾ inch thick

2 teaspoons Jamaican jerk seasoning

1. For melon salsa, in a medium bowl combine honeydew, cantaloupe, mint, and honey. Cover and chill until ready to serve.

2. Preheat indoor electric grill*. Trim fat from chops. Sprinkle Jamaican jerk seasoning evenly over both sides of chops; rub in with your fingers. Place chops on grill rack. If using a covered grill, close lid. Grill until an instant-read thermometer inserted in the center of the pork registers 160°F. For a covered grill, allow 6 to 8 minutes. For an uncovered grill, allow 12 to 15 minutes, turning once halfway through grilling. Serve chops with melon salsa.

Per serving: 261 cal., 9 g total fat (3 g sat. fat), 78 mg chol., 228 mg sodium, 12 g carbo., 1 g fiber, 31 g pro.

> *NOTE: If you do not have an indoor grill, you can broil the pork chops. Preheat broiler. Place seasoned chops on the unheated rack of a broiler pan. Broil 3 to 4 inches from the heat for 9 to 11 minutes or until 160°F, turning chops once halfway through broiling.

MENU

Hot cooked couscous

Mixed greens with vinaigrette dressing

French baguette slices

Mu Shu-Style Pork Roll-Ups

293

START TO FINISH:
20 MINUTES

OVEN:
350°F

MAKES:
4 SERVINGS

4   10-inch flour tortillas

1   teaspoon toasted sesame oil

12 ounces packaged pork stir-fry strips or lean boneless pork, cut into strips

2   cups frozen stir-fry vegetables (any combination)

¼   cup bottled plum or hoisin sauce

1. Wrap tortillas tightly in foil. Heat in a 350°F oven about 10 minutes or until softened. (Or wrap tortillas in white, microwave-safe paper towels; microwave on high [100%] power for 15 to 30 seconds or until tortillas are softened.)

2. Meanwhile, in a large skillet heat sesame oil over medium-high heat. Add pork; stir-fry for 2 to 3 minutes or until no longer pink. Add stir-fry vegetables. Cook and stir for 3 to 4 minutes or until vegetables are crisp-tender.

3. Spread each tortilla with 1 tablespoon of the plum sauce; place a quarter of the meat mixture just below the center of each tortilla. Fold the bottom edge of each tortilla up and over the filling. Fold in the sides until they meet; roll up over the filling.

Per serving: 302 cal., 8 g total fat (2 g sat. fat), 53 mg chol., 311 mg sodium, 34 g carbo., 2 g fiber, 22 g pro.

MENU

Sweet pepper strips and pickled baby corn

Multigrain chips

Fortune cookies

294 Jamaican Pork Stir-Fry

START TO FINISH:
20 MINUTES

MAKES:
4 SERVINGS

2   tablespoons cooking oil

1   16-ounce package frozen stir-fry vegetables (carrots, snap peas, mushrooms, and onion)

12 ounces packaged pork stir-fry strips or lean boneless pork, cut into strips

2   to 3 teaspoons Jamaican jerk seasoning

¾   cup bottled plum sauce

2   cups hot cooked rice or pasta

2   tablespoons chopped peanuts

1. In a wok or large skillet heat cooking oil over medium-high heat. Add frozen vegetables; cook and stir for 5 to 7 minutes or until vegetables are crisp-tender. Remove vegetables from the wok.

2. Toss pork strips with Jamaican jerk seasoning; add the pork strips to the wok. (Add more cooking oil during cooking, if necessary.) Cook and stir for 2 to 5 minutes or until meat is no longer pink.

3. Add plum sauce to the wok. Return vegetables to the wok. Gently toss all ingredients together to coat. Heat through. Serve over hot cooked rice. Sprinkle with peanuts.

Per serving: 445 cal., 14 g total fat (3 g sat. fat), 46 mg chol., 804 mg sodium, 54 g carbo., 3 g fiber, 24 g pro.

MENU
Multigrain rolls
Pound cake with lemon curd and blueberries

Ham and Potato Stuffed Peppers

295

START TO FINISH:
15 MINUTES

MAKES:
4 SERVINGS

2 medium green sweet peppers

1 pint deli potato salad

1 cup diced cooked ham

½ cup frozen whole kernel corn, thawed

1 to 2 tablespoons dill pickle relish

1. Cut sweet peppers in half; remove and discard stems, seeds, and membranes. In a large saucepan cook pepper halves in a large amount of boiling water for 3 minutes. Drain. Put pepper halves in bowl of ice water to chill.

2. Meanwhile, stir together potato salad, ham, corn, and pickle relish. Invert pepper halves onto paper towels to drain. Set pepper halves cut sides up. Spoon potato mixture into pepper halves.

Per serving: 280 cal., 14 g total fat (3 g sat. fat), 106 mg chol., 1,229 mg sodium, 23 g carbo., 3 g fiber, 12 g pro.

MENU
Whole grain bread
Fresh fruit plate

296 Pizza-Style Salad

START TO FINISH:
15 MINUTES

MAKES:
4 SERVINGS

1 10-ounce package Italian-style torn mixed salad greens

1 3.5-ounce package sliced pepperoni

1 cup onion-and-garlic flavor croutons

1 cup finely shredded Parmesan or mozzarella cheese (4 ounces)

1 2.25-ounce can sliced pitted ripe olives, drained

½ cup bottled Italian salad dressing

1. In a large salad bowl combine torn mixed greens, pepperoni, croutons, cheese, and olives. Add dressing; toss gently to coat. Serve immediately.

Per serving: 461 cal., 36 g total fat (11 g sat. fat), 45 mg chol., 1,364 mg sodium, 17 g carbo., 2 g fiber, 17 g pro.

MENU
Garlic bread
Ice cream sandwiches made with sugar cookies and peach ice cream

B L T and More

¼ cup mayonnaise or salad dressing

8 slices whole grain bread, toasted

12 slices bacon or turkey bacon, cooked and drained

2 medium tomatoes, sliced

4 to 8 leaf lettuce leaves or 8 to 12 fresh spinach leaves

1. Spread mayonnaise on one side of each slice of toasted bread. To assemble sandwiches, top 4 bread slices with bacon, tomato, lettuce, and remaining bread slices, mayonnaise-side-down. Cut in half to serve.

Per sandwich: 345 cal., 21 g total fat (5 g sat. fat), 26 mg chol., 771 mg sodium, 27 g carbo., 4 g fiber, 13 g pro.

- B L T WITH GUACAMOLE: Prepare as above, except substitute thawed, frozen guacamole for the mayonnaise or salad dressing.

Per sandwich: 268 cal., 12 g total fat (3 g sat. fat), 21 mg chol., 717 mg sodium, 28 mg carbo., 5 g fiber, 13 g pro.

- B L T WITH TURKEY: Prepare as above, adding 1 or 2 thin slices cooked turkey breast (2 to 4 ounces) to each sandwich.

Per sandwich: 358 cal., 21 g total fat (5 g sat. fat), 31 mg chol., 926 mg sodium, 27 mg carbo., 4 g fiber, 16 g pro.

- B L T WITH CHEESE: Prepare as above, adding a slice of cheese (such as Havarti with dill, white cheddar, or Jarlsburg) to each sandwich.

Per sandwich: 435 cal., 29 g total fat (5 g sat. fat), 52 mg chol., 876 mg sodium, 27 mg carbo., 4 g fiber, 17 g pro.

- B L T WITH PESTO-MAYONNAISE: Reduce mayonnaise or salad dressing to 2 tablespoons. In a small bowl stir together the mayonnaise and 3 tablespoons purchased pesto. Spread pesto-mayonnaise on 1 side of each slice of toasted bread. Continue as above.

Per sandwich: 377 cal., 23 g total fat (4 g sat. fat), 25 mg chol., 820 mg sodium, 29 mg carbo., 4 g fiber, 14 g pro.

MENU
Potato chips
Pasta salad (from a deli)
Strawberry or raspberry shakes

298 Honey-Mustard Lamb Chops

PREP:
10 MINUTES

BROIL:
10 MINUTES

MAKES:
4 SERVINGS

8   lamb rib or loin chops, cut 1 inch thick (about 1½ to 2 pounds)

2   medium zucchini and/or yellow summer squash, quartered lengthwise

2   tablespoons Dijon-style mustard

2   tablespoons honey

1   tablespoon snipped fresh rosemary or 1 teaspoon dried rosemary, crushed

1. Preheat broiler. Trim fat from chops. Sprinkle chops and zucchini with *salt* and *black pepper.* Arrange chops and zucchini, cut sides down, on the unheated rack of a broiler pan. In a small bowl stir together mustard, honey, and rosemary. Brush half of the mustard mixture on top of the chops.

2. Broil chops and zucchini 3 to 4 inches from the heat for 5 minutes. Turn chops and zucchini; brush remaining mustard mixture over the chops and zucchini. Broil for 5 to 10 minutes more or until lamb is medium doneness (160°F) and zucchini is tender.

Per serving: 181 cal., 5 g total fat (2 g sat. fat), 60 mg chol., 302 mg sodium, 12 g carbo., 1 g fiber, 20 g pro.

MENU
Toasted pita bread
Hot cooked orzo with feta cheese and chopped tomato
Purchased baklava

299

Lamb and Sweet Peppers

START TO FINISH:
25 MINUTES

MAKES:
4 SERVINGS

8   lamb rib or loin chops, cut 1 inch thick (1½ to 2 pounds)
1   tablespoon olive oil or cooking oil
3   green, red, and/or yellow sweet peppers, cut into 1-inch pieces
1   tablespoon snipped fresh oregano or 1 teaspoon dried oregano, crushed
1   teaspoon bottled minced garlic (2 cloves)
¼   cup sliced pitted green or ripe olives

1. Preheat broiler. Trim fat from chops. If desired, sprinkle chops with *salt* and *black pepper.* Place chops on the unheated rack of a broiler pan. Broil chops 3 to 4 inches from the heat for 10 to 15 minutes for medium (160°F), turning once halfway through broiling.

2. Meanwhile, in a large skillet heat oil over medium-high heat. Add sweet peppers, oregano, and garlic to hot oil. Cook for 8 to 10 minutes or until peppers are crisp-tender. Add olives. Cook and stir until heated through. Spoon pepper mixture over chops.

Per serving: 216 cal., 13 g total fat (3 g sat. fat), 64 mg chol., 264 mg sodium, 4 g carbo., 1 g fiber, 20 g pro.

MENU
Hot cooked linguine
Caesar salad
Crusty Italian bread

300 Lemon-Dill Butter Chicken and Cucumbers

PREP:
10 MINUTES

BROIL:
12 MINUTES

MAKES:
4 SERVINGS

4   skinless, boneless chicken breast halves

3   tablespoons butter

½   teaspoon finely shredded lemon peel

2   tablespoons lemon juice

½   teaspoon dried dill

¼   teaspoon salt

¼   teaspoon black pepper

1½ cups coarsely chopped cucumber or zucchini

1. Preheat broiler. Place chicken on the unheated rack of a broiler pan. Broil 4 to 5 inches from heat for 12 to 15 minutes or until no longer pink (170°F), turning once halfway through broiling.

2. Meanwhile, in a small skillet melt butter over medium heat. Stir in lemon peel, lemon juice, dill, salt, and pepper. Stir in cucumber. Cook and stir over medium heat for 3 to 4 minutes or just until cucumber begins to soften. Spoon sauce over chicken.

Per serving: 244 cal., 11 g total fat (6 g sat. fat), 107 mg chol., 477 mg sodium, 2 g carbo., 0 g fiber, 33 g pro.

MENU
Hot cooked angel hair pasta
Sliced tomatoes
Angel food cake with fresh berries

Sweet Pepper and Peach Chicken

301

START TO FINISH:
30 MINUTES

MAKES:
4 SERVINGS

4   skinless, boneless chicken breast halves

1½ teaspoons fajita seasoning

2   tablespoons olive oil or butter

1½ cups red, yellow, and/or green sweet pepper strips

1   medium fresh peach or nectarine, peeled and cut into thin slices, or 1 cup frozen peach slices, thawed

1. Sprinkle both sides of chicken breast halves with fajita seasoning. In a large skillet heat 1 tablespoon of the oil over medium-high heat. Add chicken; reduce heat to medium. Cook for 8 to 10 minutes or until chicken is no longer pink (170°F), turning occasionally to brown evenly. Remove chicken from skillet; cover to keep warm.

2. Add remaining olive oil to skillet; add sweet pepper strips. Cook and stir about 3 minutes or until pepper strips are crisp-tender. Gently stir in peach slices. Cook and stir for 1 to 2 minutes more or until heated through. Spoon peach mixture over chicken.

Per serving: 243 cal., 9 g total fat (1 g sat. fat), 82 mg chol., 150 mg sodium, 7 g carbo., 2 g fiber, 33 g pro.

MENU
Roasted potato wedges
Corn on the cob
Ice cream cake

302

Pesto Chicken Breasts with Summer Squash

START TO FINISH:
25 MINUTES

MAKES:
4 SERVINGS

4   skinless, boneless chicken breast halves

1   tablespoon olive oil

2   cups coarsely chopped zucchini and/or yellow summer squash

3   tablespoons purchased pesto

2   tablespoons finely shredded Asiago or Parmesan cheese

1. Sprinkle chicken with *salt* and *black pepper*. In a large nonstick skillet heat oil over medium-high heat. Add chicken; reduce heat to medium. Cook chicken for 8 to 12 minutes or until the chicken is no longer pink (170°F), turning occasionally to brown evenly. Remove chicken from skillet; cover to keep warm.

2. Add squash to hot skillet. Cook and stir for 2 to 3 minutes or until squash is crisp-tender. Transfer chicken and squash to 4 dinner plates. Spread pesto over chicken; sprinkle with cheese.

Per serving: 269 cal., 12 g total fat (3 g sat. fat), 90 mg chol., 371 mg sodium, 4 g carbo., 1 g fiber, 36 g pro.

MENU
Breadsticks
Hot cooked tortellini
Sliced tomatoes

Quick Thai Chicken

303

START TO FINISH:
20 MINUTES

MAKES:
4 SERVINGS

1 tablespoon cooking oil

4 skinless, boneless chicken breast halves

¾ cup unsweetened coconut milk

¼ cup peanut butter

¼ teaspoon ground ginger

¼ teaspoon black pepper

4 green onions, cut into 1-inch pieces

¼ cup honey-roasted peanuts, coarsely chopped

1. In a large skillet heat oil over medium-high heat. Add chicken; reduce heat to medium. Cook for 8 to 12 minutes or until chicken is no longer pink (170°F), turning occasionally to brown evenly. Remove chicken from skillet; cover to keep warm.

2. In a small bowl whisk together coconut milk, peanut butter, ginger, and pepper; set aside. Add green onion to skillet. Cook and stir about 2 minutes or until tender. Stir in coconut milk mixture. Cook and stir until bubbly. Spoon over chicken; sprinkle with peanuts.

Per serving: 415 cal., 25 g total fat (11 g sat. fat), 82 mg chol., 192 mg sodium, 8 g carbo., 2 g fiber, 39 g pro.

MENU
Hot cooked rice
Toasted pita bread
Pineapple sorbet with toasted coconut

304

Chicken with Brandied Fruit

START TO FINISH:
30 MINUTES

MAKES:
4 SERVINGS

4   skinless, boneless chicken breast halves
¼   cup all-purpose flour
¼   teaspoon salt
¼   teaspoon black pepper
2   tablespoons olive oil
3   cups thinly sliced nectarines, peeled peaches, plums, or pears
3   tablespoons brandy, orange juice, or apple juice
2   tablespoons water
1   tablespoon lemon juice
2   tablespoons sliced almonds, toasted

1. Place each chicken breast half between 2 pieces of plastic wrap. Using the flat side of a meat mallet, pound chicken lightly to about ¼ inch thick.*

2. In a shallow dish combine flour, salt, and pepper. Lightly coat chicken pieces on both sides with flour mixture; shake off excess.

3. In a large skillet heat oil over medium-high heat. Add chicken; reduce heat to medium. Cook for 6 to 8 minutes or until chicken is no longer pink, turning occasionally to brown evenly. Remove skillet from heat. Remove chicken from skillet; cover to keep warm.

4. Add fruit, brandy, water, and lemon juice to the skillet. Return skillet to heat and cook for 1 minute, stirring gently. Spoon fruit mixture over chicken. Sprinkle with almonds.

Per serving: 346 cal., 12 g total fat (2 g sat. fat), 82 mg chol., 242 mg sodium, 18 g carbo., 3 g fiber, 36 g pro.

*Note: If you like, skip pounding the chicken in step 1. Prepare as above, except cook the chicken in the hot oil over medium heat for 10 to 12 minutes or until no longer pink (170°F), turning occasionally to brown evenly.

MENU

Rice pilaf
(from a mix)

Mixed greens
salad with
desired dressing

Plum cobbler

20-Minute Chicken Fettuccine

305

START TO FINISH:
20 MINUTES

MAKES:
4 SERVINGS

1   9-ounce package refrigerated red sweet pepper or plain fettuccine

¼   of a 7-ounce jar oil-packed dried tomato strips or pieces (¼ cup)

1   large zucchini or yellow summer squash, halved lengthwise and sliced (about 2 cups)

8   ounces packaged skinless, boneless chicken breast strips (stir-fry strips)

2   tablespoons olive oil

½   cup finely shredded Parmesan, Romano, or Asiago cheese (2 ounces)

1. Using kitchen scissors, cut fettuccine strands in half. Cook fettuccine according to package directions; drain. Return fettuccine to hot pan.

2. Meanwhile, drain dried tomatoes, reserving 2 tablespoons of the oil from the jar. Set drained tomatoes aside. In a large skillet heat 1 tablespoon of the reserved tomato oil over medium-high heat. Add zucchini; cook and stir for 2 to 3 minutes or until crisp-tender. Remove zucchini from the skillet. Add remaining 1 tablespoon reserved oil to skillet. Add chicken; cook and stir for 2 to 3 minutes or until no longer pink.

3. Add chicken, zucchini, drained tomatoes, and olive oil to cooked fettuccine; toss gently to combine. Sprinkle individual servings with cheese. Season to taste with *salt* and *black pepper.*

Per serving: 384 cal., 14 g total fat (4 g sat. fat), 93 mg chol., 356 mg sodium, 37 g carbo., 4 g fiber, 28 g pro.

MENU
Garlic bread
Romaine salad with vinaigrette dressing
Cantaloupe and honeydew melon wedges

306 Chicken Soup with Spinach and Orzo

START TO FINISH:
20 MINUTES

MAKES:
6 SERVINGS

4   14-ounce cans reduced-sodium chicken broth

1   cup dried orzo

12   ounces fresh asparagus spears, trimmed and bias-sliced into 1½-inch pieces

3   cups chopped fresh spinach, Swiss chard, or kale, or one 10-ounce package frozen chopped spinach, thawed

1½   cups chopped fresh tomato (3 medium)

1½   cups shredded cooked chicken (8 ounces)

⅓   cup cubed cooked ham

     Snipped fresh chives and/or parsley (optional)

1. **In a covered 5- to 6-quart Dutch oven bring chicken broth to boiling. Add orzo. Return to boiling; reduce heat. Simmer, uncovered, for 6 minutes. Add asparagus; simmer about 2 minutes more or until orzo is tender and asparagus is crisp-tender.**

2. **Stir in spinach, tomato, chicken, and ham; heat through. Season to taste with *salt* and *black pepper*. If desired, sprinkle individual servings with chives.**

Per serving: 221 cal., 4 g total fat (1 g sat. fat), 35 mg chol., 837 mg sodium, 28 g carbo., 3 g fiber, 20 g pro.

MENU
Sourdough rolls
Fudge brownies

307

Thai Chicken in Lettuce Cups

START TO FINISH:
25 MINUTES

MAKES:
4 SERVINGS

12 ounces chicken breast tenders

¼ cup bottled Thai ginger salad dressing and marinade

½ cup thinly sliced red onion (1 medium)

4 Boston or Bibb lettuce cups

3 tablespoons coarsely chopped dry-roasted peanuts

1. In a medium bowl combine chicken and marinade; toss to coat. Let stand at room temperature for 10 minutes.

2. Heat a large skillet over medium-high heat for 2 minutes; add undrained chicken mixture and onion. Cook and stir for 3 to 5 minutes or until chicken is no longer pink and onion is tender.

3. Divide chicken mixture among lettuce cups. Sprinkle with peanuts.

Per serving: 156 cal., 5 g total fat (1 g sat. fat), 49 mg chol., 392 mg sodium, 6 g carbo., 0 g fiber, 22 g pro.

MENU
Hot cooked curly noodles
Spring rolls
(frozen or takeout)
Lemon sorbet with honey

308 Tequila-Lime Chicken

START TO FINISH:
15 MINUTES

MAKES:
4 SERVINGS

1   9-ounce package refrigerated fettuccine
1   10-ounce container refrigerated Alfredo pasta sauce
¼   cup tequila or milk
1   teaspoon finely shredded lime peel
2   5.5-ounce packages refrigerated cooked grilled chicken breast strips
     Lime wedges

1. Cook the fettuccine according to package directions; drain.

2. In a medium saucepan combine Alfredo sauce, tequila, and lime peel; cook and stir just until boiling. Stir in chicken strips; heat through. Toss chicken mixture with hot fettuccine. Serve with lime wedges.

Per serving: 547 cal., 24 g total fat (1 g sat. fat), 133 mg chol., 981 mg sodium, 39 g carbo., 2 g fiber, 11 g pro.

MENU
Tomato and avocado slices
Corn muffins
Key lime pie

Southwestern Chicken Wraps

309

½   cup dairy sour cream

2   tablespoons purchased guacamole

4   10-inch dried tomato, spinach, and/or plain flour tortillas

2   5.5-ounce packages Southwestern-flavor refrigerated cooked chicken breast strips

2   roma tomatoes, sliced

2   cups shredded lettuce

1. In a small bowl stir together sour cream and guacamole. Divide sour cream mixture among tortillas, spreading over 1 side of each tortilla. Divide chicken, tomatoes, and lettuce among tortillas. Roll up.

Per wrap: 395 cal., 13 g total fat (4 g sat. fat), 49 mg chol., 1,015 mg sodium, 45 g carbo., 2 g fiber, 25 g pro.

MENU
Baked beans
Corn chips
Root beer floats

310 Chicken with Orzo

START TO FINISH:
15 MINUTES

MAKES:
4 SERVINGS

8   ounces dried orzo pasta (1½ cups)

2   cups shredded packaged prewashed fresh spinach leaves

½   cup crumbled feta cheese (2 ounces)

1   teaspoon finely shredded lemon peel

1   hot rotisserie chicken, cut into serving-size pieces

1   medium tomato, cut in wedges

1. **Prepare orzo according to package directions. Drain well. Return the orzo to saucepan.**

2. **Add spinach, half of the feta cheese, and lemon peel to orzo in the saucepan, tossing to mix. Divide orzo mixture among 4 dinner plates. Arrange chicken pieces and tomato wedges on top of orzo mixture. Sprinkle with the remaining feta cheese.**

Per serving: 528 cal., 19 g total fat (7 g sat. fat), 112 mg chol., 267 mg sodium, 45 g carbo., 3 g fiber, 41 g pro.

MENU
Toasted pita bread

Sliced peaches and blueberries with vanilla yogurt

Chicken and Pasta Salad with Tomatoes

311

START TO FINISH:
30 MINUTES

MAKES:
4 SERVINGS

1   16-ounce package frozen pasta and vegetables in a seasoned sauce (such as pasta, broccoli, peas, and carrots in onion and herb seasoned sauce)
1   cup chopped cooked chicken or turkey (about 5 ounces)
½   cup dairy sour cream dip with chives
1   cup coarsely chopped tomato (2 medium)
½   cup shredded cheddar cheese (2 ounces)

1. In a 2-quart saucepan cook frozen pasta and vegetables in sauce according to package directions.

2. Meanwhile, in a large bowl stir together chicken and sour cream dip. Gently fold the undrained cooked pasta mixture and the tomato into the chicken mixture. Cover and chill in the freezer for 10 minutes.

3. Sprinkle individual servings with cheddar cheese.

Per serving: 335 cal., 17 g total fat (10 g sat. fat), 67 mg chol., 785 mg sodium, 24 g carbo., 5 g fiber, 21 g pro.

MENU
Whole wheat rolls
Praline ice cream with
caramel sauce

312 Asian Chicken Salad

START TO FINISH:
15 MINUTES

MAKES:
4 SERVINGS

1   10-ounce package torn mixed salad greens

1½ cups chopped cooked chicken (8 ounces)

⅓   cup bottled Asian vinaigrette salad dressing

1   11-ounce can mandarin orange sections, drained

3   tablespoons sliced almonds, toasted

1. **In a large bowl combine salad greens and chicken. Add salad dressing; toss to coat. Divide greens mixture among 4 salad plates. Top with mandarin orange sections and almonds.**

Per serving: 218 cal., 9 g total fat (1 g sat. fat), 50 mg chol., 502 mg sodium, 15 g carbo., 2 g fiber, 19 g pro.

MENU
Crusty bread
Fresh plums and apricots

Cool-as-a-Cucumber Chicken Salad

313

START TO FINISH:
25 MINUTES

MAKES:
4 TO 6 SERVINGS

2 cups shredded cooked chicken (10 ounces)

2 cups halved seedless red grapes or cut-up cantaloupe

1 cup chopped cucumber

⅓ cup orange juice

3 tablespoons salad oil

1 tablespoon snipped fresh mint or cilantro

4 cups shredded romaine or leaf lettuce

1. In a large bowl toss together chicken, cantaloupe, and cucumber.

2. For dressing, in a screw-top jar combine orange juice, oil, and cilantro. Cover and shake well. Season to taste with *salt* and *black pepper.* Drizzle over chicken mixture; toss lightly to coat.

3. Arrange lettuce on 4 salad plates. Top with chicken mixture.

Per serving: 269 cal., 16 g total fat (3 g sat. fat), 62 mg chol., 114 mg sodium, 11 g carbo., 1 g fiber, 22 g pro.

MENU
Soft breadsticks
Pound cake with fresh
berries and whipped cream

314 Chicken Salad Sandwiches

START TO FINISH:
20 MINUTES

MAKES:
4 SANDWICHES

1   cup chopped cooked chicken (5 ounces)

⅓   cup chopped apple, cucumber, or celery

1   hard-cooked egg, peeled and chopped

2   tablespoons plain low-fat yogurt

2   tablespoons light mayonnaise or salad dressing

8   slices whole wheat bread

1. In a medium bowl stir together chicken, apple, and egg. Add yogurt and mayonnaise; stir to combine. Season to taste with *salt* and *black pepper.*

2. Spread chicken mixture on half of the bread slices. Top with the remaining bread slices. If desired, cut off crusts. Cut each sandwich into 2 or 4 triangles or squares.

Per sandwich: 244 cal., 9 g total fat (2 g sat. fat), 87 mg chol., 432 mg sodium, 26 g carbo., 4 g fiber, 17 g pro.

MENU
Corn chips
Carrot and sweet pepper
strips with veggie dip
Chocolate cupcakes

Dried Tomato and Basil Chicken Wraps

315

½ of a 3-ounce package (about ¾ cup) dried tomatoes (not oil-packed)
3 cups shredded roasted or grilled chicken (about 1 pound)
1 cup shredded mozzarella or Monterey Jack cheese (4 ounces)
½ cup chopped pecans, toasted
⅓ cup bottled creamy Italian or ranch salad dressing
6 10-inch dried tomato, spinach, and/or plain flour tortillas, warmed*
1 cup large fresh basil leaves

1. Soak dried tomatoes in enough hot water to cover for 10 minutes. Drain and chop tomatoes.

2. In a large bowl combine dried tomato, chicken, cheese, pecans, and salad dressing.

3. Line each tortilla with some of the basil leaves. Divide chicken mixture among the tortillas. Fold in sides and roll up. Cut each wrap diagonally in half.

Per wrap: 449 cal., 24 g total fat (6 g sat. fat), 73 mg chol., 701 mg sodium, 29 g carbo., 3 g fiber, 30 g pro.

*NOTE: To warm tortillas, wrap them in white microwave-safe paper towels; microwave on 100% power (high) for 15 to 30 seconds or until tortillas are softened. (Or preheat oven to 350°F. Wrap tortillas in foil. Heat in preheated oven for 10 to 15 minutes or until warmed.)

MENU
Pasta salad (from a deli)
Kettle-cooked potato chips
Fresh fruit shakes

316 Chicken Focaccia Sandwiches

START TO FINISH:
15 MINUTES

MAKES:
4 SANDWICHES

1   8- to 10-inch tomato or onion Italian flatbread (focaccia) or 1 loaf sourdough bread
⅓   cup mayonnaise dressing or salad dressing
1   cup lightly packed fresh basil
8   ounces sliced or shredded cooked chicken
½   cup bottled roasted red sweet peppers. drained and cut into strips

1. Using a long serrated knife, cut bread in half horizontally. Spread cut sides of bread halves with mayonnaise.

2. Layer basil leaves, chicken, and roasted sweet peppers between bread halves. Cut into quarters.

Per sandwich: 435 cal., 22 g total fat (3 g sat. fat), 65 mg chol., 486 mg sodium, 38 g carbo., 1 g fiber, 24 g pro.

MENU
Marinated vegetable salad
(from a deli)
Corn chips
Parfaits made with layers
of sliced peaches, vanilla
yogurt, and granola

Chicken and Prosciutto Sandwiches

317

PREP:
10 MINUTES

BAKE:
12 MINUTES

OVEN:
450°F

MAKES:
6 SANDWICHES

⅓   cup refrigerated basil pesto

6   ½-inch bias-cut slices Italian bread (about one-third of a 1-pound loaf)

3   ounces thinly sliced prosciutto

1   14-ounce can artichoke hearts, drained and thinly sliced

1   cup bottled roasted red sweet peppers, drained and cut into strips

12 ounces cooked chicken or turkey, cut into bite-size strips (about 2¼ cups)

1   to 1½ cups shredded provolone cheese (4 to 6 ounces)

1. Preheat oven to 450°F. Lightly spread pesto on 1 side of each bread slice. Top slices with prosciutto, artichoke slices, red pepper strips, and chicken strips.

2. Place sandwiches on a large foil-lined cookie sheet. Cover loosely with foil.

3. Bake about 8 minutes or until nearly heated through. Uncover sandwiches and sprinkle with cheese. Bake for 4 to 5 minutes more or until cheese melts.

Per open-face sandwich: 387 cal., 20 g total fat (6 g sat. fat), 67 mg chol., 855 mg sodium, 20 g carbo., 1 g fiber, 31 g pro.

MENU
Fruit salad (from a deli)
Potato chips
Watermelon wedges

318 Sweet Chicken Tostadas

START TO FINISH:
20 MINUTES

MAKES:
4 SERVINGS

8   tostada shells

½   cup dairy sour cream

1   cup bottled fruit salsa

1½ cups finely chopped cooked chicken (8 ounces)

1   cup shredded Monterey Jack cheese with jalapeño chile peppers (4 ounces)

1. Preheat broiler. Spread one side of each tostada shell with 1 tablespoon of the sour cream, spreading to edges. Spread 2 tablespoons of the salsa evenly on top of sour cream on each tostada. Top each with 3 tablespoons of the chopped chicken and 2 tablespoons of the shredded cheese.

2. Place 4 of the tostadas on a large cookie sheet. Place on a broiler rack. Broil 4 to 5 inches from the heat for 1 to 1½ minutes or until cheese is melted. Repeat with remaining tostadas. Serve warm.

Per serving (2 tostadas): 511 cal., 26 g total fat (12 g sat. fat), 89 mg chol., 488 mg sodium, 42 g carbo., 4 g fiber, 27 g pro.

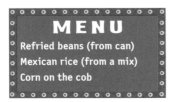

MENU
Refried beans (from can)
Mexican rice (from a mix)
Corn on the cob

Ranch-Style Chicken Pockets

319

START TO FINISH:
15 MINUTES

MAKES:
4 SANDWICHES

¼ cup plain yogurt

¼ cup bottled reduced-fat ranch salad dressing

1½ cups chopped cooked chicken or turkey (8 ounces)

½ cup chopped broccoli

¼ cup shredded carrot

¼ cup chopped pecans or walnuts (optional)

2 6- to 7-inch whole wheat pita bread rounds, halved crosswise

1. In a small bowl stir together yogurt and ranch salad dressing.

2. For filling, in a medium bowl combine chicken, broccoli, carrot, and, if desired, nuts. Pour yogurt mixture over chicken mixture; toss to coat.

3. Spoon filling into pita halves.

Per sandwich: 231 cal., 8 g total fat (1 g sat. fat), 53 mg chol., 392 mg sodium, 21 g carbo., 3 g fiber, 20 g pro.

MENU
Dill pickles
Fruit salad (from a deli)
Fudge brownies

320 Balsamic Turkey with Zucchini

START TO FINISH:
25 MINUTES

MAKES:
4 SERVINGS

2   tablespoons balsamic vinegar

2   tablespoons cooking oil

1   tablespoon honey

⅛   to ¼ teaspoon crushed red pepper

2   turkey breast tenderloins (about 1¼ pounds)

2   medium zucchini, halved lengthwise and cut into ¼-inch slices

2   cups hot cooked pasta or rice

½   cup chopped tomato (1 medium) (optional)

Shredded fresh basil (optional)

1. For dressing, in a small bowl stir together balsamic vinegar, 1 tablespoon of the oil, the honey, and crushed red pepper; set aside.

2. Split each turkey breast in half horizontally to make 4 turkey steaks. Lightly sprinkle turkey with *salt* and *black pepper.* In a large nonstick skillet heat the remaining 1 tablespoon oil over medium-high heat. Add turkey; reduce heat to medium. Cook for 8 to 10 minutes or until turkey is no longer pink (170°F), turning occasionally to brown evenly. Remove turkey from skillet; cover to keep warm.

3. Add zucchini to skillet; cook and stir about 3 minutes or until crisp-tender. Cut turkey into bite-size pieces. In a large bowl combine turkey, zucchini, and dressing. Spoon over hot pasta. If desired, sprinkle with tomato and basil.

Per serving: 358 cal., 10 g total fat (2 g sat. fat), 85 mg chol., 224 mg sodium, 29 g carbo., 2 g fiber, 38 g pro.

MENU

Spinach salad with balsamic vinaigrette

Focaccaia

Peach pie

Turkey Tenderloin with Bean and Corn Salsa

321

START TO FINISH:
25 MINUTES

MAKES:
4 SERVINGS

2   turkey breast tenderloins (about 1 pound)

¼   cup red jalapeño chile pepper jelly

1¼ cups purchased black bean and corn salsa

2   tablespoons snipped fresh cilantro

1. Preheat broiler. Split each turkey breast tenderloin in half horizontally to make 4 turkey steaks. Place turkey on the unheated rack of a broiler pan. Sprinkle with *salt* and *black pepper.* Broil 4 to 5 inches from heat for 5 minutes.

2. Meanwhile, in a small saucepan melt the jelly. Remove 2 tablespoons of the jelly. Turn turkey and brush with the 2 tablespoons jelly. Discard any remaining jelly used as brush-on. Broil for 4 to 6 minutes more or until turkey is no longer pink (170°F).

3. In another small saucepan heat salsa. Transfer turkey to 4 dinner plates. Spoon jelly remaining in saucepan over turkey. Spoon salsa over the turkey. Sprinkle with cilantro.

Per serving: 196 cal., 2 g total fat (1 g sat. fat), 66 mg chol., 377 mg sodium, 16 g carbo., 1 g fiber, 27 g pro.

MENU
Tomato slices
Hot cooked rice
Cherry cobbler

322

Turkey Steaks and Vegetables

PREP:
6 MINUTES

GRILL:
5 MINUTES
(COVERED)
OR 9 MINUTES
(UNCOVERED)

MAKES:
4 SERVINGS

2 tablespoons vegetable juice

2 tablespoons mayonnaise or salad dressing

1½ teaspoons snipped fresh chives or green onion tops

1 teaspoon snipped fresh thyme or ½ teaspoon dried thyme, crushed

1 1-inch-thick turkey breast tenderloin (about 8 ounces)

1 small zucchini, halved lengthwise

2 roma tomatoes, halved lengthwise

1. For sauce, in a small bowl gradually stir vegetable juice into mayonnaise; stir in chives and thyme. Set aside.

2. Lightly grease the rack of an indoor electric grill. Preheat grill. Sprinkle turkey with *salt* and *black pepper.* Place turkey and zucchini, cut sides down, on the grill rack. If using a covered grill, close lid. Grill until turkey is no longer pink (170°F) and zucchini is crisp-tender. For a covered grill, allow 4 to 6 minutes, brushing once with sauce the last 1 minute of grilling. For an uncovered grill, allow 8 to 12 minutes, turning once halfway through grilling and brushing occasionally with sauce the last 4 minutes of grilling. Remove turkey and zucchini from grill; cover to keep warm.

3. Add tomatoes, cut sides down, to the grill rack. If using a covered grill, close lid. For a covered or uncovered grill, grill for 1 to 2 minutes or until tomatoes are heated through. Serve turkey with zucchini and tomatoes.

Per serving: 187 cal., 6 g total fat (1 g sat. fat), 50 mg chol., 91 mg sodium, 3 g carbo., 1 g fiber, 18 g pro.

MENU
Crusty Italian bread
Hot cooked tortellini
Blueberry ice cream

Apple-Glazed Turkey

323

PREP:
10 MINUTES

BROIL:
8 MINUTES

MAKES:
4 SERVINGS

2   turkey breast tenderloins (about 1 pound)

1   tablespoon olive oil or cooking oil

1   tablespoon lemon juice

½   teaspoon seasoned salt

½   teaspoon dried sage leaves, crushed

2   teaspoons bottled minced garlic (4 cloves)

2   tablespoons apple jelly, melted

1. Preheat broiler. Split each turkey breast tenderloin in half horizontally to make 4 turkey steaks. In a small bowl combine oil, lemon juice, seasoned salt, sage, and garlic. Place turkey on the unheated rack of a broiler pan. Brush oil mixture on both sides of each turkey steak.

2. Broil turkey 4 to 5 inches from the heat for 4 minutes. Turn turkey; broil for 2 minutes more. Brush turkey with apple jelly. Broil for 2 to 4 minutes more or until turkey is no longer pink (170°F). Slice the turkey steaks before serving.

Per serving: 192 cal., 5 g total fat (1 g sat. fat), 68 mg chol., 247 mg sodium, 8 g carbo., 0 g fiber, 27 g pro.

MENU

Steamed green beans

Hot cooked noodles tossed with butter and parsley

Raspberries and ice cream

324 Thai Turkey Burgers

PREP:
15 MINUTES

BROIL:
14 MINUTES

MAKES:
4 SERVINGS

1   egg, lightly beaten
¼   cup fine dry bread crumbs
1   teaspoon Thai seasoning
1   pound uncooked ground turkey
4   kaiser rolls or hamburger buns, split and toasted
¾   cup fresh basil leaves
2   tablespoons bottled peanut dipping sauce
     Bias-sliced green onion (optional)

1. Preheat broiler. In a medium bowl combine egg, bread crumbs, and Thai seasoning. Add ground turkey; mix well. Shape turkey mixture into four ¾-inch-thick patties.

2. Place patties on the unheated rack of a broiler pan. Broil 4 to 5 inches from the heat for 14 to 18 minutes or until no longer pink (165°F), turning once halfway through broiling.

3. To serve burgers, top bottom halves of buns with basil. Add burgers. Spoon peanut dipping sauce over patties. If desired, sprinkle with green onion. Add bun tops.

Per serving: 389 cal., 13 g total fat (3 g sat. fat), 123 mg chol., 739 mg sodium, 36 g carbo., 2 g fiber, 31 g pro.

MENU

Spinach salad with mandarin oranges and desired vinaigrette

Spring rolls (frozen or takeout)

Pineapple sorbet with toasted coconut

Italian-Style Turkey Burgers

325

1   egg, lightly beaten

¼   cup seasoned fine dry bread crumbs

¼   teaspoon salt

1   pound uncooked ground turkey

4   slices provolone or mozzarella cheese (4 ounces)

4   kaiser rolls or hamburger buns, split and toasted

    Fresh basil leaves or shredded lettuce

¼   cup dried tomato-flavored light mayonnaise dressing

1. Preheat broiler. In a medium bowl combine egg, bread crumbs, and salt. Add ground turkey; mix well. Shape turkey mixture into four ¾-inch-thick patties.

2. Place patties on the unheated rack of a broiler pan. Broil 4 to 5 inches from the heat for 14 to 18 minutes or until no longer pink (165°F), turning once halfway through broiling time. Top each patty with a slice of cheese; broil about 30 seconds more or until cheese melts.

3. To serve, top bottom halves of buns with basil. Add burgers. Spread mayonnaise dressing on bun tops; place on burgers.

Per serving: 531 cal., 26 g total fat (9 g sat. fat), 172 mg chol., 1,087 mg sodium, 37 g carbo., 1 g fiber, 35 g pro.

MENU

Corn on the cob

Pasta salad (from a deli)

Cantaloupe and honeydew melon wedges

326

Turkey Sub with Citrus Mayonnaise

START TO FINISH:
15 MINUTES

MAKES:
4 SANDWICHES

½ cup mayonnaise or salad dressing

1 teaspoon finely shredded orange peel

2 tablespoons orange juice

4 sourdough rolls, split

8 to 12 ounces thinly sliced cooked peppered turkey or cooked smoked turkey

4 slices Swiss or provolone cheese (3 to 4 ounces)

1. For citrus mayonnaise, in a small bowl stir together mayonnaise, orange peel, and orange juice; set aside.

2. If desired, toast rolls. Spread citrus mayonnaise on the cut sides of rolls. Place bottom halves of rolls on a serving platter, mayonnaise sides up. Layer turkey and cheese on rolls. Top with remaining halves of rolls, mayonnaise sides down.

Per sandwich: 436 cal., 30 g total fat (7 g sat. fat), 61 mg chol., 1,123 mg sodium, 21 g carbo., 1 g fiber, 21 g pro.

MENU
Multigrain chips
Baked beans .
Marinated vegetable salad
(from a deli)

Smoked Turkey and Blue Cheese Pasta Salad

327

START TO FINISH:
25 MINUTES

MAKES:
4 SERVINGS

1   cup dried medium farfalle (bow ties) or medium shell macaroni (about 2½ ounces)
½   cup crumbled blue cheese (2 ounces)
⅓   cup bottled balsamic vinaigrette or oil and vinegar salad dressing
6   ounces smoked turkey, cut into bite-size pieces
3   cups packaged torn mixed salad greens
¼   cup walnut or pecan pieces, toasted
1   11-ounce can mandarin orange sections, drained

1. Cook pasta according to package directions. Drain in colander. Rinse with cold water; drain again.

2. Meanwhile, in a large bowl toss blue cheese with salad dressing. Add turkey, salad greens, and nuts. Add pasta; toss gently to coat. Top individual servings with orange sections.

Per serving: 284 cal., 16 g total fat (4 g sat. fat), 29 mg chol., 887 mg sodium, 25 g carbo., 2 g fiber, 14 g pro.

MENU
Sourdough bread
Assorted fruit plate

328 Brats with Onion-Pepper Relish

PREP:
15 MINUTES

COOK:
15 MINUTES

MAKES:
4 SERVINGS

4   uncooked turkey bratwurst
½   cup water
2   teaspoons butter or margarine
1   small onion, thinly sliced
1   small red or green sweet pepper, cut into thin strips
¼   teaspoon black pepper
⅛   teaspoon salt
4   bratwurst buns, split and toasted
3   tablespoons spicy brown mustard

1. In a large nonstick skillet cook bratwurst over medium heat about 5 minutes or until brown, turning frequently. Carefully add the water. Bring to boiling; reduce heat. Simmer, covered, for 15 to 20 minutes or until internal temperature registers 165°F. Drain bratwurst on paper towels.

2. Meanwhile, in a medium saucepan melt butter. Add onion, sweet pepper, black pepper, and salt. Cover and cook for 3 minutes. Stir onion mixture. Cook, covered, for 3 to 4 minutes more or until onion is golden.

3. Spread cut sides of toasted buns with mustard. Place bratwurst in buns; top with onion mixture.

Per serving: 284 cal., 12 g total fat (4 g sat. fat), 43 mg chol., 1,100 mg sodium, 27 g carbo., 2 g fiber, 17 g pro.

MENU
Potato salad (from a deli)
Steamed broccoli spears
Banana splits

Sea Bass with Lemon-Caper Butter

329

PREP:
10 MINUTES

BROIL:
8 MINUTES

MAKES:
4 SERVINGS

4   5- to 6-ounce fresh or frozen sea bass steaks, cut 1 inch thick
¼   cup butter, softened
1   tablespoon capers, drained
1   teaspoon finely shredded lemon peel
2   teaspoons lemon juice
½   teaspoon bottled minced garlic (1 clove)
    Lemon wedges (optional)

1. Thaw fish, if frozen. Preheat broiler. Rinse fish steaks; pat dry with paper towels. Sprinkle fish with *salt* and *black pepper.* Place fish on the greased unheated rack of a broiler pan. Broil 4 inches from heat for 8 to 12 minutes or until fish begins to flake when tested with a fork, turning once halfway through broiling.

2. Meanwhile, for lemon-caper butter, in a small bowl stir together butter, capers, lemon peel, lemon juice, and garlic. To serve, top fish with lemon-caper butter. If desired, garnish with lemon wedges.

Per serving: 277 cal., 16 g total fat (8 g sat. fat), 102 mg chol., 449 mg sodium, 2 g carbo., 1 g fiber, 32 g pro.

MENU
Wild and brown rice pilaf (from a mix)
Steamed green beans
Apricot bars

330

Swordfish with Tomato Relish

PREP:
20 MINUTES

GRILL:
4 MINUTES
(COVERED)
OR 8 MINUTES
(UNCOVERED)

MAKES:
4 SERVINGS

2   5- to 6-ounce fresh or frozen swordfish or halibut steaks, cut 1 inch thick

4   teaspoons olive oil

¼   cup chopped leek (1 small) or green onion (2)

1   cup chopped, seeded tomato (2 medium)

¼   cup snipped fresh basil

1   tablespoon drained capers

¼   teaspoon black pepper

⅛   teaspoon salt

1. Thaw fish, if frozen. Rinse fish; pat dry with paper towels. Lightly grease the grill rack of an indoor electric grill. Preheat electric indoor grill.

2. For tomato relish, in a small saucepan heat 2 teaspoons of the oil over medium heat. Add leek; cook and stir for 2 to 3 minutes or just until tender. Remove from heat. Stir in tomato, basil, capers, pepper, and salt. Set aside.

3. Brush the remaining 2 teaspoons oil over fish steaks. Place fish on grill rack. If using a covered grill, close lid. Grill until fish begins to flake when tested with a fork. For a covered grill, allow 4 to 6 minutes. For an uncovered grill, allow 8 to 12 minutes, carefully turning once halfway through grilling. To serve, cut each fish steak into 2 serving pieces. Top each serving with tomato relish.

Per serving: 154 cal., 8 g total fat (2 g sat. fat), 32 mg chol., 217 mg sodium, 3 g carbo., 1 g fiber, 17 g pro.

MENU

Roasted zucchini and sweet pepper chunks

Boiled new potatoes with butter

Cherry pie

Tuna Steaks with Jalapeño Mayo

331

PREP:
20 MINUTES

GRILL:
4 MINUTES
(COVERED)
OR 8 MINUTES
(UNCOVERED)

MAKES:
4 SERVINGS

4   5- to 6-ounce fresh or frozen tuna or halibut steaks, cut 1 inch thick
1   tablespoon olive oil or cooking oil
    Dash cayenne pepper
⅓   cup mayonnaise or salad dressing
1   fresh jalapeño chile pepper, finely chopped*
1   tablespoon Dijon-style mustard
1   teaspoon lemon juice

1. Thaw fish, if frozen. Rinse fish; pat dry with paper towels. In a small bowl combine oil and cayenne pepper; brush over both sides of fish. Sprinkle both sides of fish with *salt* and *black pepper.*

2. For jalapeño mayo, in a small bowl combine mayonnaise, jalapeño pepper, mustard, and lemon juice. Cover; chill until serving time.

3. Lightly grease the rack of an indoor electric grill. Preheat grill. Place fish on grill rack. If using a covered grill, close lid. Grill until fish begins to flake when tested with a fork. For a covered grill, allow 4 to 6 minutes. For an uncovered grill, allow 8 to 12 minutes, gently turning fish once. Serve with jalapeño mayo.

Per serving: 350 cal., 19 g total fat (3 g sat. fat), 89 mg chol., 300 mg sodium, 1 g carbo., 0 g fiber, 41 g pro.

*NOTE: Because chile peppers contain volatile oils that can burn your skin and eyes, avoid direct contact with them as much as possible. When working with chile peppers, wear plastic or rubber gloves. If your bare hands do touch the peppers, wash your hands and nails well with soap and warm water.

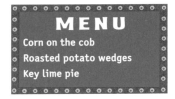

MENU
Corn on the cob
Roasted potato wedges
Key lime pie

332

Halibut with Tomatoes and Olives

PREP:
15 MINUTES

BROIL:
8 MINUTES

MAKES:
4 SERVINGS

4   5- to 6-ounce fresh or frozen halibut steaks, cut 1 inch thick

2   tablespoons olive oil

⅓   cup chopped tomato (1 small)

⅓   cup Greek black olives, pitted and chopped

2   tablespoons snipped fresh Italian parsley or 1 tablespoon snipped fresh
     oregano or thyme

1. Thaw fish, if frozen. Rinse fish; pat dry with paper towels. Brush fish with
   1 tablespoon of the oil; sprinkle with *salt* and *black pepper.*

2. Preheat broiler. Place fish on the greased unheated rack of a broiler pan. Broil
   fish 4 inches from heat for 8 to 12 minutes or until fish begins to flake when
   tested with a fork, turning once halfway through broiling.

3. Meanwhile, in a small bowl stir together the remaining 1 tablespoon oil,
   tomato, olives, and parsley. To serve, spoon tomato mixture over fish.

Per serving: 262 cal., 12 g total fat (2 g sat. fat), 54 mg chol., 264 mg sodium, 2 g carbo., 1 g fiber, 36 g pro.

MENU

Hot cooked orzo

Spinach salad with feta and
vinaigrette dressing

Toasted pita bread

Salmon with Pesto Mayo

333

START TO FINISH:
15 MINUTES

MAKES:
4 SERVINGS

4   5- to 6-ounce fresh or frozen skinless salmon fillets
¼   cup mayonnaise or salad dressing
3   tablespoons purchased basil pesto
     Shaved Parmesan cheese (optional)

1. Thaw fish, if frozen. Rinse fish; pat dry with paper towels. Measure thickness of fish. Preheat broiler.

2. Place fish fillets on the greased unheated rack of a broiler pan, tucking under any thin edges to make the fish of uniform thickness. Broil 4 inches from heat until fish begins to flake when tested with a fork. (Allow 4 to 6 minutes per ½-inch thickness of fish. If fillets are 1 inch or more thick, turn once halfway through broiling.)

3. Meanwhile, for pesto mayo, in a small bowl stir together mayonnaise and pesto. Spoon pesto mayo over fillets. Broil 1 minute more or until topping is bubbly. If desired, top with shaved Parmesan cheese.

Per serving: 440 cal., 34 g total fat (5 g sat. fat), 94 mg chol., 256 mg sodium, 2 g carbo., 0 g fiber, 30 g pro.

MENU
Marinated vegetable salad
(from a deli)
Focaccia
Peach pie

334 Lime-Poached Mahi Mahi

START TO FINISH:
20 MINUTES

MAKES:
4 SERVINGS

4   5- to 6-ounce fresh or frozen mahi mahi or catfish fillets, ½ to ¾ inch thick
2   teaspoons seasoned pepper
1   tablespoon olive oil
⅓   cup frozen margarita mix concentrate, thawed
2   cups hot cooked rice

1. Thaw fish, if frozen. Skin fish, if necessary. Rinse fish; pat dry with paper towels. Sprinkle both sides of fillets with seasoned pepper.

2. In a large nonstick skillet heat oil over medium-high heat. Add fish; cook for 2 to 4 minutes or until light brown on both sides, turning once. Reduce heat to medium-low. Carefully add margarita mix concentrate to skillet. Cook, covered, for 6 to 8 minutes more or until fish begins to flake when tested with a fork. Serve with hot cooked rice.

Per serving: 336 cal., 5 g total fat (1 g sat. fat), 124 mg chol., 150 mg sodium, 41 g carbo., 0 g fiber, 34 g pro.

MENU
Avocado and tomato slices
Tortilla chips and salsa
Raspberry sorbet

Sesame Seared Tuna 335

START TO FINISH:
20 MINUTES

MAKES:
4 SERVINGS

4   5- to 6-ounce fresh or frozen tuna fillets, about ¾ inch thick
1   tablespoon olive oil
⅓   cup bottled hoisin sauce
3   tablespoons orange juice
1   tablespoon sesame seeds, toasted*

1. Thaw fish, if frozen. Rinse fish; pat dry with paper towels. In a large skillet heat oil over medium-high heat. Add fish; cook about 8 minutes or until tuna begins to flake when tested with a fork (tuna may be slightly pink in the center), turning once halfway through cooking.

2. Meanwhile, for sauce, in a small saucepan stir together hoisin sauce and orange juice; heat through.

3. Transfer fish to 4 dinner plates; drizzle with sauce and sprinkle with toasted sesame seeds.

Per serving: 271 cal., 7 g total fat (1 g sat. fat), 76 mg chol., 297 mg sodium, 9 g carbo., 0 g fiber, 41 g pro.

*NOTE: To toast the sesame seeds, place them in a single layer in a glass pie plate or on a baking sheet. Bake in a preheated 350°F oven for 2 to 4 minutes or until seeds are a golden color and smell toasted. Watch closely as they will burn easily.

MENU
Hot cooked rice
Spinach salad with mandarin oranges and vinaigrette dressing
Honeydew melon wedges

336 Red Snapper Veracruz

START TO FINISH:
20 MINUTES

MAKES:
4 SERVINGS

4   4- to 5-ounce fresh or frozen skinless red snapper or orange roughy fillets,
       ½ to 1 inch thick
1   14-ounce can vegetable broth
1   cup quick-cooking couscous
¼   cup thinly sliced green onion (2) or coarsely chopped fresh cilantro
⅓   cup bottled salsa
     Lemon wedges (optional)

1. Thaw fish, if frozen. Preheat broiler. In a medium saucepan bring vegetable broth to boiling. Stir in couscous. Cover saucepan and remove from heat. Let stand about 5 minutes or until liquid is absorbed. Stir in green onion.

2. Meanwhile, rinse fish; pat dry. Sprinkle fish with *salt* and *black pepper.* Place fish on the greased unheated rack of a broiler pan, tucking under any thin edges to make pieces of uniform thickness. Measure thickness of the fish. Broil 4 to 5 inches from the heat until fish begins to flake when tested with a fork. (Allow 4 to 6 minutes per ½-inch thickness of fish; if fillets are 1 inch thick, turn once halfway through broiling.) Spoon the salsa over fish; broil 1 minute more or until salsa is heated through.

3. To serve, arrange fish on couscous mixture. If desired, serve with lemon wedges.

Per serving: 298 cal., 2 g total fat (0 g sat. fat), 42 mg chol., 603 mg sodium, 38 g carbo., 3 g fiber, 29 g pro.

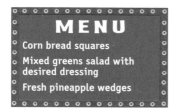

MENU
Corn bread squares
Mixed greens salad with desired dressing
Fresh pineapple wedges

Flounder with Roma Tomatoes

337

1 pound fresh or frozen flounder fillets or other thin, mild fish fillets

1 tablespoon olive oil

1 cup finely chopped onion (2 medium)

1 medium fresh mild green chile pepper, such as Anaheim, seeded and chopped (½ cup)

2 cups chopped roma tomato (4 medium)

2 tablespoons capers, drained

¼ cup sliced, pitted imported black olives, such as kalamata or niçoise

¼ teaspoon salt

⅛ teaspoon black pepper

Fresh Italian parsley sprigs (optional)

1. Thaw fish, if frozen. Rinse fish; pat dry with paper towels. Cut fish into 4 serving-size pieces, if necessary. Set fish aside.

2. In a large skillet heat oil over medium heat. Add onion and chile pepper; cook about 4 minutes or until tender. Stir in tomato, drained capers, olives, and ⅛ teaspoon of the salt. Arrange fish on top of the vegetables. Sprinkle fish with the remaining ⅛ teaspoon salt and the black pepper. Cook, covered, over medium heat for 4 to 5 minutes or until fish begins to flake when tested with a fork. If desired, garnish with fresh parsley.

Per serving: 188 cal., 6 g total fat (1 g sat. fat), 54 mg chol., 500 mg sodium, 10 g carbo., 2 g fiber, 23 g pro.

MENU
Crusty Italian bread
Hot cooked fettuccine
Tiramisu (frozen)

338

Crunchy Catfish and Zucchini Sticks

PREP:
15 MINUTES

BAKE:
12 MINUTES

OVEN:
425°F

MAKES:
4 SERVINGS

1   pound fresh or frozen catfish fillets

1   medium zucchini or yellow summer squash

4   cups cornflakes

1   cup bottled ranch salad dressing

2   teaspoons bottled hot pepper sauce

1. Thaw fish, if frozen. Rinse fish; pat dry with paper towels. Bias-cut fish into 1-inch strips. Cut zucchini in half crosswise. Cut each zucchini half lengthwise into 6 wedges.

2. Preheat oven to 425°F. Grease a 15x10x1-inch baking pan; set aside. Place the cornflakes in a large resealable plastic bag. Seal and crush slightly; set aside. In a large bowl combine ranch dressing and hot pepper sauce. Set aside half of the dressing mixture for dipping sauce. Add catfish and zucchini strips to remaining dressing mixture in bowl; stir gently to coat.

3. Add one-third of the zucchini strips to the bag with the crushed cornflakes. Seal; shake to coat. Remove zucchini and place in a single layer in prepared baking pan. Repeat to coat remaining zucchini and the fish.

4. Bake for 12 to 15 minutes or until fish begins to flake when tested with a fork and crumbs are golden brown. Serve with reserved dipping sauce.

Per serving: 545 cal., 40 g total fat (7 g sat. fat), 58 mg chol., 779 mg sodium, 24 g carbo., 0 g fiber, 20 g pro.

MENU
Baked beans
Corn chips
Brownies

Fish Fillets with Salsa Verde

339

PREP:
10 MINUTES

BROIL:
4 TO 6 MINUTES
PER ½-INCH
THICKNESS

MAKES:
4 SERVINGS

1 pound fresh or frozen cod or orange roughy fillets

1 tablespoon lime juice

1 tablespoon olive oil

⅛ teaspoon salt

⅛ teaspoon black pepper

½ cup bottled green salsa

3 tablespoons snipped fresh cilantro

Lime wedges (optional)

1. Thaw fish, if frozen. Rinse fish; pat dry with paper towels. Preheat broiler. In a small bowl combine lime juice, oil, salt, and pepper. Brush both sides of fish with lime juice mixture.

2. Measure thickness of fish. Place fish on the greased unheated rack of a broiler pan, tucking under any thin edges to make fish of uniform thickness. Broil 4 inches from heat until fish begins to flake when tested with a fork. (Allow 4 to 6 minutes per ½-inch thickness of fish. If fish is 1 inch or more thick, turn once halfway through broiling.)

3. Meanwhile, stir together salsa and 2 tablespoons of the cilantro. To serve, top fish with salsa mixture; sprinkle with the remaining 1 tablespoon cilantro. If desired, garnish with lime wedges.

Per serving: 125 cal., 4 g total fat (1 g sat. fat), 42 mg chol., 157 mg sodium, 1 g carbo., 0 g fiber, 20 g pro.

MENU

Spanish rice (from a mix)

Black beans seasoned with fresh lime juice

Warm flour tortillas

340 Vegetable-Topped Fish

PREP:
15 MINUTES

BAKE:
4 TO 6 MINUTES
PER ½-INCH
THICKNESS
OF FISH

OVEN:
450°F

MAKES:
4 SERVINGS

1   pound fresh or frozen fish fillets

2   teaspoons butter or margarine, melted

⅛   teaspoon salt

⅛   teaspoon black pepper

1   cup bottled salsa

1   small yellow summer squash or zucchini, halved lengthwise and cut into ¼-inch slices

1. **Thaw fish, if frozen. Preheat oven to 450°F. Rinse fish; pat dry with paper towels. Measure thickness of fish. Place fish in a greased shallow baking pan, tucking under any thin edges to make fish of uniform thickness. Brush fish with melted butter. Sprinkle with salt and pepper.**

2. **Bake, uncovered, until fish begins to flake when tested with a fork. (Allow 4 to 6 minutes per ½-inch thickness.)**

3. **Meanwhile, in a small saucepan stir together salsa and summer squash. Bring to boiling; reduce heat. Simmer, covered, for 5 to 6 minutes or until squash is crisp-tender. Serve squash mixture over fish.**

Per serving: 131 cal., 3 g total fat (0 g sat. fat), 48 mg chol., 403 mg sodium, 5 g carbo., 1 g fiber, 22 g pro.

MENU
Mashed potatoes
Buttermilk biscuits
Chocolate ice cream with raspberries

Orange-Sauced Fish with Broccoli

341

START TO FINISH:
30 MINUTES

MAKES:
4 SERVINGS

1   pound fresh or frozen fish fillets, ½ to ¾ inch thick
1   10-ounce package frozen chopped broccoli
1   tablespoon water
1   cup water
½   cup orange marmalade
¼   teaspoon salt
1   cup quick-cooking couscous
1   tablespoon butter or margarine
2   teaspoons lemon juice

1. Thaw fish, if frozen. Rinse fish; pat dry with paper towels. Cut fish into 4 serving-size pieces, if necessary; set aside.

2. Place broccoli in a microwave-safe 2-quart square baking dish. Sprinkle with the 1 tablespoon water. Cover with vented plastic wrap. Microwave on 100% power (high) for 4 to 6 minutes or until crisp-tender, giving the dish a half-turn and stirring broccoli halfway through cooking. Stir in the 1 cup water, 2 tablespoons of the orange marmalade, and the ¼ teaspoon salt. Stir in couscous. Spread couscous mixture evenly in dish. Arrange fish on top of the couscous mixture, folding under any thin edges to make fish of uniform thickness; sprinkle fish with additional salt and black pepper.

4. Cover with vented plastic wrap. Microwave on 100% power (high) for 7 to 9 minutes or until fish begins to flake when tested with a fork, giving the dish a half-turn halfway through cooking.

5. For sauce, in a small microwave-safe bowl combine remaining marmalade, the butter, and lemon juice. Microwave on high about 1 minute or until butter is melted and sauce is bubbly. Stir sauce; drizzle over fish.

Per serving: 420 cal., 5 g total fat (2 g sat. fat), 62 mg chol., 312 mg sodium, 66 g carbo., 5 g fiber, 29 g pro.

MENU
Multigrain rolls
Fresh apricots and plums

342 Sweet Pepper and Salsa Fish

START TO FINISH:
25 MINUTES

MAKES:
4 SERVINGS

1 pound fresh or frozen skinless fish fillets, about ¾ inch thick
    Nonstick cooking spray
1½ cups packaged sliced fresh mushrooms
1 cup coarsely chopped green and/or yellow sweet pepper (1 large)
1 small onion, halved lengthwise and sliced
1 cup bottled salsa

1. Thaw fish, if frozen. Rinse fish; pat dry with paper towels. Cut fish into 4 serving-size pieces, if necessary; set aside.

2. Coat a large nonstick skillet with nonstick cooking spray. Heat skillet over medium-high heat. Add mushrooms, sweet pepper, and onion to skillet; cook about 5 minutes or until vegetables are tender. Remove vegetables with a slotted spoon; set aside.

3. Reduce heat to medium. Add fish to skillet. Cook, covered, for 6 to 9 minutes or until fish begins to flake when tested with a fork, turning once.

4. Spoon cooked vegetables on top of fish in skillet; top with salsa. Cook, covered, over low heat about 2 minutes more or until heated through.

Per serving: 108 cal., 1 g total fat (0 g sat. fat), 22 mg chol., 213 mg sodium, 7 g carbo., 2 g fiber, 18 g pro.

MENU
Hot cooked rice
Spinach and tomato salad with desired dressing
Banana split

Tuna and Slaw Cups

343

START TO FINISH:
15 MINUTES

MAKES:
4 SERVINGS

1½ cups purchased creamy coleslaw
⅓ cup chopped, seeded tomato (1 small)
1 6-ounce can tuna, drained and flaked
4 large butterhead (Bibb or Boston) lettuce leaves
¼ cup chopped peanuts
Dairy sour cream dip with chives (optional)

1. In a small bowl stir together coleslaw and tomato. Gently fold in tuna.

2. To serve, spoon the tuna mixture onto lettuce leaves. Sprinkle with peanuts. If desired, top with dip.

Per serving: 148 cal., 7 g total fat (1 g sat. fat), 21 mg chol., 213 mg sodium, 9 g carbo., 2 g fiber, 14 g pro.

MENU
Toasted pita bread
Fresh tropical fruit plate
with toasted coconut

344 Tuna on Greens

START TO FINISH:
15 MINUTES

MAKES:
4 SERVINGS

⅓   cup bottled Caesar salad dressing

2   teaspoons snipped fresh tarragon or thyme or ¼ teaspoon dried tarragon
     or thyme, crushed

1   10-ounce package torn mixed salad greens (8 cups)

1   6.5-ounce can chunk white tuna (water pack), drained and broken into chunks

1   large tomato, cut into thin wedges

1. For dressing, in a small bowl, stir together salad dressing and tarragon; set
   dressing aside.

2. Arrange salad greens on 4 salad plates. Top with tuna and tomato wedges.
   Drizzle with dressing.

Per serving: 178 cal., 13 g total fat (2 g sat. fat), 20 mg chol., 396 mg sodium, 4 g carbo., 1 g fiber, 12 g pro.

MENU
Soft breadsticks
Watermelon wedges

Scallops with Orange-Anise Tapenade

345

START TO FINISH:
20 MINUTES

MAKES:
4 SERVINGS

12 fresh or frozen sea scallops (about 1¼ pounds)

⅓ cup pitted kalamata olives, coarsely chopped

2 tablespoons sliced green onion (1)

½ teaspoon finely shredded orange peel

2 teaspoons orange juice

¼ teaspoon anise seeds, crushed

⅛ teaspoon cayenne pepper (optional)

Nonstick cooking spray

1. Thaw scallops, if frozen. Rinse scallops; pat dry with paper towels. Set aside.

2. For tapenade, in a small bowl combine olives, green onion, orange peel, orange juice, anise seeds, and, if desired, cayenne pepper. Set aside.

3. Coat an unheated large nonstick skillet with nonstick cooking spray. Preheat skillet over medium-high heat. Add scallops to skillet; cook, stirring frequently, for 3 to 6 minutes or until scallops turn opaque. Serve scallops with tapenade.

Per serving: 145 cal., 3 g total fat (0 g sat. fat), 47 mg chol., 353 mg sodium, 5 g carbo., 1 g fiber, 24 g pro.

MENU

Mixed greens salad with fennel bulb strips and vinaigrette dressing

Hot cooked spinach fettuccine

Carrot cake

346 Seared Scallops with Ginger Sauce

START TO FINISH:
15 MINUTES

MAKES:
4 SERVINGS

1 pound fresh or frozen sea scallops

4 teaspoons butter or margarine

⅓ cup chicken broth

¼ cup frozen pineapple-orange juice concentrate, thawed

1 teaspoon grated fresh ginger

1. Thaw scallops, if frozen. Rinse scallops; pat dry with paper towels. In a large skillet melt butter over medium-high heat. Add scallops to skillet. Cook, stirring frequently, for 2 to 3 minutes or until scallops turn opaque. Remove scallops from skillet; cover to keep warm.

2. For ginger sauce, add chicken broth, juice concentrate, and ginger to skillet. Bring to boiling. Boil, uncovered, until sauce is reduced by about half. Spoon sauce over scallops.

Per serving: 168 cal., 5 g total fat (3 g sat. fat), 48 mg chol., 311 mg sodium, 10 g carbo., 0 g fiber, 19 g pro.

MENU
Japanese curly noodles
Steamed snow pea pods
Pineapple sherbet

Shrimp Kabobs

347

PREP:
20 MINUTES

BROIL:
8 MINUTES

MAKES:
4 SERVINGS

1   pound fresh or frozen medium to large shrimp in shells
1   small red or green sweet pepper, cut into 16 pieces
¼   of a medium fresh pineapple, cut into chunks
4   green onions, cut into 1-inch pieces
¼   cup bottled barbecue sauce

1. Thaw shrimp, if frozen. Preheat broiler. Peel and devein shrimp, leaving tails intact, if desired. Rinse shrimp; pat dry with paper towels. On 8 skewers alternately thread shrimp, sweet pepper, pineapple, and green onion, leaving ¼-inch space between pieces.

2. Place skewers on the greased unheated rack of a broiler pan. Broil about 4 inches from the heat for 8 to 10 minutes or until shrimp are opaque, turning skewers once and brushing with barbecue sauce halfway through broiling.

Per serving: 134 cal., 2 g total fat (0 g sat. fat), 129 mg chol., 258 mg sodium, 10 g carbo., 1 g fiber, 18 g pro.

MENU
Hot cooked rice
Broccoli salad (from a deli)
Fudge brownies

348 Coconut-Curry Shrimp

START TO FINISH:
25 MINUTES

MAKES:
4 SERVINGS

1   pound fresh or frozen peeled, cooked large shrimp

1   13.5-ounce can unsweetened coconut milk

1   to 3 teaspoons red curry paste

1   16-ounce package frozen broccoli, green beans, pearl onions, and red peppers

2   tablespoons snipped fresh cilantro or chopped peanuts

1. Thaw shrimp, if frozen. Rinse shrimp; pat dry with paper towels. Set aside.

2. In a large skillet stir together coconut milk and red curry paste. Add vegetables. Bring to boiling; reduce heat. Simmer, covered, for 6 to 8 minutes or until vegetables are crisp-tender, stirring occasionally. Add shrimp; heat through. Sprinkle individual servings with cilantro.

Per serving: 336 cal., 20 g total fat (16 g sat. fat), 172 mg chol., 306 mg sodium, 11 g carbo., 3 g fiber, 26 g pro.

MENU
Hot cooked basmati rice
Warm pita bread
Pineapple upside-down cake

Shrimp Capellini with Pesto Sauce

349

START TO FINISH:
20 MINUTES

MAKES:
4 SERVINGS

12 ounces fresh or frozen peeled and deveined shrimp

8 ounces dried tomato-flavor angel hair pasta (capellini), fettuccine, or linguine
Nonstick cooking spray

2 medium yellow summer squash and/or zucchini, cut into ½-inch chunks (about 2 cups)

⅓ cup purchased pesto

½ cup chopped roma tomato (1 medium)

1. Thaw shrimp, if frozen. Rinse shrimp; pat dry with paper towels. Set shrimp aside. Cook pasta according to package directions; drain and keep warm.

2. Meanwhile, coat an unheated large nonstick skillet with nonstick cooking spray (or, brush it with a little oil drained from the pesto). Heat skillet over medium-high heat. Add shrimp; cook and stir for 2 minutes. Add squash; cook and stir about 2 minutes more or until shrimp are opaque and squash is crisp-tender. Remove skillet from heat. Add pesto; toss gently to coat.

   Serve shrimp mixture over pasta; sprinkle with chopped tomato.

Per serving: 428 cal., 16 g total fat (0 g sat. fat), 134 mg chol., 316 mg sodium, 47 g carbo., 3 g fiber, 25 g pro.

MENU
Crusty Italian bread
Caesar salad
Chocolate gelato
with coffee liqueur

350 Scandinavian Shrimp Salad

START TO FINISH:
25 MINUTES

MAKES:
4 SERVINGS

12 ounces peeled, deveined, cooked shrimp
6 cups packaged torn mixed salad greens
1 cup chopped tomato (1 large)
¾ cup thinly sliced cucumber
½ of a small red onion, thinly sliced
½ cup bottled olive oil vinaigrette salad dressing
2 tablespoons snipped fresh dill or 1 teaspoon dried dill
  Party rye bread, toasted*, or rye crackers (optional)
  Fresh dill (optional)

1. If desired, remove tails from shrimp. Set shrimp aside.

2. Arrange salad greens on 4 salad plates. Top with tomato, cucumber, onion, and shrimp. Stir together salad dressing and the 2 tablespoons snipped dill; drizzle over salads. If desired, serve with toasted party rye bread and garnish with fresh dill sprigs.

Per serving with 2 slices party rye: 261 cal., 17 g total fat (1 g sat. fat), 166 mg chol., 352 mg sodium, 7 g carbo., 2 g fiber, 19 g pro.

*NOTE: To toast party rye bread, place slices on a baking sheet. Bake in a preheated 425°F oven about 5 minutes or until lightly toasted.

MENU
Cantaloupe and watermelon chunks
Assorted pastries

Tossed Shrimp Salad

351

START TO FINISH:
10 MINUTES

MAKES:
4 SERVINGS

2 8-ounce packages frozen peeled, cooked shrimp, thawed

1 10-ounce package torn mixed salad greens (about 8 cups)

¼ cup thinly sliced green onion (2)

⅓ cup bottled Italian salad dressing

¼ cup sliced almonds, toasted

1. Drain shrimp; pat dry with paper towels.

2. In a large salad bowl combine shrimp, salad greens, and green onion. Drizzle dressing over salad; toss to coat. Season to taste with *salt* and *black pepper*. Sprinkle with almonds.

Per serving: 301 cal., 20 g total fat (2 g sat. fat), 185 mg chol., 483 mg sodium, 6 g carbo., 2 g fiber, 26 g pro.

MENU
Sourdough rolls
Lemon sorbet with
fresh berries

352

Salsa-Topped Crab Cakes

PREP:
20 MINUTES

COOK:
6 MINUTES

MAKES:
4 SERVINGS

½ cup finely chopped water chestnuts

¼ cup mayonnaise or salad dressing

2 tablespoons seasoned fine dry bread crumbs

2 6-ounce cans crabmeat, drained, flaked, and cartilage removed

Nonstick cooking spray

¼ cup bottled salsa

1. In a medium bowl combine water chestnuts, 3 tablespoons of the mayonnaise, and bread crumbs. Stir in crabmeat. Shape into eight ½-inch-thick patties.

2. Coat a large nonstick skillet with nonstick cooking spray. Heat skillet over medium heat. Add crab patties. Cook for 6 to 8 minutes or until light brown and heated through, turning once.

3. Meanwhile, in a small bowl, stir together salsa and remaining mayonnaise. Spoon salsa mixture on top of crab cakes.

Per serving: 208 cal., 12 g total fat (2 g sat. fat), 81 mg chol., 522 mg sodium, 6 g carbo., 1 g fiber, 18 g pro.

MENU
Steamed green beans
Rice pilaf (from a mix)
Raspberry shakes

Fettuccine-Vegetable Toss

353

START TO FINISH:
20 MINUTES

MAKES:
4 SERVINGS

1   9-ounce package refrigerated spinach or plain fettuccine
1   tablespoon olive oil
2   tablespoons chopped green onion (1)
2   cups chopped red and/or yellow tomato (4 small)
½   cup finely chopped carrot (1 medium)
¼   cup oil-packed dried tomatoes, drained and snipped
½   cup crumbled garlic-and-herb feta cheese, peppercorn feta cheese, or plain feta cheese
      (2 ounces)

1. Cook pasta according to package directions; drain well. Return to hot pan; cover to keep warm.

2. Meanwhile, in a large skillet heat oil over medium heat. Add green onion; cook for 30 seconds. Stir in fresh tomato, carrot, and dried tomato pieces. Cook, covered, for 5 minutes, stirring once. Spoon tomato mixture over cooked pasta. Sprinkle with feta cheese; toss gently to mix.

Per serving: 311 cal., 11 g total fat (4 g sat. fat), 73 mg chol., 250 mg sodium, 44 g carbo., 2 g fiber, 13 g pro.

MENU
Steamed green beans
Whole wheat bread
Raspberry sorbet

354 Rotini and Sweet Pepper Primavera

START TO FINISH:
25 MINUTES

MAKES:
4 SERVINGS

1 pound fresh asparagus

8 ounces dried rotini or gemelli pasta

2 small red and/or yellow sweet peppers, cut into 1-inch pieces

1 cup halved baby pattypan squash or sliced yellow summer squash

1 10-ounce container refrigerated light Alfredo pasta sauce

2 teaspoons snipped fresh thyme or ¾ teaspoon dried thyme, crushed

⅛ to ¼ teaspoon crushed red pepper

Coarsely cracked black pepper (optional)

1. Snap off and discard woody bases from asparagus. If desired, scrape off scales. Bias-cut asparagus into 1-inch pieces. (You should have about 2 cups.)

2. Cook pasta according to package directions, adding asparagus, sweet pepper, and squash to the pasta for the last 3 minutes of cooking. Drain well. Return the pasta and vegetables to hot pan; cover to keep warm.

3. Meanwhile, in a small saucepan stir together Alfredo sauce, thyme, and crushed red pepper. Cook and stir over medium heat about 5 minutes or until mixture is heated through. Pour over pasta and vegetables; toss gently to coat. If desired, sprinkle with cracked black pepper.

Per serving: 421 cal., 12 g total fat (6 g sat. fat), 31 mg chol., 622 mg sodium, 66 g carbo., 2 g fiber, 15 g pro.

MENU
Soft breadsticks
Tiramisu (frozen)

Beans, Barley, and Tomatoes

355

1   14-ounce can vegetable broth or chicken broth

1   teaspoon Greek seasoning or garam masala

1   cup frozen green soybeans (shelled edamame)

¾   cup quick-cooking barley

½   cup packaged shredded carrot (1 medium)

4   cups packaged prewashed fresh spinach leaves

4   small to medium tomatoes, sliced

1. In a medium saucepan bring broth and seasoning to boiling. Add soybeans and barley. Return to boiling; reduce heat. Simmer, covered, for 12 minutes. Stir carrot into barley mixture.

2. Meanwhile, arrange spinach on 4 salad plates; top with tomato slices. Using a slotted spoon, spoon barley mixture over tomatoes (or drain barley mixture; spoon over tomato slices).

Per serving: 171 cal., 3 g total fat (0 g sat. fat), 0 mg chol., 484 mg sodium, 33 g carbo., 10 g fiber, 9 g pro.

MENU
Multigrain rolls
Watermelon wedges

356 Mediterranean Couscous with Tofu

START TO FINISH:
15 MINUTES

MAKES:
4 SERVINGS

1   5.7-ounce package curry-flavor or roasted garlic and olive oil-flavor couscous mix
½   of a 12- to 16-ounce package extra-firm tofu (fresh bean curd), well drained
1   tablespoon olive oil
½   cup sliced pitted ripe olives or sliced pitted Greek black olives
½   cup crumbled feta cheese or finely shredded Parmesan cheese (2 ounces)

1. **Prepare couscous according to package directions, except omit oil. Meanwhile, cut tofu into ½-inch cubes. Pat tofu dry with paper towels.**

2. **In a large skillet heat oil over medium-high heat. Add tofu; stir-fry for 5 to 7 minutes or until tofu is brown. Stir tofu and olives into couscous. Transfer to 4 dinner plates. Top with cheese.**

Per serving: 259 cal., 10 g total fat (4 g sat. fat), 17 mg chol., 763 mg sodium, 33 g carbo., 3 g fiber, 11 g pro.

MENU
Spinach and tomato salad with desired dressing
French baguette slices
Cheesecake with fresh berries

Polenta with Fresh Tomato Sauce

357

START TO FINISH:
18 MINUTES

MAKES:
4 SERVINGS

4 teaspoons olive oil

½ teaspoon bottled minced garlic (1 clove)

2 cups coarsely chopped roma tomato (6 medium)

¼ cup pitted halved kalamata olives or sliced pitted ripe olives

2 teaspoons snipped fresh rosemary or 2 tablespoons snipped fresh thyme

1 16-ounce tube refrigerated prepared polenta

½ cup shredded smoked Gouda or Swiss cheese (2 ounces)

1. For sauce, in a medium saucepan heat 2 teaspoons of the oil and the garlic over medium heat. Add tomato; cook for 2 minutes. Stir in olives and rosemary. Bring to boiling; reduce heat. Simmer, uncovered, for 8 minutes, stirring occasionally. Season to taste with *salt* and *black pepper.*

2. Meanwhile, cut polenta into 8 slices. In a large nonstick skillet or on a griddle heat the remaining 2 teaspoons oil. Add polenta; cook over medium heat about 6 minutes or until golden brown, turning once. Remove from heat and sprinkle with cheese. Top polenta with tomato sauce.

Per serving: 226 cal., 10 g total fat (3 g sat. fat), 16 mg chol., 608 mg sodium, 27 g carbo., 5 g fiber, 8 g pro.

MENU

Warm cannellini beans with baby spinach and vinaigrette dressing

Crusty Italian bread

Cookies and cream ice cream

358 Cheese and Vegetable Focaccia

START TO FINISH:
20 MINUTES

MAKES:
4 SERVINGS

⅓ cup mayonnaise or salad dressing

2 tablespoons honey mustard

1 8- to 10-inch tomato or onion focaccia bread, halved horizontally

1 cup packaged prewashed fresh spinach leaves

6 ounces dilled Havarti cheese, very thinly sliced

1 16-ounce jar pickled mixed vegetables, drained and chopped

1. **In a small bowl stir together mayonnaise and honey mustard. Spread mayonnaise mixture over bottom half of focaccia. Top with spinach leaves and half of the cheese. Spoon vegetables over cheese; top with remaining cheese. Replace bread top. Cut into quarters.**

Per serving: 364 cal., 32 g total fat (2 g sat. fat), 67 mg chol., 1,251 mg sodium, 10 g carbo., 0 g fiber, 10 g pro.

MENU

Three-bean salad
(from a deli)

Corn chips

Watermelon and honeydew
melon wedges

Italian Veggie Burger Bites

359

START TO FINISH:
15 MINUTES

MAKES:
4 SERVINGS

4   refrigerated or frozen meatless burger patties

¼   cup tomato paste

4   to 5 tablespoons water

2   teaspoons snipped fresh basil

8   slices firm-textured whole wheat or oatmeal bread, toasted if desired

4   slices mozzarella cheese (1 ounce)

16 small fresh basil leaves

1. Cook burger patties according to package directions. Meanwhile, for sauce, in a small bowl combine tomato paste, water, and snipped basil.

2. To serve, place each burger patty on 1 slice of bread. Top with sauce, cheese, and basil leaves. Top with another slice of bread. If desired, cut each sandwich into quarters.

Per serving: 332 cal., 12 g total fat (2 g sat. fat), 25 mg chol., 819 mg sodium, 33 g carbo., 8 g fiber, 26 g pro.

- **TOMATO-MAYO VEGGIE BURGER BITES:** Prepare as above except omit tomato paste, water, basil, and cheese. In a small bowl combine ¼ cup mayonnaise or salad dressing, 3 tablespoons ketchup, and dash garlic powder. Top each burger with some of the ketchup mixture and a lettuce leaf. Serve as above.

Per serving: 289 cal., 11 g fat (2 g sat fat), 8 mg chol., 805 mg sodium, 33 g carbo., 7 g fiber, 19 g pro.

- **BARBECUE VEGGIE BURGER BITES:** Prepare as above except omit tomato paste, water, basil, and cheese. Top each burger with 1 rounded tablespoon bottled barbecue sauce and a lettuce leaf. Serve as above.

Per serving: 253 cal., 6 g fat (2 g sat fat), 3 mg chol., 736 mg sodium, 32 g carbo., 8 g fiber, 20 g pro.

MENU
Multigrain chips
Pasta salad (from a deli)
Root beer floats with chocolate ice cream

360 Fresh Tomato Pizza

START TO FINISH:
25 MINUTES

MAKES:
4 SERVINGS

4   6- to 7-inch individual-size packaged focaccia or prebaked pizza crusts
1½ cups shredded pizza cheese
½   cup finely shredded fresh basil
4   fresh roma tomatoes or 2 medium tomatoes, cut into thin wedges or slices
2   to 3 teaspoons olive oil
¼   cup pine nuts (optional)

1. **Preheat oven to 425°F. Place focaccia on a very large baking sheet. Bake for 5 minutes.**

2. **Remove focaccia from oven; sprinkle with cheese. Top with fresh basil. Arrange the tomato wedges in a circular pattern on top. Drizzle with olive oil and, if desired, sprinkle with pine nuts. Bake for 10 minutes more.**

Per serving: 369 cal., 15 g total fat (9 g sat. fat), 30 mg chol., 631 mg sodium, 41 g carbo., 5 g fiber, 19 g pro.

MENU

Romaine salad with creamy Italian dressing

Marinated vegetable salad (from a deli)

Brownie sundaes

Tomato Barley Soup with Garden Vegetables

361

START TO FINISH:
30 MINUTES

MAKES:
4 SERVINGS

2 14-ounce cans vegetable broth
¾ cup quick-cooking barley
¾ cup thinly sliced carrot
1 teaspoon dried thyme, crushed
⅛ teaspoon black pepper
1 19-ounce can ready-to-serve tomato basil soup
2 cups coarsely chopped zucchini and/or yellow summer squash (2 small)
1 cup frozen cut green beans

1. In a large saucepan combine vegetable broth, barley, carrot, thyme, and pepper. Bring to boiling; reduce heat. Simmer, covered, for 10 minutes.

2. Stir in tomato basil soup, zucchini, and green beans. Return to boiling; reduce heat. Simmer, covered, for 8 to 10 minutes more or until vegetables and barley are tender.

Per serving: 197 cal., 3 g total fat (0 g sat. fat), 0 mg chol., 1,265 mg sodium, 40 g carbo., 6 g fiber, 7 g pro.

MENU
Crusty dinner rolls
Red and green grapes
Assorted cheese plate

362 Italian Mozzarella Salad

START TO FINISH:
20 MINUTES

MAKES:
4 SERVINGS

1   15-ounce can black beans or garbanzo beans, rinsed and drained

1   15-ounce can butter beans or Great Northern beans, rinsed and drained

1   small cucumber, quartered lengthwise and sliced (1 cup)

2   red and/or yellow tomatoes, cut into thin wedges

¼   cup thinly sliced green onion (2)

½   cup bottled oil-and-vinegar salad dressing

8   ounces round- or log-shape fresh mozzarella

1. **In a large bowl combine beans, cucumber, tomato, and green onion. Add salad dressing; toss lightly to coat. Cut cheese into thin slices; gently toss into bean mixture.**

Per serving: 462 cal., 28 g total fat (11 g sat. fat), 40 mg chol., 954 mg sodium, 34 g carbo., 10 g fiber, 20 g pro.

MENU
Focaccia
Spumoni ice cream with
crushed amaretti cookies

Open-Face Portobello Sandwiches

363

START TO FINISH:
25 MINUTES

MAKES:
4 SERVINGS

⅔ cup chopped tomato (1 medium)

2 teaspoons snipped fresh basil, thyme, and/or oregano

⅛ teaspoon salt

2 fresh medium portobello mushrooms (about 4 inches in diameter)

1 teaspoon balsamic vinegar or red wine vinegar

½ teaspoon olive oil

½ of a 12-inch Italian flat bread (focaccia), quartered, or ½ of a 12-inch thin-crust Italian bread shell

Finely shredded Parmesan cheese (optional)

1. Preheat broiler. In a small bowl combine tomato, basil, and salt; set aside.

2. Clean mushrooms; cut off stems even with caps. Discard stems. Combine vinegar and oil; gently brush mixture over the mushrooms. Place mushrooms on the unheated rack of the broiler pan.

3. Broil mushrooms 4 to 5 inches from the heat for 6 to 8 minutes or just until tender, turning once. Drain mushrooms on paper towels. Thinly slice mushrooms.

4. Place bread on a baking sheet. Place under broiler for 2 to 3 minutes or until heated through.

5. To serve, top toasted bread with mushroom slices and tomato mixture. If desired, top with Parmesan cheese.

Per serving: 161 cal., 3 g total fat (1 g sat. fat), 2 mg chol., 71 mg sodium, 29 g carbo., 3 g fiber, 7 g pro.

MENU
Spinach salad with desired dressing
Orange sherbet

364

Fontina and Melon Salad

START TO FINISH:
25 MINUTES

MAKES:
4 SERVINGS

1½ cups dried large farfalle (bow ties) (about 6 ounces)

2 cups purchased cantaloupe and/or honeydew melon chunks

1 cup cubed fontina or Swiss cheese (4 ounces)

⅓ cup bottled nonfat poppy seed salad dressing

1 to 2 tablespoons snipped fresh mint

2 cups watercress, stems removed

Cantaloupe slices (optional)

1. **Cook pasta according to package directions. Drain in a colander; rinse with cold water. Drain.**

2. **In a large bowl toss together pasta, cantaloupe chunks, and cheese. Combine salad dressing and mint; pour over pasta mixture, tossing gently to coat.**

3. **Stir watercress into pasta mixture. If desired, garnish with cantaloupe slices.**

Per serving: 219 cal., 10 g total fat (6 g sat. fat), 37 mg chol., 355 mg sodium, 23 g carbo., 1 g fiber, 10 g pro.

MENU
Sourdough bread
Vanilla ice cream
with sliced peaches

Pasta and Portobello Mushroom Salad

365

1   16-ounce package frozen herb-seasoned or Italian-style pasta-and-vegetable mix

3   tablespoons olive oil

5   ounces packaged sliced portobello mushrooms (about 2 cups)

½   teaspoon crushed red pepper

8   ounces mozzarella cheese, cubed

3   tablespoons balsamic vinegar or red wine vinegar

3   cups packaged torn mixed greens

1. Prepare pasta mix according to package directions. Transfer to a bowl. Quick-chill the pasta mixture in the freezer, stirring mixture occasionally.

2. Meanwhile, in a large nonstick skillet heat 1 tablespoon of the oil over medium heat. Add mushrooms and red pepper; cook and stir for 2 minutes.

3. Add mushroom mixture, cubed mozzarella, the remaining 2 tablespoons oil, and the vinegar to pasta mixture in bowl. Toss to mix. Arrange greens on 4 salad plates. Spoon pasta mixture over greens.

Per serving: 400 cal., 14 g total fat (5 g sat. fat), 59 mg chol., 1,270 mg sodium, 20 g carbo., 1 g fiber, 18 g pro.

MENU

Multigrain bread

Fresh berry shortcakes made with purchased shortcakes, whipped cream, and choice of berries

NOTE: Boldfaced page numbers indicate photographs.

NOTE: Boldfaced page numbers indicate photographs.

NOTE: Boldfaced page numbers indicate photographs.

NOTE: Boldfaced page numbers indicate photographs.

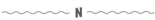

NOTE: Boldfaced page numbers indicate photographs.

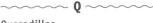
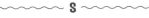

NOTE: Boldfaced page numbers indicate photographs.

NOTE: Boldfaced page numbers indicate photographs.

NOTE: Boldfaced page numbers indicate photographs.

METRIC INFORMATION

The charts on this page provide a guide for converting measurements from the U.S. customary system, which is used throughout this book, to the metric system.

PRODUCT DIFFERENCES

Most of the ingredients called for in the recipes in this book are available in most countries. However, some are known by different names. Here are some common American ingredients and their possible counterparts:

- Sugar (white) is granulated, fine granulated, or castor sugar.
- Powdered sugar is icing sugar.
- All-purpose flour is enriched, bleached or unbleached white household flour. When self-rising flour is used in place of all-purpose flour in a recipe that calls for leavening, omit the leavening agent (baking soda or baking powder) and salt.
- Light-colored corn syrup is golden syrup.
- Cornstarch is cornflour.
- Baking soda is bicarbonate of soda.
- Vanilla or vanilla extract is vanilla essence.
- Green, red, or yellow sweet peppers are capsicums or bell peppers.
- Golden raisins are sultanas.

VOLUME AND WEIGHT

The United States traditionally uses cup measures for liquid and solid ingredients. The chart below shows the approximate imperial and metric equivalents. If you are accustomed to weighing solid ingredients, the following approximate equivalents will be helpful.

- 1 cup butter, castor sugar, or rice = 8 ounces = ½ pound = 250 grams
- 1 cup flour = 4 ounces = ¼ pound = 125 grams
- 1 cup icing sugar = 5 ounces = 150 grams

Canadian and U.S. volume for a cup measure is 8 fluid ounces (237 ml), but the standard metric equivalent is 250 ml.

1 British imperial cup is 10 fluid ounces.

In Australia, 1 tablespoon equals 20 ml, and there are 4 teaspoons in the Australian tablespoon.

Spoon measures are used for smaller amounts of ingredients. Although the size of the tablespoon varies slightly in different countries, for practical purposes and for recipes in this book, a straight substitution is all that's necessary. Measurements made using cups or spoons always should be level unless stated otherwise.

COMMON WEIGHT RANGE REPLACEMENTS

IMPERIAL / U.S.	METRIC
½ ounce	15 g
1 ounce	25 g or 30 g
4 ounces (¼ pound)	115 g or 125 g
8 ounces (½ pound)	225 g or 250 g
16 ounces (1 pound)	450 g or 500 g
1¼ pounds	625 g
1½ pounds	750 g
2 pounds or 2¼ pounds	1,000 g or 1 Kg

OVEN TEMPERATURE EQUIVALENTS

FAHRENHEIT SETTING	CELSIUS SETTING*	GAS SETTING
300°F	150°C	Gas Mark 2 (very low)
325°F	160°C	Gas Mark 3 (low)
350°F	180°C	Gas Mark 4 (moderate)
375°F	190°C	Gas Mark 5 (moderate)
400°F	200°C	Gas Mark 6 (hot)
425°F	220°C	Gas Mark 7 (hot)
450°F	230°C	Gas Mark 8 (very hot)
475°F	240°C	Gas Mark 9 (very hot)
500°F	260°C	Gas Mark 10 (extremely hot)
Broil	Broil	Grill

*Electric and gas ovens may be calibrated using celsius. However, for an electric oven, increase celsius setting 10 to 20 degrees when cooking above 160°C. For convection or forced air ovens (gas or electric) lower the temperature setting 25°F/10°C when cooking at all heat levels.

BAKING PAN SIZES

IMPERIAL / U.S.	METRIC
9×1½-inch round cake pan	22- or 23×4-cm (1.5 L)
9×1½-inch pie plate	22- or 23×4-cm (1 L)
8×8×2-inch square cake pan	20×5-cm (2 L)
9×9×2-inch square cake pan	22- or 23×4.5-cm (2.5 L)
11×7×1½-inch baking pan	28×17×4-cm (2 L)
2-quart rectangular baking pan	30×19×4.5-cm (3 L)
13×9×2-inch baking pan	34×22×4.5-cm (3.5 L)
15×10×1-inch jelly roll pan	40×25×2-cm
9×5×3-inch loaf pan	23×13×8-cm (2 L)
2-quart casserole	2 L

U.S. / STANDARD METRIC EQUIVALENTS

⅛ teaspoon = 0.5 ml

¼ teaspoon = 1 ml

½ teaspoon = 2 ml

1 teaspoon = 5 ml

1 tablespoon = 15 ml

2 tablespoons = 25 ml

¼ cup = 2 fluid ounces = 50 ml

⅓ cup = 3 fluid ounces = 75 ml

½ cup = 4 fluid ounces = 125 ml

⅔ cup = 5 fluid ounces = 150 ml

¾ cup = 6 fluid ounces = 175 ml

1 cup = 8 fluid ounces = 250 ml

2 cups = 1 pint = 500 ml

1 quart = 1 litre